Building a Sustainable Political Economy: SPERI Research & Policy

Series Editors
Colin Hay
SPERI
University of Sheffield
Sheffield, UK

Anthony Payne
SPERI
University of Sheffield
Sheffield, UK

The Sheffield Political Economy Research Institute (SPERI) is an innovation in higher education research and outreach. It brings together leading international researchers in the social sciences, policy makers, journalists and opinion formers to reassess and develop proposals in response to the political and economic issues posed by the current combination of financial crisis, shifting economic power and environmental threat. Building a Sustainable Political Economy: SPERI Research & Policy will serve as a key outlet for SPERI's published work. Each title will summarise and disseminate to an academic and postgraduate student audience, as well as directly to policy-makers and journalists, key policy-oriented research findings designed to further the development of a more sustainable future for the national, regional and world economy following the global financial crisis. It takes a holistic and interdisciplinary view of political economy in which the local, national, regional and global interact at all times and in complex ways. The SPERI research agenda, and hence the focus of the series, seeks to explore the core economic and political questions that require us to develop a new sustainable model of political economy at all times and in complex ways.

speri.

More information about this series at
http://www.palgrave.com/gp/series/14879

Scott Lavery

British Capitalism After the Crisis

palgrave
macmillan

Scott Lavery
Sheffield Political Economy Research
Institute (SPERI)
University of Sheffield
Sheffield, UK

Building a Sustainable Political Economy: SPERI Research & Policy
ISBN 978-3-030-04045-1 ISBN 978-3-030-04046-8 (eBook)
https://doi.org/10.1007/978-3-030-04046-8

Library of Congress Control Number: 2018961182

This Palgrave Macmillan imprint is published by the registered company Springer Nature Switzerland AG
The registered company address is: Gewerbestrasse 11, 6330 Cham, Switzerland

To my grandma, Helen Burnett

Acknowledgements

This book would not have been possible without the intellectual input and personal support of a great many people. The book began its life as a Ph.D. thesis. I would like to thank my Ph.D. supervisor and Co-Director of the Sheffield Political Economy Research Institute (SPERI), Colin Hay, for his invaluable engagement with my work. It was a great privilege to be supervised by Colin, and I have benefited immeasurably from his generous support throughout the research and writing process. I would also like to thank my second supervisor, Jonathan Joseph, for his encouragement and for his many insightful thoughts on the project. I would also like to extend my warmest thanks to Tony Payne, the co-founder and former Co-Director of the Sheffield Political Economy Research Institute (SPERI). I was fortunate enough to receive funding for the Ph.D. from SPERI, and I am incredibly grateful to Tony and to SPERI for this opportunity.

Other colleagues at SPERI also strongly merit a mention. During the first five years of SPERI's life, I was fortunate enough to share my workspace with a fantastic group of people. Craig Berry, Martin Craig, Adam Barber, Hannah Lambie-Munford, Tom Hunt, Sarah Boswell and Laure Astill all deserve a special mention in this regard. Jeremy Green, a former colleague at SPERI, has become an intellectual collaborator and good friend over the course of writing the thesis and this book. It has also been a pleasure to work alongside other colleagues—notably SPERI's new Co-Directors Genevieve le Baron and Adam Leaver—as well as Andrew Baker, Liam Stanley, Kaisa Pietila, Patrick Kaczmarczyk, Edward

Pemberton and many others within the SPERI office over the past few years. All these people make the institute a brilliant and highly collegial place to pursue research.

Andrew Gamble and Matthew Watson examined the original Ph.D. thesis and provided erudite feedback which helped me to transform the thesis into a book. I thank them both for their intellectual engagement and for the professional support which they provided me with throughout the early stages of my academic career. During my time at the University of York, it was my MA supervisor, Chris Rogers, who encouraged me to consider embarking upon a Ph.D. I would like to thank him for his support and advice during this period. The Department of Politics at the University of Sheffield has also been an excellent place to study and to develop both intellectually and professionally. Thanks to the academic and administrative staff who make the Department such a good place to work. Matt Bishop, Owen Parker, Burak Tansel, Simon Bulmer and Andy Hindmoor all merit a special mention, alongside colleagues at SPERI who I mentioned above. Each has provided invaluable feedback on my work at various stages for which I am hugely grateful. I also made a number of very good friends within the Ph.D. community at Sheffield who helped to shape my thinking in important ways. In particular, the neo-Gramscian reading group was a source of great inspiration and enjoyment for me. Davide Schmid, James Chamberlain, Robbie Pye, Sam Morecroft, Vanessa Bilancetti, Rasmus Hovedskov and Jonathan Webb have all engaged in this group in a highly collaborative spirit.

I couldn't hope for a better partner than Stephanie Wardle who has been a source of incredible support, companionship and love over the past few years. Finally I thank my family—Fiona, Colin, Gavin, Gillian and Helen—for all the love and encouragement they have given to me over the years. Without them, this book would not have been possible. I dedicate this book to my grandma, Helen Burnett.

Contents

List of Figures

CHAPTER 1

Introduction

The global financial crisis of 2008 embodied the biggest shock to the capitalist system since the Great Depression. Crises on this scale have historically produced large transformations. The 1930s crisis destroyed the gold standard and eventually ushered in the Bretton Woods settlement. The 1970s 'stagflationary' crisis unravelled the compromise of post-war capitalism and was followed by a far-reaching project of neoliberal restructuring. Many observers expected a similar transformation to occur in the wake of the 2008 crisis. The decade which followed the crash has been one of profound turbulence. But whether this 'post-crisis' conjuncture will give rise to a new capitalist order remains an open question.

There is evidence of both continuity and change within post-crisis capitalism. On the one hand, deep public expenditure cuts, sustained real wage decline and welfare retrenchment intensified across many advanced capitalist states. Neoliberal policy ideas proved markedly resilient whilst inequality intensified (Schmidt & Thatcher, 2013). However, important shifts were also afoot in this post-crisis era. Central banks engaged in sustained programmes of 'loose' monetary policy, exemplified by sustained low interest rates and the unorthodox monetary policy of Quantitative Easing (Green & Lavery, 2018). Despite these efforts, low growth and the danger of deflation endured as threats to the advanced capitalist order. At the same time, anti-establishment forces and political parties on both the right and the left emerged, challenging some of the core tenets of the pre-crisis order (Blyth & Matthijs, 2017; Watkins, 2016).

S. Lavery, *British Capitalism After the Crisis*, Building a Sustainable Political Economy: SPERI Research & Policy,
https://doi.org/10.1007/978-3-030-04046-8_1

This book focuses on the case of British capitalism after the crisis. It examines the extent to which British capitalism has been transformed by the 2008 crash and its aftermath. Four distinct phases of development can be identified in the prelude to and the fallout from the 2008 crisis in Britain. First, between September 1992 and the 2008 crash, the British economy underwent a phase of relatively sustained economic expansion. During this period, unemployment fell, inflation remained low and economic output expanded at a steady annual rate. At the height of this period, political elites claimed that Britain's liberalised market economy demonstrated how economic dynamism and sustained non-inflationary growth could be secured under conditions of globalisation. In 2006, the then-Chancellor of the Exchequer, Gordon Brown, infamously proclaimed that 'boom and bust' had been effectively abolished under his watch. Tight counter-inflationary policy, 'light touch' regulation of the financial services sector, labour market flexibilisation and 'prudential' macroeconomic management had produced, he claimed, a period of sustained and apparently stable economic expansion within Britain.

With the 2008 crisis, this phase of economic expansion came to an abrupt halt. From March 2008, the UK entered the deepest economic downturn which it had experienced in the post-war period. Subsequently, under the newly formed Coalition government, Britain narrowly averted a 'double dip' recession in 2012. Economic growth throughout this period was consistently low. This phase of protracted economic stagnation had a profound impact on the structure of the British economy. Between 2008 and 2013, productivity growth flatlined, as the UK recorded its worst productivity performance in over 45 years (Jones, 2013: 2). Private investment fell by 10.5% between 2010 and 2013 (Lee, 2015: 23), whilst public investment simultaneously collapsed by 40% (Van Reenen, 2015: 3). Real wages fell by 10% between 2008 and 2015, meaning that Britain experienced the largest real terms wage cut of any European economy with the exception of Greece (TUC, 2016). At the same time, attempts to eliminate the budget deficit—the annual amount of borrowing required to finance the difference between government revenues and expenditure—were consistently frustrated due to weak tax receipts and lower than expected economic growth. Sixteen years of economic 'boom' were followed—contrary to the expectations of New Labour's 'Iron Chancellor'—by the largest 'bust' which the British economy had experienced since the Great Depression.

Throughout the latter half of the 2010–2015 parliament, it appeared that the British economy had finally entered into a phase of economic recovery. By the spring of 2013, relatively strong GDP growth became established once again, registering at 1.7% in the second quarter of this year. This increase was then sustained for eight successive quarters, such that by April 2015, GDP per capita finally returned to its pre-crisis peak. On a range of headline economic indicators, the British economy began to strongly outperform many comparator states within the European Union (EU). Employment increased markedly—the Coalition government claimed by around 2 million—making Britain, in the words of the Prime Minister David Cameron, the 'jobs factory of Europe' (Cameron, 2015). By 2015, the budget deficit—although not abolished as had been initially promised by the Chancellor George Osborne—had been reduced by half. Confidence seemed to be returning to the British economy, as consumer spending increased and business investment began to pick up. After half a decade of relative stagnation, the British economy had returned—or so it was claimed—to a renewed wave of economic expansion and private sector-led growth.

The Coalition had implemented a deep programme of public expenditure cuts. But in the aftermath of the 2015 election, it appeared that the crisis had been contained. Growth and employment were rising. The architects of Britain's austerity experiment—the Conservative Party under David Cameron and George Osborne—unexpectedly secured a parliamentary majority. Under the surface, however, a new wave of turbulence was emerging. Cameron had committed to holding an 'in-out' referendum on the UK's membership of the European Union (EU). In 2016, the British electorate voted to 'leave' the EU, ending forty years of membership and pitching the UK into a prolonged period of political and constitutional crisis. In its aftermath, Cameron resigned and was replaced by Theresa May. The May government committed to a 'hard' Brexit, leaving the Single Market and the Customs Union, ending the jurisdiction of the European Court of Justice and ending budgetary contributions to the EU. Statist interventionism re-emerged in the early phase of the May government, as she sought to colonise seats in Labour's heartlands (Pabst, 2017). At the same time, the Labour Party—under the leadership of Jeremy Corbyn—advanced a populist left economic programme which secured a high level of support during the 2017 general election. A distinctive post-crisis British politics had emerged. A decade after the 2008 crisis, a potential transformation in British capitalism was in the making.

Theorising Continuity and Change in British Capitalism

The four phases of development outlined above provide the temporal backdrop to this book. Throughout, the first phase of development, from 1992 to 2008, will be referred to as the '*pre-crisis conjuncture*'. The second, third and fourth phases, from 2008 to 2018, will be referred to as the '*post-crisis conjuncture*'. The core objective of this book is to determine the extent to which Britain's model of capitalism in the post-crisis conjuncture embodied a *continuation of* or a *rupture with* the model of capitalism which had been in place throughout the 'pre-crisis conjuncture'. The extent to which institutional or policy change can be identified of course depends on which policy area or institutional complex one isolates in one's analysis (Marsh & Stoker, 2010: 228). Insofar as the existing literature has attempted to examine continuity and change in Britain in the post-crisis period, there has been a tendency to focus on a range of distinct policy spheres in relative isolation from one another. For example, existing research has examined *inter alia* reforms to Britain's post-crisis financial regulatory architecture (Baker, 2013; Bell & Hindmoor, 2015), changes to social policy and public service provision (Grimshaw & Rubery, 2012) and shifts in the strategic positioning of political parties under conditions of fiscal austerity (Hayton, 2013). Whilst these approaches offer valuable accounts of continuity and change in this period, this book advances an analysis of post-crisis British capitalism from a different perspective. Specifically, it deploys a conceptual framework which seeks to identify the ways in which seemingly disparate spheres of social activity are in fact embedded within—and are in turn constitutive of—emergent, relatively unified and integrated *regimes* of capitalist development. This approach is broadly in line with the understanding of political economy as advanced by Andrew Gamble and his collaborators, who propose that, 'social orders and the institutions which make them up need to be studied as *complex wholes* rather than as analytically distinct parts' (cited in Clift, 2014: 5). This commitment to studying the political economy *holistically* requires that we deploy a conceptual framework capable of moving beyond analysis of distinct policy areas studied in isolation from one another. Rather, we must advance a theoretical framework which can identify the emergent properties and underlying tendencies of a given social and economic order.

Within political economy, a number of approaches have been advanced with this basic objective in mind. For example, comparative political economists have attempted to map the distinct 'varieties of capitalism' (VoC) which are in evidence across Western nation states (Hall & Soskice, 2001). The VoC approach draws attention to the ways in which distinct national institutional configurations can give rise to divergent logics of economic development which tend to endure over time. Other approaches of a 'regulationist' orientation have attempted to distinguish between distinct 'regimes of accumulation' whereby underlying economic models become embedded within and effectively stabilised by complementary institutional forms (Aglietta, 1976; Boyer, 1990; Jessop & Sum, 2006; Overbeek, 1989). In each case, the objective is to transcend a narrow focus on distinct policy areas in order to identify the underlying social, economic and institutional mechanisms which give rise to relatively coherent patterns of capitalist development over time.

In this vein, this book draws upon and develops a literature which emerged in the aftermath of the 2008 crisis which I term the *growth model perspective* (Crouch, 2009; Finlayson, 2009; Watson, 2010; see also Engelen et al., 2011). This literature argues that although the British economy generated (seemingly) stable economic growth throughout the pre-crisis conjuncture, it simultaneously incubated a series of deep structural weaknesses which rendered it peculiarly exposed to the 2008 crisis (Hay, 2013; Hay & Payne, 2015). Advocates of this growth model perspective argue that British capitalism had been underpinned by a distinctive—and ultimately unsustainable—dynamic of 'privatised Keynesianism' throughout the pre-crisis conjuncture (Crouch, 2009; Hay, 2013). At its core, this growth model rested upon relative real wage stagnation, financial market liberalisation and asset-price inflation. This gave rise to a situation whereby economic growth became increasingly tied to rising levels of private indebtedness, debt-fuelled consumption and persistent current account deficits (Crouch, 2011; see also Engelen et al., 2011; Stockhammer, 2015). In contrast to dominant narrations of the crisis—which argued that the crash was caused primarily by 'profligate' borrowing on the part of the New Labour government—the growth model perspective argues that the large increase in Britain's budget deficit and public debt levels were symptoms of a deeper failure, namely the country's over-reliance on expanding levels of private debt and on economic activity concentrated in and around the financial services sector (Hay, 2013; see also Streeck, 2014).

The growth model perspective provides us with a good framework through which to identify and analyse the mechanisms which underpinned British capitalism throughout the pre-crisis conjuncture. However, the approach is also limited in a number of respects. In particular, it tends to privilege analytically those forms of state intervention which were 'functional' to—or in other words actively facilitated—the financialisation of the British economy throughout the pre-crisis conjuncture. The growth model perspective tends to focus on state interventions which encouraged finance-led expansion either through macroeconomic policy or through cultivating the emergence of 'financialised subjectivities' amongst citizens (Finlayson, 2009; Langley, 2007; Watson, 2010). As a result, the growth model perspective deploys a highly *limited conception of the state* which fails to account for the ways in which government actors are typically oriented towards securing a range of divergent—and often incompatible—social and political objectives. Between 2000 and 2008, Britain's finance-led growth model was flanked by the largest real terms increases in expenditure on public services in the post-war period (Smith, 2014: 618). This expansion in public spending helped to stabilise British capitalism in a variety of ways, not least through increasing levels of public sector employment and in sustaining aggregate demand in regions which would otherwise have been excluded from the dominant growth dynamic (Ertürk et al., 2011). However, these developments are *not* reducible to the 'logic' of Britain's finance-led growth model. They were the outcome of a range of social and political pressures and strategic considerations on the part of state actors. The growth model perspective—in its current form—is not sufficiently developed to grasp these dynamics.

This book overcomes this limitation by integrating a more robust theory of the state into the growth model perspective. In this regard, the book draws upon and develops the neo-Marxist tradition of state theory (Jessop, 1990). Neo-Marxist state theory begins from the premise that capitalist states are typically driven to simultaneously secure two related—but often contradictory—objectives. First, states must secure the conditions for continued *accumulation* over time (Offe, 1984). Advanced capitalist states are formally separated from the economy in the sense that there are certain (socially determined and often legally codified) limits on the extent to which government can intervene within the 'private sphere' of economic activity. This means that the capitalist state is in essence a *tax state* (Gamble, 2014; O'Connor, 1973). If it is to perform its core functions—for example to provide basic services or to maintain social order—it must ensure that the conditions for continued taxable economic activity are in place. On the other hand, state managers must at the same time secure the conditions for continued *legitimation* over time. This means that government actors—in particular those who operate within the political constraints of the modern democratic state form—are not exclusively concerned with securing continued economic growth. Rather, policymakers are persistently driven to engage in patterns of state intervention which are oriented towards securing a degree of popular support within society. These dual accumulation/legitimation imperatives can in certain conditions complement one another. However, they can also conflict. The analytical implication is that analysis of advanced capitalist state interventions should not—as is the case with the growth model perspective—focus narrowly on the ways in which the state can actively support particular growth models over time. Analysis should also interrogate the ways in which the state is typically oriented towards securing other social and political objectives, including the need to secure legitimation. In turn, analysis should account for how these alternative patterns of interventions can either stabilise or compromise the developmental logic of the dominant growth model.

It is here where the book makes a break with the growth model perspective and offers an alternative conceptual framework for tracing the evolution of British capitalism throughout the pre- and post-crisis conjunctures. The existing growth model perspective focuses on what can be termed the *accumulation strategy* pursued by state managers throughout the pre-crisis conjuncture (Jessop, 1990: 216). It identifies how state intervention throughout this period actively encouraged the development of certain economic sectors and 'financialised' subjectivities over others. However, this means that the *legitimation strategies*—or in Gramscian terms the 'hegemonic projects'—advanced by actors operating within the state remain relatively neglected in the analysis. The result is that the growth model perspective neglects the ways in which core state functions—such as its capacity to impose tax liabilities or to increase social expenditure—are typically deployed in order to secure the support of strategically significant social groups. The growth model perspective therefore misses the ways in which these interventions can 'flank' and stabilise growth models over time. Drawing upon neo-Marxist state theory improves upon the 'growth model' perspective in three ways. First, it offers a more compelling account of how phases of capitalist stability can be secured within a given conjuncture. Second, it allows us to distinguish analytically between forms of state intervention oriented towards facilitating the expansion of a given growth model and forms of state intervention oriented towards securing a popular base of support within society. Third, and crucially, it allows us to identify analytically and to periodise *continuity and change* across different phases of capitalist development in terms of the accumulation and legitimation strategies deployed by state managers (Jessop, 1990; Jessop & Sum, 2006). This reformulated 'growth model' perspective provides us with the conceptual framework around which the subsequent comparative analysis of the political economy of New Labour and the Coalition is organised.

Core Arguments of the Book

This book examines the extent to which British capitalism has been reconfigured since the 2008 crisis. In line with the periodisation outlined above, the book is organised around an examination of two broad periods: the 'pre-crisis' conjuncture (1992–2008) and the 'post-crisis' conjuncture (2008–2018). The core argument is that whilst the Coalition government re-established Britain's pre-crisis growth model, it broke with legitimation strategy which New Labour had advanced in office. This re-embedded a series of structural weaknesses which are likely to shape the future trajectory of British capitalism. The emergence of a distinctive and volatile post-crisis British politics—exemplified by Brexit, May and Corbyn—are symptoms of this deeper structural malaise. Whether these post-crisis developments are likely to lead to transformation or a consolidation of British capitalism remains an open question. In advancing this thesis, five distinct arguments are made throughout the course of the book. It is worthwhile anticipating these briefly here.

1. *New Labour established a 'hybrid' regime of social and economic development which—temporarily—stabilised British capitalism throughout the pre-crisis conjuncture*

New Labour presided over a period of relatively stable economic expansion. In this period, New Labour advanced a distinctive *hybrid* regime of social and economic development. On the one hand, New Labour's approach was underpinned by a finance-led *accumulation strategy*. As argued by advocates of the growth model perspective, the New Labour government sought to embed a model of economic development which systematically privileged the preferences of international creditor institutions whilst further advancing the financialisation of the British economy. On the other hand, New Labour's political economy was also organised around a distinctive—albeit imperfect and limited—'One Nation' *hegemonic project.* This sought to secure and extend New Labour's popular base of support by channelling material concessions and symbolic rewards to the social base. This dimension of the New Labour project was driven by a range of political considerations, including internal party pressures, electoral calculations and a residual commitment to some redistributive social goals. In accordance with this political orientation, New Labour substantially boosted spending on public services from 2000 onwards—in particular on health and education—which resulted in substantially increased levels of public sector and state-supported employment particularly across the ex-industrial regions (Tomlinson, 2012). Additionally, this dynamic was flanked by a series of (often covertly employed) redistributive social policies which channelled resources to low- to middle-income households. These policies played a key role in reducing relative poverty, constraining the growth of income inequality and mitigating the uneven development of 'Anglo-liberal' capitalism throughout the pre-crisis conjuncture (Joyce & Sibieta, 2013). In contrast to existing accounts of New Labour—which have tended to characterise the Blair and Brown governments as *either* 'neoliberal' or 'social democratic'—New Labour established a distinctive *hybrid* regime of social and economic development which effectively, but only temporarily, stabilised Britain's model of capitalism throughout the pre-crisis conjuncture.

2. *The Coalition effectively re-established the conditions for a renewed wave of 'finance-led' growth in Britain, albeit in a modified form*

This conception of New Labour's 'hybrid' regime of development provides us with a benchmark against which to conceptualise continuity and change under the Coalition in the post-crisis conjuncture. To this end, the evolution of the Coalition's economic programme in office is traced in order to establish the extent to which this represented a continuation of or a rupture with the accumulation strategy which had been pursued by New Labour. In this regard, it is shown that from 2010, the Coalition's economic policy was underpinned by two ostensible objectives: to eliminate Britain's budget deficit within one parliament and to 'rebalance' the British economy in favour of exports and savings. However, in each case, the Coalition failed. The Coalition's austerity programme eroded tax receipts and undermined deficit reduction. Growth, when it returned, was driven by rising consumption and the collapse of household savings. At key strategic moments, the Conservative-led government abandoned key elements of its programme in the light of political calculations. The result was that by the end of the parliament, the Coalition had not substantially transformed Britain's finance-led growth model. Rather, it effectively re-established, albeit in a modified form, the basic conditions for a renewed wave of 'privatised Keynesian' growth in the future.

3. *The Coalition deployed a distinctive 'two nations' hegemonic project which aimed to secure a limited but durable base of support for further fiscal consolidation and private sector-led recovery in the future*

Whilst we can identify *continuity* in the re-establishment of Britain's finance-led growth model, the Coalition effectively broke with the legitimation strategy or 'One Nation' hegemonic project which New Labour had advanced in government. In a context of fiscal austerity and reduced tax revenues, the capacity of the Coalition to build support through channelling material concessions and symbolic rewards to the social base was highly constrained. Instead, we can identify the emergence of a distinctive '*two nations*' hegemonic project under the Coalition which sought to secure a limited but durable base of support for its governing programme. The immediate post-crisis context generated a series of relatively novel distributional trends. In particular, the incomes of non-working households were protected relative to 'in-work' households and public sector pay was protected, for a period of time, relative to private sector pay. In response to this, the Coalition successfully constructed and entrenched a series of 'moralised antagonisms' between workers/working-age benefit claimants and private/public sector employees. In this way, the Coalition government sought to secure a limited but durable base of support for its economic and social programme under conditions of fiscal austerity.

4. *The emergent regime of development established under the Coalition has consolidated a series of structural weaknesses and imbalances at the heart of British capitalism. These are likely to destabilise social and economic development in the future*

Taking the above four points together, then, the core argument of this book is as follows: that whilst the Coalition effectively re-established the finance-led growth model which had been placed throughout the pre-crisis conjuncture, it effectively broke with the legitimation strategy which New Labour had pursued in office. This has a number of important implications. First, contrary to the initial claims of the Coalition, British capitalism was not fundamentally 'rebalanced' away from the finance-led growth model which had been in place in the pre-crisis conjuncture. As a result, the structural weaknesses associated with that growth model are likely to endure and even intensify into the future. Second, Britain's pre-crisis model of capitalism had been stabilised—temporarily and imperfectly—by enhanced public expenditure and state-led employment creation (particularly in the ex-industrial regions) as a result of New Labour's 'One Nation' hegemonic project. In contrast, under the Coalition these flanking mechanisms were no longer in place to the same extent by the end of the 2010–2015 parliament. As a result, new forms of capitalist instability, social antagonism and uneven development are likely to emerge within British capitalism in the future.

5. *A distinctive form of post-crisis British politics has emerged since 2015, exemplified by the evolving politics of Brexit, the May government and Corbyn's Labour Party. Whilst each of these contains the potential to precipitate a transformation in British capitalism, profound structural barriers to reform remain*

The final sections of the book examine the period after the Coalition. In 2015, it looked like the Conservatives had effectively contained the fall-out from the 2008 crisis. Britain's finance-led growth model had been re-established and the Conservatives now held a small majority in parliament. However, trouble was bubbling under the surface. Three political developments emerged in this period which set unleashed a period of deep volatility within British capitalism. The emergence of Brexit, the evolution of the May government and the rise of Corbyn's Labour Party together arose out of the deep structural malaise which had set in during Britain's post-crisis conjuncture. Each of these forms of post-crisis British politics promised to transform various aspects of British capitalism. However, profound structural barriers to reform remain in place. Whether post-crisis British politics brings about a transformation or consolidation of Britain's dysfunctional model of capitalism remains an open question. Thinking through the conditions which could bring about a transformation of British capitalism remains a crucial task, both intellectually and politically.

References

Aglietta, M. (1976). *A Theory of Capitalist Regulation: The US Experience.* London: Verso.

Baker, A. (2013). The New Political Economy of the Macroprudential Ideational Shift. *New Political Economy, 18*(1), 112–139.

Bell, S., & Hindmoor, A. (2015). Taming the City? Ideas, Structural Power and the Evolution of British Banking Policy Amidst the Great Financial Meltdown. *New Political Economy, 20*(3), 454–474.

Blyth, M., & Matthijs, M. (2017). Black Swans, Lame Ducks, and the Mystery of IPE's Missing Macroeconomy. *Review of International Political Economy, 24*(2), 203–231.

Boyer, R. (1990). *The Regulation School: A Critical Introduction.* Columbia: Columbia University Press.

Cameron, D. (2015). *David Cameron Speech on the Jobs Miracle.* Retrieved February 16, 2016, from http://press.conservatives.com/post/116631921185/david-cameron-speech-on-the-jobs-miracle.

Clift, B. (2014). *Comparative Political Economy: States, Markets and Global Capitalism.* Basingstoke: Palgrave Macmillan.

Crouch, C. (2009). Privatised Keynesianism: An Unacknowledged Policy Regime. *British Journal of Politics and International Relations, 11*(3), 382–399.

Crouch, C. (2011). *The Strange Non-death of Neoliberalism.* Cambridge: Polity Press.

Engelen, E., Erturk, I., Froud, J., Johal, S., Leaver, A., Moran, M., & Nilsson, A. (2011). *After the Great Complacence: Financial Crisis and the Politics of Reform.* Oxford: Oxford University Press.

Ertürk, I., Froud, J., Johal, S., Leaver, A., Moran, M., & Williams, K. (2011). *City State Against National Settlement UK Economic Policy and Politics After the Financial Crisis.* Manchester. Retrieved from http://scholar.googleusercontent.com/scholar?q=cache:nET8YD5SM50J:scholar.google.com/&hl=en&as_sdt=0,5.

Finlayson, A. (2009). Financialisation, Financial Literacy and Asset-Based Welfare. *The British Journal of Politics & International Relations, 11*(3), 400–421.

Gamble, A. (2014). *Crisis Without End? The Unravelling of Western Prosperity.* Basingstoke: Palgrave Macmillan.

Green, J., & Lavery, S. (2018). After Neoliberalisation? Monetary Indiscipline, Crisis and the State. *Transactions of the Institute of British Geographers, 43*(1), 79–94.

Grimshaw, D., & Rubery, J. (2012). The End of the UK's Liberal Collectivist Social Model? The Implications of the Coalition Government's Policy During the Austerity Crisis. *Cambridge Journal of Economics, 36*(1), 105–126.
Hall, P., & Soskice, D. (2001). *Varieties of Capitalism: The Institutional Foundations of Comparative Advantage*. Oxford: Oxford University Press.
Hay, C. (2013). *The Failure of Anglo-Liberal Capitalism*. Basingstoke: Palgrave Macmillan.
Hay, C., & Payne, A. (2015). *Civic Capitalism*. Cambridge: Polity Press.
Hayton, R. (2013). Conservative Party Statecraft and the Politics of Coalition. *Parliamentary Affairs, 67*(1), 6–24.
Jessop, B. (1990). *State Theory: Putting the Capitalist State in Its Place*. Cambridge: Polity Press.
Jessop, B., & Sum, N.-L. (2006). *Beyond the Regulation Approach*. Cheltenham: Edward Elgar.
Jones, R. (2013). *The UK's Innovation Deficit and How to Repair It* (SPERI Paper No. 6). Sheffield Political Economy Research Institute.
Joyce, R., & Sibieta, L. (2013). An Assessment of Labour's Record on Income Inequality and Poverty. *Oxford Review of Economic Policy, 29*(1), 178–202.
Langley, P. (2007). Uncertain Subjects of Anglo-American Financialization. *Cultural Critique, 65*, 67–91.
Lee, S. (2015). Indebted and Unbalanced: The Political Economy of the Coalition. In M. Beech & S. Lee (Eds.), *The Conservative-Liberal Coalition: Examining the Cameron-Clegg Government* (pp. 16–35). Basingstoke: Palgrave Macmillan.
Marsh, D., & Stoker, G. (2010). *Theory and Methods in Political Science*. Basingstoke: Palgrave Macmillan.
O'Connor, J. (1973). *The Fiscal Crisis of the State*. New York: St. Martin's Press.
Offe, C. (1984). *Contradictions of the Welfare State*. Cambridge: MIT Press.
Overbeek, H. (1989). *Global Capitalism and National Decline*. London: Routledge.
Pabst, A. (2017). Postliberalism: The New Centre Ground of British Politics. *The Political Quarterly, 88*(3), 500–509.
Schmidt, V., & Thatcher, M. (2013). *Resilient Liberalism in Europe's Political Economy*. Cambridge: Cambridge University Press.
Smith, M. (2014). Globalisation and the Resilience of Social Democracy: Reassessing New Labour's Political Economy. *The British Journal of Politics & International Relations, 16*(4), 597–623.
Stockhammer, E. (2015). Rising Inequality as a Cause of the Present Crisis. *Cambridge Journal of Economics, 39*(3), 935–958. https://doi.org/10.1093/cje/bet052.

Streeck, W. (2014). *Buying Time: The Delayed Crisis of Democratic Capitalism*. London: Verso.
Tomlinson, J. (2012). From "Distribution of Industry" to "Local Keynesianism": The Growth of Public Sector Employment in Britain. *British Politics, 7*(3), 204–223.
TUC. (2016). *Trades Union Congress—UK Workers Experienced Sharpest Wage Fall of Any Leading Economy*. TUC Analysis Finds. Retrieved from https://www.tuc.org.uk/economic-issues/labour-market/uk-workers-experienced-sharpest-wage-fall-any-leading-economy-tuc.
Van Reenen, J. (2015). *Austerity: Growth Costs and Post-election Plans*. Centre for Economic Perfomance. Retrieved from cep.lse.ac.uk/pubs/download/ea020.pdf.
Watkins, S. (2016). Oppositions. *New Left Review, 98*, 5–30.
Watson, M. (2010). House Price Keynesianism and the Contradictions of the Modern Investor Subject. *Housing Studies, 25*(3), 413–436.

CHAPTER 2

British Capitalism Before the Crisis

Between 1992 and 2008, British capitalism experienced a phase of relatively stable economic expansion. Inflationary pressures were contained, growth rose consistently, and unemployment remained low across the country. However, under the surface, deep structural weaknesses endured within British capitalism. This chapter engages with a body of literature—the 'growth model perspective'—which argues that Britain's pre-crisis growth model was underpinned by a dangerous dynamic of 'privatised Keynesianism' (Crouch, 2009; Hay, 2013b). This growth model emerged out of the breakdown of the post-war settlement of 'democratic capitalism'. It generated high levels of private debt across the economy which in turn underpinned aggregate demand and economic growth. This rendered the British economy peculiarly vulnerable to the 2008 financial crisis. However, the growth model perspective is underpinned by two weaknesses. First, it deploys a *limited conception of the state* which privileges analytically forms of intervention which were 'functional' to financialisation processes. Second, the growth model perspective struggles to explain how British capitalism was *stabilised* throughout the pre-crisis conjuncture. A broader theory of the state is therefore needed if we are to adequately capture the distinctive regime which underpinned British capitalism throughout the pre-crisis conjuncture.

S. Lavery, *British Capitalism After the Crisis*, Building a Sustainable Political Economy: SPERI Research & Policy, https://doi.org/10.1007/978-3-030-04046-8_2

The Long Transformation of British Capitalism

In the pre-crisis conjuncture, British capitalism was underpinned by a distinctive growth model of 'privatised Keynesianism' (Crouch, 2009). This growth model had its origins in the long transformation of British capitalism which had taken place during the post-war era. Since the crisis of the 1970s, Britain along with other Western capitalist states had experienced the breakdown of what Wolfgang Streeck has termed 'democratic capitalism' (Streeck, 2014). 'Democratic capitalism' refers to the distinctive ensemble of social, political and economic institutions which emerged in the aftermath of the Second World War and which laid the foundations for rapid economic expansion throughout the USA and Western Europe. This settlement was underpinned by a distinctive mode of economic development—characterised elsewhere as a 'Fordist' accumulation regime—which effectively combined mass production with mass consumption (Overbeek, 1989: 55). Productivity increases—driven by an intensified division of labour, 'rational' state planning and the utilisation of new production techniques—generated a 'virtuous' growth dynamic, whereby rising real wages and government expenditure underpinned rising aggregate demand and economic expansion.

This framework represented far more than just a 'technical' economic framework; it was at the same time fundamentally *political* in the sense that it relied upon an unwritten social accord between capital, labour and the state. On the one hand, the organised working class accepted markets and property rights in exchange for a range of democratic rights and social entitlements. This settlement guaranteed citizens a minimum level of social security as well as rising living standards (Streeck, 2011: 10). On the other hand, markets were embedded within a system of social regulation which established definite limits on the legitimate scope of the commodification process (Streeck, 2011: 16). For example, fixed exchange rates and capital controls limited the mobility of speculative capital flows across national borders, the growth of the welfare state softened the disciplinary effect of unemployment, and the development of free 'collective bargaining' arrangements placed limits on capital's control over wage rates and the labour process.

In the immediate post-war period, this framework generated impressive economic growth, full employment and rising living standards across the advanced capitalist societies. In turn, this consolidated the legitimacy of the post-war social order from the perspective of both labour and capital (Streeck, 2014: 79). However, whilst this model of development temporarily *displaced* distributional and social conflict, it did not abolish it permanently. Rather, this regime rested upon a 'forced marriage' between democracy and capitalism (Streeck, 2014: 4). It effectively—but only temporarily—reconciled two competing principles of resource allocation, 'one operating according to marginal productivity…[the] 'free play of market forces', and the other based on social need or entitlement, as certified by the collective choices of democratic politics' (Streeck, 2011: 7). Insofar as democratic capitalism continued to generate economic growth, these latent conflicts could be managed through macroeconomic intervention. However, from the late 1960s onwards, profit rates began to decline rapidly amidst rising inflation, growing turbulence in the international commodity markets, an upsurge in labour militancy and falling rates of private investment. In an effort to restore profitability and to regain control over the labour process, business interests increasingly agitated for policies which would discipline the rising expectations and the political power of the organised working class. As a result, those institutions which had hitherto limited the scope of the market—powerful trade unions, extensive systems of social protection and the public ownership of key firms and sectors—were increasingly subject to politically coordinated retrenchment (Glyn, 2006: 122; Harvey, 2005).

The 2008 crash and its aftermath can be read as the most recent phase in this ongoing, long decomposition of 'democratic capitalism' (Streeck, 2014). Since the late 1970s, 'market justice' has increasingly emerged as the dominant principle of resource allocation. However, attempts to establish and maintain this 'market liberal' distributional framework tend to be hugely disruptive (Polanyi, 2001). As capital progressively extricated itself from the parameters imposed on it by the post-war settlement, government officials were increasingly faced with the question of how to ensure that this process did not provoke a wider legitimation crisis or political crisis of the state (Burnham, 2011; Habermas, 1975). Streeck's argument is that from the mid-1970s onwards, the institution of *money* played a key role in containing the effects of the breakdown of 'democratic capitalism' by displacing the social and distributional conflicts which might otherwise have destabilised this process into the future. On this basis, Streeck periodises capitalist development since the 1970s in terms of three distinctive 'monetary fixes' which have 'bought time' for—or avoided a social crisis of—the emergent market liberal order.

First, from the early 1970s onwards, *inflation* played a key role in temporarily preventing distributional conflicts from undermining the political basis of the state (Streeck, 2014: 33). Since Second World War, successive Western governments had based their legitimacy on securing the conditions for full employment and on ensuring rising living standards for their citizens. Consequently, as economic stagnation began to set in, governments across the West calculated that it would be highly risky to impose deflationary policies on their citizens. Rather than implementing rapid cuts or abandoning their commitment to full employment, governments instead adopted a monetary policy which allowed wage increases to outstrip productivity growth (Streeck, 2014: 32). In the first half of the 1970s, this allowed for relatively high levels of employment to continue and for nominal wages (at least in highly unionised sectors) to be protected in relative terms despite the economic downturn (Sachs & Gordon, 1983: 257). However, this dynamic could not endure indefinitely. Rising inflation devalued national currencies and eroded the confidence of international and domestic creditor institutions. As a result, private investors increasingly withdrew their capital from circulation, compounding the deflationary spiral and increasing the social and political pressures on the Keynesian national state in the process (Jessop, 2002).

By the early 1980s, Western governments—led by the administrations of Ronald Reagan and Margaret Thatcher—began to implement radically deflationary policies (Jessop, Bonnett, Bromley, & Ling, 1988). After the 'Volcker Shock' of 1981, interest rates were hiked further and unemployment rose across Anglo-America (Hall, 1993: 283). Although this served to discipline the wage demands and political power of organised labour, the huge increase in unemployment simultaneously increased pressure on governments' welfare budgets (Farrall, 2006: 272). At the same time, the tax base contracted as corporations and high-income earners successfully agitated for large tax cuts. Consequently, public debt increased rapidly from the late 1970s onwards across the advanced capitalist states (Streeck, 2014: 8). This process benefited holders of capital in two ways. Lower rates of taxation meant that corporations and wealthy households held onto far larger portions of their after-tax income. At the same time, increased levels of public debt meant that these same social groups could lend their savings back to the state—through purchasing government bonds—at a considerable profit (Blyth, 2013; Hager, 2015). Growing *public indebtedness* therefore represented the second 'monetary fix' which emerged in the period after the 1970s, as the costs of rapid deflation were displaced into the future via the public balance sheet (Streeck, 2011: 14).

This mechanism could not be deployed indefinitely. By the late 1980s, government deficit and debt levels had ballooned. International creditors increasingly began to question the creditworthiness of sovereign debt (Streeck, 2014: 36). There were also concerns that large levels of government borrowing would 'crowd out' private investment by artificially raising the cost of credit. As a result, by the early 1990s, Western governments—led by Bill Clinton in the USA and by John Major in Britain—set out to reduce their budget deficits through further rounds of expenditure cuts. This programme of fiscal consolidation could have provoked a social crisis, not least because the substantial cuts proposed occurred in a context of constrained wage growth and growing inequality. As such, fiscal consolidation could have seriously undermined household spending power and aggregate demand. However, once again, a 'monetary fix' came to the rescue. As deficit reduction was implemented across Britain and America, the systemic importance of the financial sector—which had already expanded rapidly throughout the 1980s—increased further still (Streeck, 2011: 17). Thus, although public debt as proportion of GDP was held relatively constant or even declined across Anglo-America in the 1990s and 2000s, total debt continued to rise rapidly, driven by huge increases in financial services and household debt. The 'delayed crisis of democratic capitalism' thus entered a third phase whereby rising *private indebtedness* increasingly came to underpin rising consumption and economic growth. These distributional shifts—as we shall see in the following section—formed the backdrop to the regime of 'privatised Keynesianism' which formed the core of Britain's growth model in the pre-crisis conjuncture (Crouch, 2009).

As the above summary suggests, Streeck's argument traces the prolonged *decomposition* of a relatively stable institutional order—what he terms 'democratic capitalism'. This captures what has been referred to elsewhere as the 'deconstructive' elements of the restructuring process which followed the 1970s crisis (Cafruny & Ryner, 2003). However, this process was of course flanked by and was closely related to the emergence of an alternative, more 'constructive' political programme: that of *neoliberalisation* (Brenner, Peck, & Theodore, 2010; Peck, 2010). The meaning of 'neoliberalism' is hugely contested and has generated a gargantuan academic literature. The concept will be engaged with at greater length in the following chapter. However, for present purposes, we can state three interrelated distributional shifts which are commonly associated with neoliberalisation processes and which are of particular relevance to the argument of this chapter. First, neoliberalisation has been associated with a declining 'wage share'—the proportion of overall output which goes to workers—across the advanced capitalist states (Bengtsson & Ryner, 2014). For example, across Europe, the 'wage share' fell from 72.5% in the early 1980s to 63.3% in 2007 (Stockhammer, 2011: 10). Second, this distributional shift was linked to a marked decline in the power of organised labour across the advanced capitalist economies (Machin, 2004). Third, there was a rapid growth of financialisation from the 1980s onwards, understood as the increasing role of 'financial motives, financial markets, financial actors and financial institutions in the operation of the domestic and international economies' (Epstein, 2005: 3; Krippner, 2011).

In combination, these distributional processes produced a structural shortfall in aggregate demand across the Western economies (Crotty, 2000). As real wages slowed relative to productivity growth, this created a conundrum for policymakers seeking to shore-up the emergent market liberal order: How would economic growth continue as domestic demand was constrained through real wage repression? Two distinctive responses emerged in response to this conundrum. Some countries—notably Germany and other Northern European states—increasingly came to rely upon externally induced demand through increasing exports (Johnston & Regan, 2016). Whilst wage rates were repressed relative to productivity growth in these 'export-led' economies, growth was achieved through generating large trade and current account surpluses (Crouch, 2009: 384). Other countries—in particular the USA and Britain—pursued 'debt-led' growth models (Stockhammer, 2012: 63). Whilst real wage growth fell in these economies relative to productivity—for example, in the USA, output per hour increased by 2.24% per annum between 1990 and 2007 whilst average hourly earnings increased by only 0.49%—domestic demand was increasingly sustained through burgeoning current account deficits and through rising levels of private indebtedness (Kotz, 2009: 17; Stockhammer, 2011: 20). The rise of neoliberalism and the corresponding decline of 'democratic capitalism' therefore produced two distinctive but interdependent growth models across the advanced capitalist states in the pre-crisis conjuncture (Stockhammer, 2011: 20). Britain's regime of privatised Keynesianism should be understood as the articulation of one such 'debt-led' growth model under a distinctive set of conjunctural conditions. It is to the key features of Britain's pre-crisis growth model of 'privatised Keynesianism' that we shall now turn.

Privatised Keynesianism in Britain

Between 1992 and 2008, the British economy experienced a period of relatively stable economic expansion. For advocates of the growth model perspective, this was generated by a distinctive regime of 'privatised Keynesianism' (Gamble, 2011: 47; Watson, 2010: 415). The core claim of the 'privatised Keynesianism' thesis is that in a context of restrained real wage growth and public expenditure, private debt increasingly became a driver of aggregate demand (Crouch, 2009: 390). The emergence of 'privatised Keynesian' growth model emerged out of the broader decomposition of democratic capitalism across the Western world outlined in the previous section. However, its emergence was also shaped by a series of specific dynamics which had taken root in Britain since the crisis of the 1970s.

Structural Shift from Manufacturing to Services

Since the 1970s, British capitalism underwent a marked shift away from manufacturing and towards services (Coutts, Glyn, & Rowthorn, 2007). In 1983—in the wake of the first Thatcher government's first squeeze on domestic industry—Britain became a net importer of manufactured goods for the first time in over two hundred years (Coates, 2001: 44). The 'shock therapy' of monetarism—pushed through with a combination of high interest rates, the abolition of exchange controls and a tightening of the public finances—resulted in a 17% increase in the real exchange rate (Keegan, 1985: 36). This hit exporters particularly hard as credit conditions tightened and the competitiveness of industrial exports weakened abroad. As a result, manufacturing output fell by 18% between 1979 and 1981 (Landesman & Snell, 1989: 3). This squeeze on manufacturing output continued throughout the Thatcher period, with investment in manufacturing falling over this period. By 1990, the number of people employed in manufacturing in Britain had declined by 30% compared to 1979 (Coates, 2005: 8).

This structural shift away from manufacturing and towards services continued between 1992 and 2007 under the Major and Blair governments. For example, whilst manufacturing amounted to 20% of total British output in 1992, by 2007 its contribution had declined to 12% (Coates, 2013: 44). This decline in manufacturing output was paralleled by an increased shedding of jobs in the manufacturing sector. Indeed, employment in manufacturing contracted more rapidly under New Labour than under the previous Conservative governments, with an annual average contraction of 3.5% each year under Blair compared to 2.5% a year under the Conservatives (Coutts et al., 2007: 5). This squeeze on manufacturing in the 1990s and 2000s was caused *inter alia* by the continuation of a high exchange rate regime and by the dominance of short-term lending in the UK's capital markets as opposed to long-term lending targeted at productive investment (Coates & Hay, 2001; Engelen et al., 2011: 190; Glyn & Wood, 2001: 52; Hutton, 2011). This led to an increasing deficit on trade in goods—a trend which was only partly offset by a surplus on the balance of trade in services (House of Commons, 2012: 5). The result of this was that the overall trade deficit increased by a factor of eleven throughout the 1990s and 2000s, from £3.3 billion in 1992 to £37.6 billion in 2007 (House of Commons, 2012: 14).

Relatively Stagnant Wage Growth

In the absence of export-led growth and with an ongoing deterioration in the current account balance, the British economy became increasingly dependent on domestic consumption throughout the 1990s and 2000s (CBI, 2011: 11; Kitson & Wilkinson, 2007: 811; Lansley, 2011: 156). However, this growing reliance on domestic consumption took place against a backdrop of relatively stagnant wage growth. As Fig. 2.1 shows, from the late 1970s onwards, real wage growth in Britain successively slowed year-on-year. Whilst real wage growth averaged 2.9% per annum in the 1970s and 1980s, this slowed to 1.5% in the 1990s and dropped again to 1.2% throughout the 2000s (ONS, 2014: 3). With the reduced bargaining power of trade unions (Glyn, 2006: 122; Machin, 1997), the continuation of a regime of flexible labour markets and the continuing growth of low pay, low productivity service sector work, real wages continued along a downwards trajectory throughout the pre-crisis conjuncture (Coates, 2001: 91).

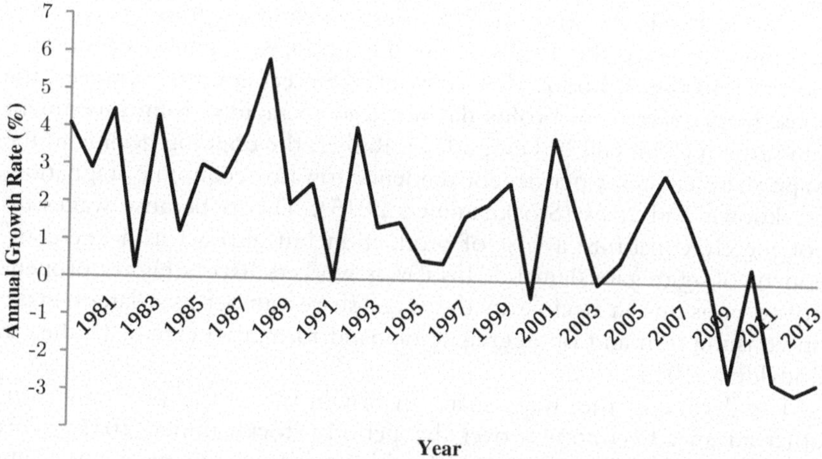

Fig. 2.1 UK real wage growth (1979–2013) (*Source* Office for national statistics [ONS, 2014]. Average weekly earnings deflated by RPI, percent change on the same quarter a year ago. Each interval point refers to Q1 of each year)

Declining 'Wage Share' and Rising Inequality

This slowdown in real wage growth contributed to a decline in the 'wage share'—the proportion of national income which accrues to labour—in Britain as in other advanced capitalist economies (Lansley, 2011: 41; Stockhammer, 2011). During the long boom of the 1950s and 1960s, and until the end of the 1970s, the wage share hovered at around 60% of national income (ibid.). This was of course partly the result of deliberate macroeconomic policymaking, as politicians sought to pump-prime the economy in order to secure full employment and rising living standards. It was also a reflection of the power of organised labour to secure wage increases broadly in line with productivity increases under the post-war Keynesian regime (Jessop, 2002). However, from the 1980s onwards, this structural coupling between productivity and wages began to unravel, and the wage share began what has been termed a 'three-decade long descent' in Britain (Lansley, 2011: 41). By 1996, it had fallen by 9% to a post-war low of 51%, recovering only slightly to 53% by 2008 (ibid.). The effect of this was that throughout the 1990s, 'wage-earners as a group were receiving around seven per cent less of national income – the equivalent of some £100 billion a year – than they were in the post-war decades' (ibid.).

This decline in the wage share has been a defining feature of economic development since the 1980s across the advanced capitalist economies. Contrary to the orthodox view of mainstream economists, however, the consequent increase in profits did not lead to rapidly rising investment and growth (Duménil & Lévy, 2011). Rather, the ongoing decline in the wage share creates a permanent tendency towards economic stagnation, breakdown and crisis (Stockhammer, 2015). This is because wages do not merely constitute a cost of production but also act as a key component of aggregate demand. Insofar as workers have a higher propensity to consume, a decline in the wage share can act as a latent brake on consumption and on aggregate demand formation (Hein, Dodig, & Budyldina, 2014).

The decline of the 'wage share' in Britain was not as pronounced in other advanced economies over this period (Stockhammer, 2015). This is where a second feature of British economic development was crucially important in constraining aggregate demand formation throughout the pre-crisis conjuncture: the growing inequality of earnings from employment across the income distribution (Plunkett, 2011). The wage share is a broad measure which takes into account the incomes of employees working in very different sectors and on very different pay scales. For example, it includes the wages of workers located in traditionally 'low pay' sectors such as food and retail as well as high-pay workers such as chief executives and senior managers. This is particularly important in the case of the UK, since 'between 1978 and 1990 household income inequality in the UK rose much more than in any other OECD state' (Glyn & Wood, 2001: 56). As a result, the earnings of workers in the top tenth of the income distribution increased substantially throughout the 1990s and 2000s relative to the median (Bell & Van Reenen, 2010). This meant that the overall fall in the wage share was experienced more sharply at the bottom of the income distribution (Lansley, 2011: 49). As a result, this can 'make the fall in the wage share look more modest than it is in reality for the majority of the wage earners' (Onaran, 2012). The implication of this is that 'the falling wage share has not been evenly distributed across the earnings range but has been borne by middle and lower paid employees. The bottom three-fifths of earners have thus faced a sustained double-edged squeeze – a shrinking share of a diminishing pool' (Lansley, 2011: 49). These trends underscore the importance of looking at the relationship between *median*-income earners and productivity rates. Indeed, focusing on median-income earners reveals that 'the wages of middle income Britain grew by an average of just 56% between 1978 and 2008, despite GDP increasing by 108% over the same period, and for some workers real income growth was far less' (Smith, 2013). From the 1970s up to 1990, median hourly earnings broadly followed increases in labour productivity. However, in the early 1990s there was a 'decoupling' between labour productivity and median wages in Britain. This meant that increasingly middle-income earners in Britain gained a smaller share of overall output.

Rising Household Debt

Between 1992 and 2007, Britain's growth model therefore internalised two pressures which had the potential to severely restrict aggregate demand: a poor export performance and a deteriorating current account balance, on the one hand, and relatively stagnant income growth resulting in a declining wage share, on the other. The privatised Keynesian thesis argues that private debt increasingly 'filled-in' for these demand shortfalls within Britain throughout the pre-crisis conjuncture (Crouch, 2011; Hay, 2013b). By looking at the data, we can see that private debt did indeed become increasingly prevalent within the British economy between 1992 and 2008. For example, household debt as a proportion of GDP stood at approximately 60% in 1987. By 1992, this figure had increased to around 70% and it remained broadly at this level until 1999. However, there was then a marked rise in household debt-to-GDP ratios between 1999 and 2007, with the figure increasing to 120% of GDP over this period (ibid.). There was also a corresponding increase in household debt as a proportion of gross disposable income. Whilst household debt stood at 100% of gross disposable income in 2000, by 2005 it had increased to approximately 150% (IMF, 2008: 18; see also Smith, 2013). There is clear evidence, then, that household debt levels increased substantially in the pre-crisis conjuncture in Britain, both as a proportion of GDP and as a proportion of gross disposable income. Two principal factors can be identified as being behind this trend. On the one hand, there was a growing demand for cheap credit (Montgomerie, 2007: 9). As gross disposable incomes stagnated—particularly for low- to middle-income earners between 2003 and 2008—there was an in-built incentive to borrow at historically low interest rates in order to maintain living standards. On the other hand, there was a boom in the *supply* of cheap credit, partly as a result of the recycling of surpluses from China and the East and partly as a result of fierce competition between creditor institutions driving commercial interest rates down (Saull, 2012).

Mortgage Equity Withdrawal and Consumption

Rising household indebtedness and appreciating property prices also played an important role in sustaining consumption throughout the pre-crisis conjuncture (Engelen et al., 2011; Hay, Smith, & Watson, 2006: 20; Watson, 2010). Mortgage credit typically accounts for approximately 80% of household debt (Stockhammer, 2012: 53). The increase in the household debt ratio from 1992 to 2008 was largely driven by households seeking to gain access to a rapidly appreciating property market. A number of factors drove this dynamic throughout the pre-crisis conjuncture. First, between 1992 and 2007, consumer price inflation fell in Britain to comparatively low and stable levels, partly as a result of counter-inflationary monetary policy but also as a result of the influx of cheap imports from China and East Asia. This created an environment in which a sustained drop in interest rates could take place, reducing the cost of borrowing for consumers and creating a powerful incentive to accumulate assets in the housing market through mortgage credit (Hay et al., 2006: 21). Second, intense competition between mortgage providers coupled with New Labour's 'light touch' regulatory approach to financial services helped to facilitate conditions under which lending conditions slackened considerably. This led to a plethora of lending practices—including rising loan-to-value ratios, a loosening in borrower eligibility requirements and ever-smaller deposit requirements—which significantly relaxed credit conditions and encouraged ever-widening access to mortgage finance. The result of this was that by the end of the New Labour period, there was a growing tendency for households to take out mortgages which were greater in value than the current valuation of the property, with an expectation that future price rises would make this a profitable investment (Watson, 2010: 418). This in turn fuelled higher levels of demand for mortgage credit which subsequently increased the upwards pressure on house prices throughout this period.

This shift towards increasing mortgage indebtedness played a crucial systemic role in sustaining British capitalism in the pre-crisis conjuncture. As Watson has written, 'private dwellings [became] quasi-public spaces positioned at the apex of political attempts to reproduce stable conditions suited to the expansion of wealth held privately within the economy' (Watson, 2010: 414). The systemic role played by rising house prices was that they effectively linked together rising levels of private indebtedness, aggregate demand and consumption. Whilst in 1995 the average house price stood at £65,000, by 2007 this had increased by over 300% to an average of £200,000 (Hamnett, 2010: 114). This increase in the value of the housing stock did not only augment the wealth portfolios of British homeowners; it also created a new reservoir of equity upon which homeowners could draw to fuel current consumption (Engelen et al., 2011: 208). Colin Hay has outlined the key link between rising house prices, equity release and consumption in some detail:

> Consider, for instance, the situation in November 2006 when the average house price in the UK topped £200,000 for the first time. At that point average annual earnings were about £30,000 and house prices were increasing at an annual rate of 11 per cent. In effect, the wealth effect associated with house price inflation was the equivalent of three quarters of pre-tax annual average earnings. Unremarkably, for many this proved an irresistible incentive to release equity to fuel consumption… such credit-based consumption was, between 2004 and 2006, typically worth between 4 and 6 per cent of GDP—or, in other words, responsible in and of itself for keeping the UK economy in growth at what most would see as a relatively high point in the economic cycle. (Hay, 2009: 469)

As mortgagers accumulated housing equity—that is as the value of their homes exceeded their outstanding mortgage debt—this led to a substantial 'wealth effect'. This allowed mortgagers to borrow against the rising value of their property in order to fuel current consumption (Hay & Wincott, 2012: 125). CRESC have calculated that of equity withdrawn in 2008, 40–50% of gross equity release was used to fuel current consumption (Ertürk et al., 2011: 33). The result of this was that, 'in the years of the Blair premiership (1997–2007), the real value of equity withdrawals was larger than the increase in gross domestic product (GDP) and in every year from 2002 to 2007 the value of housing equity withdrawal was at or above 4%' (Engelen et al., 2011: 208). This emphasis on the housing market as a source of funds for private consumption has been described by Hay as one of the key drivers of the 'Anglo-liberal' growth model (Berry & Hay, 2016: 3; see also Crouch, 2009: 391). Hay continues, 'this process of equity release…has been responsible to a significant extent for the UK's sustained period of personal debt-financed consumer-led economic growth since 1992' (Hay, 2009: 470).

Financial Market Deregulation

Easy access to credit for households and firms was an essential component of Britain's growth model in the pre-crisis conjuncture. One crucial precondition of this dynamic was the deregulation of finance and the liberalisation of capital markets across Anglo-America (Krippner, 2011; Stockhammer, 2011: 20). In Britain, the abolition of exchange controls (1979), the ending of direct control over bank lending (1980), followed by the removal of restrictions on Building Societies' lending capacities (1986) all contributed to a decline in the cost of credit for households and firms (Aoki, Proudman, & Vlieghe, 2002: 4). This trend continued throughout the 1990s and 2000s, such that the Bank of England wrote in its 2001 inflation report that, 'competition in retail credit markets has intensified in recent years which, together with product innovation, may have widened the availability of credit and reduced its price' (Bank of England, 2001: 5). In addition, financial market deregulation also played a crucial role in sustaining the international context within which Britain's growth model was embedded. The large current account deficits accumulated in Anglo-America over this period were possible only insofar as foreign creditors were willing to finance these deficits. In other words, 'debt-led' growth was possible only insofar as the export-led economies were willing to recycle the large surpluses which they had accumulated through capital markets into the debt-led economies (Stockhammer, 2011: 20). In addition, the UK's 'light touch' regulation of the financial sector led to a huge increase in corporate debt. Between 2000 and 2008, 'declared UK bank liabilities rose by 151 per cent' whilst by the end of New Labour's period in office, the UK had the highest private debt of the G7 economies (Thompson, 2013: 479).

Britain's Finance-Led Growth Model and the 2008 Crisis

The steady expansion of British capitalism came to an abrupt halt in 2008. In the immediate aftermath of the crisis, politicians in Britain advanced two competing narratives which claimed to identify the cause of—and attribute blame for—the crisis which had gripped the British economy (Hay, 2011: 24). The first narrative—promoted in particular by the incumbent Labour government under Gordon Brown—argued that the downturn had been caused by an 'external shock' emanating from the international financial markets. The 'exogenous' nature of the crisis implied that the government could not be held responsible for the downturn (Thompson, 2009: 521). According to this argument, the public finances had been in good shape under New Labour. Net public debt stood at 36.5% of GDP, and the budget deficit stood at 2.4% of GDP on the eve of the crisis (Ussher, 2010: 113). Since these debt and deficit levels were not high by historical standards and fell broadly within the Treasury's framework of 'prudent' fiscal rules (Keegan, 2003), it was argued that the crisis was caused neither by New Labour's profligacy nor by structural weaknesses within the British economy. Rather, the crisis was caused by 'exogenous' factors—namely the implosion of the subprime mortgage market in the USA and the subsequent cessation of inter-bank lending on international credit markets (Brown, 2008; Buller & Lindstrom, 2013: 400).

The second crisis narrative—promoted in particular by the Conservative Party under David Cameron and the then-Shadow Chancellor George Osborne—sought to place the blame for the crisis directly at the door of the incumbent Labour government (Cameron, 2010; see also Gamble, 2010a: 652). Specifically, the Conservatives argued that Labour had been imprudent in office, recklessly compromising the public finances by funding unsustainable expansions in public spending (Kerr, Byrne, & Foster, 2011: 203). This, so this narrative went, led to a crippling debt burden which in turn produced deep imbalances at the heart of Britain's economic model (Osborne, 2010). Labour's 'debt crisis' was therefore identified as a principal cause of the recession (The Conservative Party, 2009). This narrative was of considerable political utility to the Conservative opposition insofar as it allowed the Party to further undermine the image of Brown as a credible custodian of the public finances (Gamble, 2010b; Hay, 2011: 24). This ensured that the Conservatives enjoyed a decisive political advantage over their opponents in the run-up to the 2010 general election.

Advocates of the 'privatised Keynesianism' thesis argue that both of these characterisations ignore deep structural weaknesses which underpinned British capitalism throughout the pre-crisis conjuncture (Crouch, 2009; Hay, 2013a; see also Gamble, 2014). As Colin Hay has argued, the 2008 crisis was not simply caused by an 'external' shock or by profligate spending on the part of the New Labour government. Rather, the 'privatised Keynesian' growth model which had come to dominate British capitalism was to blame. The frailties of this growth model are numerous (Christensen, Shaxson, & Wigan, 2016). Britain's exposure to turbulence in the international financial markets had been greatly heightened by the policy of successive UK governments to consolidate the role of the City of London as an international financial hub and as the leading economic sector within Britain. Under Blair and Brown, the financial services sector grew rapidly, such that by the end of New Labour's period in office the UK had the highest private debt of the G7 economies (Thompson, 2013: 477). Consumption had emerged as a key driver of growth, but this had become increasingly tied to a rapidly appreciating housing market (Montgomerie & Büdenbender, 2015; Watson, 2010). This dependence on rapid asset (particularly house) price inflation meant that the British economy was peculiarly exposed to a downturn in international credit conditions. In addition, the revenue base of the state had become increasingly dependent on tax receipts generated from within the financial services sector, associated ancillary services and from consumption associated with this dynamic of credit expansion (Hay, 2013a: 9). As a result, by 2007 the British economy had, 'high and steeply rising mortgage and general household debt and rapid house price appreciation… [a] banking sector… reliant on wholesale funding (and hence more susceptible to the freezing-up of interbank lending)…and…a large current account deficit' (Hay, 2013a: 6). Together, these *internal* structural weaknesses rendered Britain peculiarly exposed to the 2008 crash and the recession which followed.

Limitations of the Growth Model Perspective

Although the 'privatised Keynesianism' thesis provides a useful framework through which to understand pre-crisis British capitalism, this perspective is also limited in a number of respects. First, the growth model perspective struggles to explain how *stability* was secured throughout the pre-crisis conjuncture. Insofar as it attempts to explain how stability was secured throughout this period, the growth model perspective tends to appeal to mechanisms which were *internal* to the finance-led growth model itself. As such, it tends to miss the ways in which alternative mechanisms were crucial to stabilising Britain's pre-crisis model of capitalism. Second, and relatedly, the literature employs a *limited conception of the state* in the sense that it analytically privileges forms of state intervention which were 'functional' to—or in other words actively facilitated—the financialisation of the British economy throughout the pre-crisis conjuncture. As a result, the literature tends to understate the role that alternative modes of state intervention—in particular the expansion of spending on public services in New Labour's second and third terms—played in stabilising, legitimising and sustaining British capitalism throughout the pre-crisis conjuncture.

Finance-Led Growth 'from above'

Many advocates of the growth model perspective, such as Crouch, Hay and Streeck, focus on the dynamics of finance-led growth models 'from above' or at the macro-scale of analysis (Crouch, 2011; Hay, 2013b; Streeck, 2014). Their work shares three broad premises. First, as we have seen, all three deploy the conception of 'privatised Keynesianism' to characterise Britain's pre-crisis growth model. Second, each therefore attributes a central role to rising *private indebtedness* as essential to (temporarily) resolving difficulties which otherwise might have acted as a drag on economic growth in the pre-crisis conjuncture. Third, each consequently tends to emphasise how financialisation—the growing importance of financial market institutions and the expansion of credit to firms and households—drove economic expansion throughout this period (Epstein, 2005: 5). Fourth, insofar as these contributions identify a relation between *the state* and Britain's pre-crisis growth model, they tend to analytically privilege forms of governmental intervention which actively extended and consolidated the above three 'financialisation' processes.

Crouch's depiction of privatised Keynesianism essentially relies upon an under-consumptionist premise (Bleaney, 1976). Crouch argues that wage constraint and welfare residualism throughout the neoliberal period negatively impacted on workers' spending power and on their economic security. These trends acted as a latent brake on consumption and on economic growth. As a result, Britain's finance-led growth model would have been undermined were it not for one crucial dynamic: the rapid expansion of private debt to households and firms from the late 1980s onwards (Crouch, 2009: 390). As Crouch writes, 'two things came together to rescue the neo-liberal model from the instability that would otherwise have been its fate: the growth of credit markets for poor and middle income people, and of derivatives and futures markets among the very wealthy' (Crouch, 2011: 114). Crouch goes on to argue that 'there was [therefore] a *market* solution' to neoliberalism's tendency to produce structural shortfalls of aggregate demand (Crouch, 2008: 482).

This argument undoubtedly captures a crucial aspect of pre-crisis British capitalism. However, there is a potentially serious shortfall in Crouch's formulation. Private debt expansion for Crouch served two related functions. First, it played a crucial *systemic role* in underpinning aggregate demand and economic growth. In Crouch's terms, privatised Keynesianism (temporarily) satisfied 'capitalism's own need for confident mass consumers' (Crouch, 2009: 382). Second, however, this expansion of credit also played a crucial *legitimation* function; it satisfied 'democracy's need for stability for people's lives' (ibid.). In the absence of wage increases, financial liberalisation and easy access to credit became 'collective goods' for citizens who were seeking to sustain their living standards and gain access to a (rapidly appreciating) housing market (ibid.: 394). As such, 'the collective and individual interests of everyone [became] tied to the financial markets' (Crouch, 2011: 116). The promise of rising living standards and continued access to consumer goods do indeed remain crucial sources of legitimation within advanced capitalist societies—and particularly within Anglo-America (Montgomerie, 2007). The problem is that Crouch's account of the role of the state in sustaining the regime of 'privatised Keynesianism' stops at this point. This is because—according to Crouch—the autonomy of the nation state had been largely 'eroded' by the late 1980s as a result of globalisation (Crouch, 2004, 2009: 388). The state's role is relatively passive in Crouch's formulation; it is acknowledged insofar as it enacts policies in line with the preferences of international creditor institutions, for example through attracting inwards investment or through preventing 'capital flight' by implementing counter-inflationary policy or by pump-priming asset markets in a situation where prices slump (ibid.: 392). As a result, the forms of state intervention which Crouch does highlight are largely 'functional' to the reproduction requirements of the dominant finance-led growth model.

This argument is underpinned by a limited theory of the state. The legitimacy of Britain's pre-crisis model of capitalism did not depend only on the expansion of private credit to workers and the growth of complex financial derivatives for the wealthy. Rather, as shall be argued in the following two chapters, discretionary government interventions played a critical role in channelling material concessions and symbolic rewards to social groups who might otherwise have been excluded from the benefits of 'privatised Keynesian' expansion. Furthermore, these interventions were not just the result of external pressures from international creditor institutions or the 'demands' of the global market. They were driven by a range of internal party political and electoral pressures which led New Labour to expand state spending substantially throughout the pre-crisis conjuncture. The proposition that 'privatised Keynesianism' was the key mechanism which secured the legitimacy of Britain's growth model is therefore incomplete: alternative patterns of state intervention were also crucial to stabilising and legitimising British capitalism throughout the pre-crisis conjuncture.

This tendency to privilege analytically forms of state intervention which were 'functional' to financialisation processes is also evident in Hay's account of privatised Keynesianism in Britain (Hay, 2013a; Hay & Wincott, 2012). Hay emphasises the way in which the ceding of operational independence to the Bank of England, the emergence of a 'low interest rate, low inflation equilibrium' and the 'liberalising' disposition of Anglo-liberal policymaking elites were crucial preconditions of the emergence of Britain's pre-crisis growth model (Hay, 2013a: 11). However, Hay's formulation remains incomplete and stands in need of further development. As was the case with Crouch, his focus on the relationship between state intervention and financialisation processes means that he understates the way in which alternative logics of state intervention played a crucial role in sustaining Britain's pre-crisis model of capitalism.

This can be seen if we consider the remarkable *durability and stability* of Britain's model of capitalism throughout the pre-crisis conjuncture. Between 1992 and 2007, Britain experienced a period of sustained economic growth and falling unemployment. As will be argued in the following chapter, such periods of relatively stable expansion cannot be explained through an appeal to 'economic' variables alone. Rather, as argued by regulation theorists, stable phases of accumulation can take place only insofar as these processes are embedded within a broader social framework which complements and stabilises economic expansion over time (Jessop, 2013). The implication of this is that when we interrogate different phases of capitalist development, we need to ask the question: What were the specific institutional complexes, social relations and patterns of state intervention which made stable growth possible throughout the conjuncture in question? It is here where the growth model perspective offers only a limited and partial answer. Hay's argument implicitly appeals to two channels through which 'privatised Keynesian' growth was stabilised. First, he attributes the durability of pre-crisis British capitalism to processes and mechanisms which were largely *internal* to the dominant finance-led growth model. For example, he writes, 'for so long as a low inflation-low interest rate equilibrium persisted, a virtuous and seemingly self-sustained growth dynamic endured. This is what drove the growth model' (Hay, 2013a: 13). He goes on to state that, 'it appeared that a virtuous cycle had been established, in which the preconditions of growth were mutually reinforcing' (Hay, 2013a: 12). Hay identifies a number of specific mechanisms which ensured that stable accumulation could continue throughout this period. For example, he points out that a sustained period of low interest rates created a disincentive for households to save. This—in a context of easily available credit—drove more individuals to take on mortgages, which in turn drove up the value of the housing market (Hay, 2013a: 11). This trajectory of rapid house price inflation further boosted the wealth effect for homeowners, raising their consumption levels and driving economic growth. As such, insofar as Hay seeks to account for the relative stability and (temporary) success of 'Anglo-liberal' growth, he appeals to mechanisms which were largely *internal* to the finance-led growth model. Alternative patterns of state intervention are largely excluded from the analysis.

The argument here is not that state-facilitated financialisation was not in evidence throughout this period. It clearly was—and these dynamics were clearly hugely important. However, Hay's focus on the relation between (state-facilitated) credit expansion, the housing market and equity-fuelled consumption leads him to understate the key role that alternative logics of state intervention played in incorporating subordinate social groups into the dominant growth model. To briefly take two examples, the consolidation and expansion of 'privatised Keynesianism' in the 2000s was paralleled by the largest real terms expansion in spending on public services—in particular on health and education—in the post-war period (Smith, 2014: 618). As a result, 700,000 new jobs were created in the public sector under New Labour (Cribb, Disney, & Sibieta, 2014: 7). Similarly, (relative) child poverty rates fell from 3.4 million in 1998 to 2.3 million in 2010, largely as a result of targeted tax credits and through the deployment of various redistributive mechanisms (Hope, 2015). However, these developments cannot be explained by the 'internal' developmental logic of 'privatised Keynesianism' alone. Rather, as will be argued in the following two chapters, these developments were driven by a distinctive legitimation strategy, or 'One Nation' hegemonic project, under New Labour (Jessop, 1990). This dynamic sought to channel (to a limited extent) material concessions and symbolic rewards to social groups which might otherwise have been excluded from the dividend associated with finance-led growth. At various points, Hay does acknowledge the way in which privatised Keynesian growth was flanked and 'supported by high levels of public expenditure' (Hay, 2013a: 12). However, after pointing this out, he immediately returns to the 'basic precondition' of finance-led accumulation: namely 'easy access to credit linked to a rising property market'. The danger is that Hay's analysis of Britain's pre-crisis growth model isolates those forms of state intervention which were 'functional' to financialisation processes whilst downplaying those counter-tendencies which were essential to securing its stability. In order to further develop the growth model perspective, then, the conception of *the state* and its relationship to Britain's growth model needs to be developed further. This alternative conceptualisation will be offered in the following chapter.

Finance-Led Growth 'from below'

A second current within the growth model perspective views pre-crisis British capitalism 'from below' and is best represented by contributions from Alan Finlayson, Paul Langley and Watson (Finlayson, 2008, 2009; Langley, 2007, 2008; Watson, 2009a, 2009b, 2010, 2013). This literature argues that financialisation is not simply a 'macro-structural' phenomenon, driven, for example, by the globalisation of 'finance capital' or by increased capital flows across national borders (Finlayson, 2009: 402; Langley, 2007: 7). Rather, financialisation is conceived as a process which involves the cultivation of distinctive 'investor subjectivities' at what could be termed the *micro-foundational* scale (Finlayson, 2009: 402; Langley, 2007: 75; Watson, 2010: 415). With its focus on the promotion and development of 'investor subjects', the literature seeks to capture the way in which individuals increasingly conceive of themselves as 'savers' or 'investors' and change their 'everyday' practices and spending habits in accordance with these roles (Watson, 2008: 584; see also French, Leyshon, & Wainwright, 2011: 804). However, this approach does not only seek to *describe* these 'micro-foundational' financialisation processes. It also aims to explain how the construction and expansion of everyday 'investor subjectivities' reinforces unequal power relations and contributes to the emergent structure of global financial markets (Langley, 2008; see also Seabrooke & Hobson, 2007).

The literature makes two broad arguments in this regard. First, whilst government departments, financial sector institutions and consultancy firms have presented the growth of consumer credit and spiralling mortgage debt as instruments which 'empower' citizens, post-structuralists argue that the growth of these instruments tends to (re)produce unequal power relations and entrenches new forms of social control (Finlayson, 2009: 415; Langley, 2007). For example, systems of 'asset-based welfare' (ABW)—where citizens are encouraged/disciplined to provide for their future welfare needs through securing access to the stock and property markets—are *presented* as essential means to achieving 'security' and independence from the state in later life (Prabhakar, 2008; Watson, 2010: 416). However, this 'liberation' from dependence on government welfare (e.g. through reliance on the state pension) simultaneously reinforces new patterns of dependence and exposes citizens to the uncertainties which are inherent to international financial markets (Langley, 2007; Watson, 2010). In this context of protracted welfare residualism and radical uncertainty, 'rational' citizens will increasingly discipline and govern *themselves* in line with a dominant 'financialised' logic: they will internalise 'risk management' techniques, withhold on current consumption and modify their spending behaviour so as to 'prudentially' accumulate assets (Watson, 2009a). As such, ABW encourages the 'government of the self by the self'. Individuals gain the formal freedom to expand their investment portfolios but at the same time they are compelled to govern their behaviour in line with the dominant market rationality (Watson, 2009a, 2010: 415). Second, the literature emphasises how these self-disciplining mechanisms do not simply emerge as a result of dis-embedded 'market processes'. Rather, these processes are actively cultivated by government. Through the construction of 'ideal typical' welfare citizens—for example, the conception of the worker who 'prudentially' invests in order to build-up savings for later life—governments design incentive structures and deploy a range of governing techniques which encourage the emergence of 'financialised' patterns of behaviour and modes of conduct (Finlayson, 2008: 103). As such, the state increasingly plays 'not only a supervisory role in relation to the market but also *stimulates, promotes and shapes subjects* who, self-consciously and responsibly, further their own freedom and security through the market in general and the financial market in particular' (Langley, 2007: 11).

The post-structuralist current in the 'growth model' literature identifies a number of policy tools and governing rationalities which emerged in Britain in the pre-crisis conjuncture and which conform to the logic outlined above. For example, Finlayson draws attention to one flagship ABW policy—the Child Trust Fund (CTF)—which was announced in Labour's 2001 manifesto and which came into effect in January 2005 (Finlayson, 2009: 402). The CTF provided households with a sum of money which was directed towards a savings account and which children could draw upon once they reached the age of eighteen (Finlayson, 2008). One core goal of the policy was to inculcate the 'savings habit' from an early age and to encourage 'financial literacy' amongst young people and their families (HM Treasury, 2001). Finlayson argues that the objective of the CTF, as with other forms of ABW, was therefore to bring about 'the creation of good investors and good customers of the financial services industry, in possession of the wherewithal to save, which will in turn aid them in focusing on the kinds of economically productive risk taking … the CTF is a policy concerned to change the behaviour of the poor through incentives and selective education' (Finlayson, 2008: 104).

Langley has advanced a similar argument which draws attention to the constitution of new 'investor subjects' by Anglo-American governments and finance firms (Langley, 2007, 2008). For example, he identifies how declining state contributions to UK pension funds—and their indexation to inflation as opposed to earnings—occurred in line with a concerted 'financial literacy drive', which aimed 'to reach out to those five to eight million low/middle-income individuals that are not currently saving for their own retirement' (Langley, 2007: 17). Both Langley and Finlayson therefore identify areas where government played a crucial role in encouraging financialisation at the 'micro-foundational' scale. The logic underpinning these state interventions is clear: '[investor] citizen subjectivities have been actively encouraged as a means of exposing more and more people to a brand of financialised capitalism with a view to integrating them within its structures' (Watson, 2009a: 204). The state, in the post-structuralist conception, therefore plays a key integrative role in the sense that it seeks to shape social practices and cultural norms so as to incorporate households into the dominant finance-led growth model.

This approach makes a valuable contribution to the literature because it captures the way in which financialisation is not simply a structural process which is 'imposed' on unwitting subjects from above. Rather, the cultivation of 'investor subjectivities and financially self-disciplined subjects' is an inherently provisional and partial process which is always mediated (and potentially contested) by actors 'on the ground' (French et al., 2011). It is made possible through the deployment of specific governmental programmes and through the corresponding internalisation of certain norms and attitudes in the 'everyday' practices of individual citizens. However, despite their attentiveness to the 'micro-foundational' scale, it is notable that these contributions—at least insofar as they seek to contribute to the IPE literature on finance—tend to frame the processes which they identify as complementary to broader processes of financialisation understood at the 'macro'-scale. For example, Finlayson explicitly states that, 'financialisation… is an aspect of global markets and of the internal operation of the firm. But it *also* has an individual or household dimension' (Finlayson, 2009: 401). Similarly, Watson's work has been particularly explicit in attempting to connect the micro-foundational constitution of 'financialised subjects' with broader, macro-structural shifts in the UK's growth model (Watson, 2008, 2009a, 2010, 2013). For example, he specifically identifies the emergence of ABW and corresponding financial literacy drives as key elements of Britain's changing socio-economic model in the pre-crisis conjuncture (Watson, 2008: 586; 2009b: 42). However, he then directly connects these micro-foundational processes with what he terms the emergence of a regime of 'house price Keynesianism' (Watson, 2010).

Watson's synthesis of the 'micro-foundational' dimensions of financialisation with a broader conceptualisation of the UK's growth model provides us with a compelling framework through which to understand New Labour's political economy. In particular, it uncovers a series of deep internal tensions which underpinned Britain's pre-crisis growth model.

For example, Watson argues that the 'investor subjectivities' encouraged through New Labour's ABW approach were based on a distinctively 'Smithian' conception of 'prudence'—one where the individual parsimoniously withholds on current consumption and invests their savings in the productive process (Watson, 2008: 582; 2009a). However, in a context of 'privatised Keynesianism', savers were encouraged to increasingly channel their savings into a rapidly appreciating housing market. Indeed, as Engelen and his collaborators have shown, before the 2008 crash, 79% of all British bank lending was accounted for by lending on residential and commercial property and related assets (Engelen et al., 2011: 206). As such, the 'prudential' investor subject—insofar as she was compelled to channel her savings into what was effectively a large and unsustainable housing bubble—contributed to a bout of 'collective irresponsibility' which ultimately derailed the British economy (Watson, 2010).

Watson's analyses make important contributions to both the 'post-structuralist' approach outlined above and to the broader political economy literature on 'privatised Keynesianism' in Britain. However, his attempt to synthesise the 'micro'- and the 'macro'-dimensions of the Britain's growth model is also limited in its explanatory potential. Watson acknowledges as much himself. For example, he states that his analysis of the new 'worker-saver-investor' subject is placed at a 'high level of abstraction' (Watson, 2010). He points out that his argument identifies:

> The emergent properties of a newly constituted, but still merely tendential, relationship between the model homeowner, the model welfare recipient and private financial institutions … the argument is not that this relationship now dictates the content of everyday economic experiences for everyone in the UK, only that the trajectory of recent policy changes renders exposure to this relationship much more likely. (Watson, 2010: 414)

This qualification is important. Although the system of ABW is presented as effectively incorporating sections of the population into the dominant finance-led growth model, Watson acknowledges that this dynamic is an emergent tendency or trend rather than a fully fledged system (Watson, 2010: 415). Watson goes on to comment that the ABW conception 'depicts a process that will forever be in the making and which can never be complete when viewed in aggregate across the whole of society' (ibid.). The implication of this is that large sections of the population are not included within Watson's formulation. This has broader implications for the extent to which accounts of ABW, 'financial literacy' drives and the cultivation of 'investor subjectivities' in general, can explain the development of the dynamic tensions which underpinned Britain's model of capitalism in the pre-crisis conjuncture. As Watson acknowledges, 'many people remain excluded from the trend due to a basic lack of access to resources. This means that the image of a fully realised asset-based system of welfare is still only an *ideal-type*' (Watson, 2009a: 204). Watson's analysis, as well as the more explicitly 'post-structuralist' approaches as articulated by Finlayson and Langley, is therefore limited in the kind of questions which it asks and in the kind of answers which it can provide.

Three specific limitations are worth briefly stating here. First, if we acknowledge that ABW systems only 'incorporated' certain sections of society into the dominant finance-led growth model, then the question remains: How were those social groups which were largely *excluded* from asset-ownership programmes integrated into Britain's pre-crisis model of capitalism? The ABW might identify one 'logic of incorporation' but it fails to provide an adequate explanation of how subordinate social groups—many without access to assets—were integrated into Britain's model of social and economic development in this period. Second, there is a danger that the methodological focus on the construction of 'ideal' welfare citizens as 'financialised subjects' in government documents isolates (and potentially exaggerates the importance of) policies which were overtly 'functional' to financialisation processes whilst ignoring other mechanisms which were also in place in this period. For example, as noted above, the CTF has been widely cited as a flagship example of ABW. However, if we look at actual spending on the CTF, it came in at £296 million in 2008–2009 (HM Revenue and Customs, 2013). In contrast—to take but one example—in the same financial year, £885 million was spent on Sure Start Centres, another policy field directed towards benefiting children from low-income families but which was underpinned by more traditional welfare goals (Glass, 1999; Shaw, 2007). Again, the risk is that the importance placed on the cultivation of new 'investor subjects' in the post-structuralist literature is overstated whilst alternative logics of incorporation and legitimation are unduly ignored. Third, the narrow focus on governing 'rationalities' and subjectivities means that post-structuralist accounts struggle to explain why for extended periods of time capitalist expansion assumes a relatively coherent and stable form. As highlighted above, the 'pre-crisis conjuncture' represented a decade and a half of steady economic expansion between 1992 and 2007 in Britain (McMorrow & Roger, 2007). A narrow focus on the relationship between idealised welfare subjects and financialised economic growth cannot adequately capture the ways in which economic expansion is sustained in such periods. Therefore, in order to explain the relative stability of finance-led growth in the pre-crisis conjuncture, a more expansive and holistic understanding of state intervention in the economy is needed.

The central problem with post-structuralist approaches is the same as the one which was identified in the previous section: insofar as these approaches acknowledge a relation between the state and Britain's growth model, they tend to privilege analytically those forms of intervention which were 'functional' to financialisation. As Finlayson has acknowledged, the government policies which are analysed in the ABW literature have '*as their primary goal*... the *incorporation* of individuals within the mainstream financial system' (Finlayson, 2009: 408). As Brasset, Rethel and Watson have written in the introduction to an important special issue on the subject, financialisation is often conceived as a process 'that strives for societal *incorporation* into its economic structure via the pricing trajectory of asset bubbles' (Brassett, Rethel, & Watson, 2009: 379). Crucial to this conception, then, is the argument that state interventions had an intended integrative effect; they sought to incorporate citizens into the dominant finance-led growth model through encouraging the emergence of certain behavioural traits, cultural norms and social practices.

The core argument advanced here is *not* that there is no evidence for these governing practices or that ABW did not amount to a coherent—if somewhat limited—governing strategy. Rather, the argument is that an exclusive focus on these aspects of Britain's growth model unduly restricts analysis to forms of state intervention which actively promoted, cultivated and facilitated 'financialised' dynamics, whether at the 'macro'- or the 'micro-foundational' scale. As will be argued in the following chapter, a broader conceptualisation of the state which accounts for the ways in which it is typically oriented towards securing a range of divergent social and political objectives allows us to move beyond the latent functionalism of the existing growth model perspective.

Conclusion

The crisis of 2008 represented the breakdown of a distinctive 'finance-led' growth model within Britain. Since the crisis of the 1970s, the post-war compact of 'democratic capitalism' had been steadily eroded. In its place, a new growth model of 'privatised Keynesianism' emerged in Britain, which generated growth through increasing private debt across the economy. This growth model generated steady economic expansion in the pre-crisis conjuncture. But it was also highly unstable. Rising levels of household debt, relatively stagnant wages, a dominant financial sector, a weak revenue base and growing inequalities were all features of 'privatised Keynesian' expansion. In combination, these rendered British capitalism highly vulnerable to the financial crisis of 2008.

The 'growth model' perspective illuminates important structural weaknesses of British capitalism before the crisis. But growth model theorists have also adopted a highly limited conception of the state. They tend to privilege patterns of state intervention which were 'functional' to financialisation processes in Britain. But this captures only one dimension of state interventions in capitalism: namely the *accumulation strategy* deployed by state managers. State actors are also driven to secure the conditions for continued *legitimation* over time. The following chapter advances an alternative conceptualisation of the state which captures this second form of state intervention in capitalist economies. Drawing upon neo-Marxist state theory, the chapter seeks to overcome some of the weaknesses of the growth model perspective whilst building upon some of its core insights. This alternative conceptualisation will then form the basis for the subsequent comparative chapters which examine the political economy of the New Labour and the Coalition governments, respectively.

References

Aoki, K., Proudman, J., & Vlieghe, G. (2002). Houses as Collateral: Has the Link Between House Prices and Consumption in the UK Changed? *Economic Policy Review*. Retrieved from https://pdfs.semanticscholar.org/ca3a/adb5df7436a4f311ee0cd20d1c1f3c876b03.pdf.

Bank of England. (2001). *Inflation Report: February 2001*. London: Bank of England.

Bell, B., & Van Reenen, J. (2010). *Bankers' Pay and Extreme Wage Inequality in the UK*. Centre for Economic Performance.

Bengtsson, E., & Ryner, M. (2014). The (International) Political Economy of Falling Wage Shares: Situating Working-Class Agency. *New Political Economy, 20*(3), 406–430.

Berry, C., & Hay, C. (2016). The Great British "Rebalancing" Act: The Construction and Implementation of an Economic Imperative for Exceptional Times. *The British Journal of Politics & International Relations, 18*(1), 3–25.

Bleaney, M. (1976). *Underconsumption Theories: A History and Critical Analysis.* New York: International Publishers.

Blyth, M. (2013). *Austerity: The History of a Dangerous Idea.* Oxford: Oxford University Press.

Brassett, J., Rethel, L., & Watson, M. (2009). Introduction to the Political Economy of the Sub-prime Crisis in Britain: Constructing and Contesting Competence. *British Journal of Politics & International Relations, 11*(3), 377–381.

Brenner, N., Peck, J., & Theodore, N. (2010). Variegated Neoliberalization: Geographies, Modalities, Pathways. *Global Networks, 10*(2), 182–222.

Brown, G. (2008). *Speech to the Lord Mayor's Banquet.* Retrieved March 2, 2016, from http://webarchive.nationalarchives.gov.uk/+/number10.gov.uk/news/speeches-and-transcripts/2008/11/speech-to-the-lord-mayors-banquet-17419.

Buller, J., & Lindstrom, N. (2013). Hedging Its Bets: The UK and the Politics of European Financial Services Regulation. *New Political Economy, 18*(3), 391–409.

Burnham, P. (2011). Towards a Political Theory of Crisis: Policy and Resistance Across Europe. *New Political Science, 33*(4), 493–507.

Cafruny, A. W., & Ryner, M. (2003). *A Ruined Fortress?: Neoliberal Hegemony and Transformation in Europe.* London: Rowman & Littlefield.

Cameron, D. (2010). Our Whole Country Is Crying Out for Change. Retrieved from https://toryspeeches.files.wordpress.com/2013/11/david-cameron-our-whole-country-is-crying-out-for-change.pdf.

CBI. (2011). A New Approach to Growth: A Vision for Rebalancing the Economy. Retrieved from http://www.cbi.org.uk/media/1231301/cbi_rebalancing_the_economy_report_301211.pdf.

Christensen, J., Shaxson, N., & Wigan, D. (2016). The Finance Curse: Britain and the World Economy. *The British Journal of Politics and International Relations, 18*(1), 255–269.

Coates, D. (2001). *Models of Capitalism: Growth and Stagnation in the Modern Era.* Cambridge: Polity Press.

Coates, D. (2005). *Prolonged Labour: The Slow Birth of New Labour in Britain.* Basingstoke: Palgrave Macmillan.

Coates, D. (2013). Labour After New Labour: Escaping the Debt. *British Journal of Politics and International Relations, 15*(1), 38–52.

Coates, D., & Hay, C. (2001). The Internal and External Face of New Labour's Political Economy. *Government and Opposition, 36*(4), 447–471.
Coutts, K., Glyn, A., & Rowthorn, B. (2007). Structural Change Under New Labour. *Cambridge Journal of Economics, 31*(6), 845–861. https://doi.org/10.1093/cje/bem022.
Cribb, J., Disney, R., & Sibieta, L. (2014). *The Public Sector Workforce: Past, Present and Future* (IFS Briefing Note BN145). London: IFS.
Crotty, J. (2000). Structural Contradictions of the Global Neoliberal Regime. *Review of Radical Political Economics, 32*(3), 361–368.
Crouch, C. (2004). *Post-democracy*. Cambridge: Polity Press.
Crouch, C. (2008). What Will Follow the Demise of Privatised Keynesianism? *Political Quarterly, 79*(4), 476–487.
Crouch, C. (2009). Privatised Keynesianism: An Unacknowledged Policy Regime. *British Journal of Politics and International Relations, 11*(3), 382–399.
Crouch, C. (2011). *The Strange Non-death of Neoliberalism*. Cambridge: Polity Press.
Duménil, G., & Lévy, D. (2011). *The Crisis of Neoliberalism*. Boston: Harvard University Press.
Engelen, E., Erturk, I., Froud, J., Johal, S., Leaver, A., Moran, M., & Nilsson, A. (2011). *After the Great Complacence: Financial Crisis and the Politics of Reform*. Oxford: Oxford University Press.
Epstein, G. (2005). Introduction: Financialization and the World Economy. In G. Epstein (Ed.), *Financialization and the World Economy*. Cheltenham: Edward Elgar.
Ertürk, I., Froud, J., Johal, S., Leaver, A., Moran, M., & Williams, K. (2011). *City State Against National Settlement UK Economic Policy and Politics After the Financial Crisis* (CRESC Working Paper Series No. 44).
Farrall, S. (2006). "Rolling Back the State": Mrs. Thatcher's Criminological Legacy. *International Journal of the Sociology of Law, 34*(4), 256–277.
Finlayson, A. (2008). Characterizing New Labour: The Case of the Child Trust Fund. *Public Administration, 86*(1), 95–110.
Finlayson, A. (2009). Financialisation, Financial Literacy and Asset-Based Welfare. *British Journal of Politics and International Relations, 11*(3), 400–421.
French, S., Leyshon, A., & Wainwright, T. (2011). Financializing Space, Spacing Financialization. *Progress in Human Geography, 35*(6), 798–819.
Gamble, A. (2010a). New Labour and Political Change. *Parliamentary Affairs, 63*(4), 639–652.
Gamble, A. (2010b). The Political Consequences of the Crash. *Political Studies Review, 8*(1), 3–14.
Gamble, A. (2011). Project Cameron. *Public Policy Research, 18*(3), 173–178.

Gamble, A. (2014). *Crisis Without End? The Unravelling of Western Prosperity*. Basingstoke: Palgrave Macmillan.

Glass, N. (1999). Sure Start: The Development of an Early Intervention Programme for Young Children in the United Kingdom. *Children & Society, 13*(4), 257–264. https://doi.org/10.1002/CHI569.

Glyn, A. (2006). *Capitalism Unleashed: Finance, Globalization, and Welfare*. Oxford: Oxford University Press.

Glyn, A., & Wood, S. (2001). Economic Policy Under New Labour: How Social Democratic Is the Blair Government? *The Political Quarterly, 72*(1), 50–66.

Habermas, J. (1975). *Legitimation Crisis*. Boston: Beacon Press.

Hager, S. B. (2015). Corporate Ownership of the Public Debt: Mapping the New Aristocracy of Finance. *Socio-Economic Review, 13*(3), 505–523.

Hall, P. A. (1993). Policy Paradigms, Social Learning, and the State: The Case of Economic Policymaking in Britain. *Comparative Politics, 25*(3), 275–296.

Hamnett, C. (2010). Housing and the UK Economy. In N. Coe & A. Jones (Eds.), *The Economic Geography of the UK* (pp. 110–122). London: Sage.

Harvey, D. (2005). *A Brief History of Neoliberalism*. Oxford: Oxford University Press.

Hay, C. (2009). Good Inflation, Bad Inflation: The Housing Boom, Economic Growth and the Disaggregation of Inflationary Preferences in the UK and Ireland. *British Journal of Politics and International Relations, 11*(3), 461–478.

Hay, C. (2011). Pathology Without Crisis? The Strange Demise of the Anglo-Liberal Growth Model. *Government and Opposition, 46*(1), 1–31.

Hay, C. (2013a). *The British Growth Crisis: A Crisis of and for Growth* (SPERI Paper No. 1). Sheffield: Sheffield Political Economy Research Institute. Retrieved from speri.dept.shef.ac.uk/wp-content/uploads/2013/01/SPERI-Paper-No.-1-—The-British-Growth-Crisis-FINAL1.pdf.

Hay, C. (2013b). *The Failure of Anglo-Liberal Capitalism*. Basingstoke: Palgrave Macmillan.

Hay, C., Smith, N. J., & Watson, M. (2006). Beyond Prospective Accountancy: Reassessing the Case for British Membership of the Single European Currency Comparatively. *The British Journal of Politics and International Relations, 8*(1), 101–121.

Hay, C., & Wincott, D. (2012). *The Political Economy of European Welfare Capitalism*. Basingstoke: Palgrave Macmillan.

Hein, E., Dodig, N., & Budyldina, N. (2014). *Financial, Economic and Social Systems: French Regulation School, Social Structures of Accumulation and Post-Keynesian Approaches Compared* (Working Paper No. 34). Berlin: Institute for International Political Economy.

HM Revenue and Customs. (2013). *Child Trust Fund: Statistical Report 2012.* Retrieved from https://www.gov.uk/government/uploads/system/uploads/attachment_data/file/255886/statistical-report.pdf.

HM Treasury. (2001). *Savings and Assets for All: The Modernisation of Britain's Tax and Benefit System* (No. 8). London: HM Treasury.

Hope, C. (2015, June 23). David Cameron Discusses Changing Child Poverty Target Days Before Embarrassing Figures Released. *The Telegraph.* Retrieved from http://www.telegraph.co.uk/news/politics/david-cameron/11694735/David-Cameron-discusses-changing-child-poverty-target-days-before-embarrassing-figures-released.html.

House of Commons. (2012). *UK Trade Statistics.* London: House of Commons. Retrieved from http://researchbriefings.files.parliament.uk/documents/SN06211/SN06211.pdf.

Hutton, W. (2011). *The State We're in.* London: Random House.

IMF. (2008). *Assessing Risks to Global Financial Stability.* Retrieved from http://www.imf.org/external/pubs/ft/gfsr/2008/02/pdf/chap1.pdf.

Jessop, B. (1990). *State Theory: Putting the Capitalist State in Its Place.* Cambridge: Polity Press.

Jessop, B. (2002). *The Future of the Capitalist State.* Cambridge: Polity Press.

Jessop, B. (2013). Revisiting the Regulation Approach: Critical Reflections on the Contradictions, Dilemmas, Fixes and Crisis Dynamics of Growth Regimes. *Capital & Class, 37*(1), 5–24.

Jessop, B., Bonnett, K., Bromley, S., & Ling, T. (1988). *Thatcherism: A Tale of Two Nations.* Cambridge: Polity Press.

Johnston, A., & Regan, A. (2016). European Monetary Integration and the Incompatibility of National Varieties of Capitalism. *Journal of Common Market Studies, 54*(2), 318–336.

Keegan, W. (1985). *Britain Without Oil.* London: Penguin Books.

Keegan, W. (2003). *The Prudence of Mr. Gordon Brown.* Chichester: Wiley.

Kerr, P., Byrne, C., & Foster, E. (2011). Theorising Cameronism. *Political Studies Review, 9*(2), 193–207.

Kitson, M., & Wilkinson, F. (2007). The Economics of New Labour: Policy and Performance. *Cambridge Journal of Economics, 31*(6), 805–816.

Kotz, D. (2009). The Financial and Economic Crisis of 2008: A Systemic Crisis of Neoliberal Capitalism. *Review of Radical Political Economics, 41*(3), 305–317.

Krippner, G. (2011). *Capitalizing on Crisis.* Boston: Harvard University Press.

Landesman, M., & Snell, A. (1989). The Consequences of Mrs Thatcher for U.K. Manufacturing Exports. *The Economic Journal, 99*(394), 1–27.

Langley, P. (2007). Uncertain Subjects of Anglo-American Financialization. *Cultural Critique, 65,* 67–91.

Langley, P. (2008). *The Everyday Life of Global Finance: Saving and Borrowing in Anglo-America*. Oxford: Oxford University Press.

Lansley, S. (2011). *The Cost of Inequality*. London: Gibson Square.

Machin, S. (1997). The Decline of Labour Market Institutions and the Rise in Wage Inequality in Britain. *European Economic Review, 41*(3–5), 647–657.

Machin, S. (2004). Factors of Convergence and Divergence in Union Membership. *British Journal of Industrial Relations, 42*(3), 423–438.

McMorrow, K., & Roger, W. (2007). An Analysis of EU Growth Trends, with a Particular Focus on Germany, France, Italy and the UK. *National Institute Economic Review*. Retrieved from http://journals.sagepub.com/doi/abs/10.1177/002795010719900109.

Montgomerie, J. (2007). *Financialization and Consumption: An Alternative Account of Rising Consumer Debt Levels in Anglo-America* (CRESC Working Paper Series). Retrieved from http://hummedia.manchester.ac.uk/institutes/cresc/workingpapers/wp43.pdf.

Montgomerie, J., & Büdenbender, M. (2015). Round the Houses: Homeownership and Failures of Asset-Based Welfare in the United Kingdom. *New Political Economy, 20*(3), 386–405. https://doi.org/10.1080/13563467.2014.951429.

Onaran, O. (2012). *A Wage Led Recovery Would Help Reverse Inequalities, Increase Demand, and Help the EU to Get Out of Its Crisis*. Retrieved from http://blogs.lse.ac.uk/europpblog/2012/04/18/wage-led-recovery-europe/.

ONS. (2014). *An Examination of Falling Real Wages, 2010–2013*. Retrieved from http://www.ons.gov.uk/ons/dcp171766_351467.pdf.

Osborne, G. (2010). *A New Economic Model*. Retrieved from http://www.totalpolitics.com/print/speeches/35193/george-osborne-mais-lecture-a-new-economic-model.thtml.

Overbeek, H. (1989). British Capitalism at the Crossroads. *International Journal of Political Economy, 19*(3), 36–75.

Peck, J. (2010). *Constructions of Neoliberal Reason*. Oxford: Oxford University Press.

Plunkett, J. (2011). *Growth Without Gain? The Faltering Living Standards of People on Low-to-Middle Incomes*. Resolution Foundation. Retrieved from https://www.resolutionfoundation.org/app/uploads/2014/08/Growth-without-gain.pdf.

Polanyi, K. (2001). *The Great Transformation: The Political and Economic Origins of Our Time*. Boston: Beacon Press.

Prabhakar, R. (2008). *Assets Agenda: Principles and Policy*. New York: Palgrave Macmillan. Retrieved from https://books.google.com/books?id=SunrAAAAMAAJ&pgis=1.

Sachs, J. D., & Gordon, R. J. (1983). Real Wages and Unemployment in the OECD Countries. *Brookings Papers on Economic Activity, 14*(1), 255–304. https://doi.org/10.2307/2534357.

Saull, R. (2012). Rethinking Hegemony: Uneven Development, Historical Blocs, and the World Economic Crisis. *International Studies Quarterly, 56*(2), 323–338.

Seabrooke, L., & Hobson, J. (2007). *Everyday Politics of the World Economy.* Cambridge: Cambridge University Press.

Shaw, E. (2007). *Losing Labour's Soul? New Labour and the Blair Government 1997–2007.* London: Routledge.

Smith, M. (2014). Globalisation and the Resilience of Social Democracy: Reassessing New Labour's Political Economy. *The British Journal of Politics & International Relations, 16*(4), 597–623.

Smith, N. J. (2013). The British Economy: A Crisis of Anglo-Liberal Capitalism? *Renewal, 21*(2), 65–86.

Stockhammer, E. (2011). Wage-Led Growth: An Introduction. *International Journal of Labour Research, 3*(2), 1–25.

Stockhammer, E. (2012). Financialization, Income Distribution and the Crisis. *Investigación Económica, 71*(279), 39–70.

Stockhammer, E. (2015). Rising Inequality as a Cause of the Present Crisis. *Cambridge Journal of Economics, 39*(3), 935–958. https://doi.org/10.1093/cje/bet052.

Streeck, W. (2011). The Crises of Democratic Capitalism. *New Left Review, 71,* 5–29.

Streeck, W. (2014). *Buying Time: The Delayed Crisis of Democratic Capitalism.* London: Verso.

The Conservative Party. (2009). *Labour's Debt Crisis.* London: The Conservative Party. Retrieved from https://www.conservatives.com/~/media/files/downloadablefiles/debtcrisisreport.ashx?dl=true.

Thompson, G. (2009). What's in the Frame? How the Financial Crisis Is Being Packaged for Public Consumption. *Economy and Society, 38*(3), 520–524.

Thompson, H. (2013). UK Debt in Comparative Perspective: The Pernicious Legacy of Financial Sector Debt. *British Journal of Politics and International Relations, 15*(3), 476–492.

Ussher, K. (2010). Labour's Record on the Economy. *The Political Quarterly, 81,* 108–122.

Watson, M. (2008). The Split Personality of Prudence in the Unfolding Political Economy of New Labour. *Political Quarterly, 79*(4), 578–589.

Watson, M. (2009a). Gordon Brown's Misplaced Smithian Appeal: The Eclipse of Sympathy in Changing British Welfare Norms. *Journal of Social Policy, 38*(2), 195–210.

Watson, M. (2009b). Planning for a Future of Asset-Based Welfare? New Labour, Financialized Economic Agency and the Housing Market. *Planning Practice and Research, 24*(1), 41–56.
Watson, M. (2010). *House Price Keynesianism and the Contradictions of the Modern Investor Subject, 25*(3), 413–436.
Watson, M. (2013). New Labour's "Paradox of Responsibility" and the Unravelling of Its Macroeconomic Policy. *British Journal of Politics and International Relations, 15*(1), 6–22.

CHAPTER 3

Theorising Capitalist Stability

The growth model perspective identifies a number of ways that Britain's model of 'privatised Keynesianism' was bolstered by the state. Macroeconomic policy was oriented towards containing inflation whilst creating the conditions for finance-led growth. Government programmes of 'asset-based welfare' sought to integrate citizens into Britain's growth model, by incentivising and cultivating financialised patterns of behaviour. However, as argued in the previous chapter, the growth model perspective deploys a limited conception of the state. It narrowly focuses on the ways in which government actors facilitated finance-led accumulation. As such, it disregards the ways in which state interventions are often oriented towards securing other objectives. This compromises the ability of the growth model perspective to explain how capitalist stability was secured in the pre-crisis conjuncture. In order to address these weaknesses, it is necessary to advance a theoretical framework which is capable of capturing the multifaceted character of state interventions within advanced capitalist economies. This chapter draws upon and develops two alternative approaches—neo-Marxist state theory and the Regulation Approach (RA)—which can overcome the limitations of the growth model perspective in its current form. Drawing on these approaches provides us with a conceptual framework through which to trace processes of continuity and change within post-crisis British capitalism.

S. Lavery, *British Capitalism After the Crisis*, Building a Sustainable Political Economy: SPERI Research & Policy, https://doi.org/10.1007/978-3-030-04046-8_3

Accumulation Strategies, Hegemonic Projects and the State

Neo-Marxist state theory emerged during the post-war settlement and developed in the context of the crisis of the Keynesian welfare state (Habermas, 1975; O'Connor, 1973; Offe, 1984). Since the Second World War, the state had greatly expanded its sphere of competences. Public expenditure had risen markedly as a share of GDP since the early twentieth century. Expansive welfare programmes had emerged across Western Europe. Public ownership of key industries was extensive. For neo-Marxist state theorists, these dynamics generated deep structural contradictions within capitalist societies. On the one hand, the expansion of the state helped to *stabilise* capitalist development. Public investment shored-up industry whilst the commitment to full employment and extensive welfare provision helped to contain working class militancy. On the other hand, the expansion of the public sector eroded profit rates and created the conditions for inflation. For state theorists, the core contradiction of advanced capitalism was that it *relied upon* but was also *undermined by* the expansion of the fiscal capacity of the state (O'Connor, 1973). The crisis of the 1970s embodied the crystallisation of this structural contradiction. As tax revenues collapsed, state managers faced a volatile combination of declining profitability, rampant inflation and growing worker militancy.

On first sight, this contradiction seemed insoluble. Systematic dysfunctions threatened to overwhelm the prevailing social order. However, neo-Marxist theorists—increasingly drawing on the work of Antonio Gramsci—argued that the state is not simply a passive expression of structural changes in the economy (Jessop, 1983; Poulantzas, 2014). It is also a site of *agency*. State managers were undoubtedly hemmed in by a variety of competing demands during the crisis of the Keynesian welfare state. But they also had the capacity to address the contradictions of this regime by seeking to advance far-reaching programmes of reform. Neo-Marxist theorising therefore shifted increasingly to analyse the role which *politics* could play in capitalist transformation (Bertramsen, Thomsen, & Torfing, 1991). Broader reconfigurations in society reflected this shift. By the late 1970s, radically distinct programmes on the Left and the Right were emerging within Britain as possible solutions to the downturn. On the Labour Left, the Alternative Economic Strategy advocated the embrace of import controls, deficit-financing and accelerated state ownership of the economy. On the Right, the emergent Thatcherite programme prioritised the need to contain inflation and reintroduce discipline into the labour process (Gamble, 1988). Both programmes sought to combine a transformative economic vision with an underlying strategy for securing popular support. In line with this shift, neo-Marxist state theory moved from an analysis of the *structural* contradictions of the advanced capitalist state to an analysis of the *strategic* considerations which underpinned rival political programmes during the unravelling of the Keynesian welfare state.

The work of Bob Jessop was critical in this shift from theorising structure to strategy (Jessop, 1990; Jessop & Sum, 2006) Jessop's central contribution was to advance the concept of the 'strategic selectivity' of the state (Jessop, 2002b). This started from the premise that the state is not merely an expression of underlying structural dynamics. The state is 'relatively autonomous' from competing social pressures, in the sense that it is a distinct institutional realm with its own resources, objectives and strategic capacities. However, the ability of the state to pursue its strategic objectives is always constrained by the wider structural context. Although policymakers within the state are free to exercise agency, they do so under a set of structural conditions which delimits their room for manoeuvre. To take one example, during an economic crisis, the interventions of state managers are not 'determined' by the 'form' of the economic downturn. Whether policymakers choose either a deflationary or expansionary response remains a relatively open question. However, their policy options are highly constrained. For example, expansionary responses to a downturn are constrained by the power of international creditors to withdraw capital from circulation. 'New Right' privatisation programmes had to navigate powerful domestic constituencies, such as the trade unions, whilst avoiding a backlash in public opinion. State intervention is therefore sharply constrained by the prevailing context. Over time, however, state interventions can reconfigure this background context, opening up new opportunities for reform whilst also creating new obstacles.

Neo-Marxist state theory picks up on the 'strategically selective' character of state interventions in the economy. Its central premise is that policymakers in capitalist societies are relentlessly driven to secure two distinct but often contradictory objectives. On the one hand, they must secure the conditions for continued *accumulation* over time (Block, 1981). States rely upon maintaining a healthy level of economic activity if they are to draw in a sufficient revenue base to finance their activities. In seeking to sustain economic growth, policymakers advance distinctive *accumulation strategies*. These refer to attempts by policymakers to privilege certain economic sectors, subjectivities and patterns of development over others (Jessop, 1990: 198). However, this concept captures only one dimension of state intervention in the social and economic realm. Policymakers are also driven to secure a second related but distinct objective: to maintain the conditions for continued *legitimation* over time. This involves securing a base of popular support for a given political programme. In pursuit of this objective, state managers must advance distinctive *legitimation strategies* designed to secure a popular base of support within society.

This shift towards theorising the legitimation strategies of state managers was a decisive move in neo-Marxist state theory in Britain. The move was crystallised in the 1980s, when a research programme emerged which sought to chart the emerging political economy of Thatcherism. This body of work, associated with Jessop, Gamble, Hall and others, noted that the Thatcher project was underpinned by radical ambitions (Gamble, 1988; Hall & Jaques, 1983; Jessop, Bonnett, Bromley, & Ling, 1988). Thatcherism aimed to fundamentally realign the balance of forces within British capitalism. It sought to initiate a sharp 'break' from the post-war order and to profoundly restructure the British economy. A sweeping programme of privatisation, deregulation and liberalisation lay at its heart. However, whilst this radicalism involved taking on powerful interest groups—notably the trade unions and the public sector bureaucracy—Thatcherism was also attentive to building a popular base of support amongst the population at large. In conceptualising the nature of this shift, neo-Marxist theorists of Thatcherism increasingly turned to the work of Antonio Gramsci and in particular his conception of 'hegemony' (Gramsci, 1971). This Gramscian perspective developed a framework through which to understand the ways in which state managers are driven to secure a popular base of support throughout society. The concept of hegemony can help us to overcome the limited conception of the state which underpins the growth model perspective.

In classical accounts of hegemony, two distinct modalities of state power can be identified (Gramsci, 1971). The first is the state's capacity to deploy coercive power—the police, the courts and the prison system—in order to directly dominate subordinate social groups and to secure social order. In this way, supremacy can be secured through relations of force and direct domination (Williams, 1960: 590). However, in advanced capitalist states where civil society is well developed—and where parliamentary democracy typically prevails—it is likely that this coercive dimension of state power will remain relatively latent and submerged. Under these conditions, a second form of state power typically comes to the fore. This is where leading social groups seek to secure *hegemony* by assuming 'moral and intellectual leadership' of their society (Femia, 1975: 30). This is done by constructing the 'particular' interests of privileged class fractions and social groups as embodying a 'general' interest which holds for society as a whole (Jessop, 1990: 208). In this way, subordinate social groups can be incorporated into 'national popular' programmes of action insofar as they come to actively identify with a conception of the 'national' or 'universal' interest which putatively transcends sectional interests. This second dimension of state power therefore involves 'the exercise of leadership by the dominant group over subordinate groups in and through *the construction of consent*' (Joseph, 2000).

A legitimation strategy or 'hegemonic project' can therefore be defined as a relatively coherent governing programme which seeks to secure broad-based support for a specific model of social, economic and political development. This is of course a broad definition. But two important implications follow. First, it opens up a new arena of state intervention beyond the limited scope of the growth model perspective. State managers must secure legitimation as well as ongoing accumulation which allows us to move beyond the functionalist underpinnings of the 'privatised Keynesianism' conception. Second, this raises the question of *how* state managers can attempt to secure 'broad-based support' for their favoured programmes of development. Two ways in which state managers can seek to do this is by *actively shaping* and *discursively constructing* distributional processes.

Distribution and Legitimation Strategies

The question of distribution lies at the heart of legitimation strategies. National growth models, when they are operating effectively, generate expanded output and an economic surplus. From the perspective of the state, this leads to increased revenues and enhanced fiscal capacity. The first core element of a legitimation strategy concerns the ways in which state managers choose to deploy that surplus in order to secure a broad base of popular support. Policymakers may choose to offer tax cuts or increases in public expenditure. They may choose to invest in infrastructure or to channel the surplus to specific social groups. Legitimation strategies, then, involve the channelling of 'material concessions and symbolic rewards' to strategically significant sections of the population (Jessop, 1990: 212).

Legitimation strategies of this form are strongly shaped by the dynamism of the underlying growth model. If growth is low, the scope for enhanced distribution will be limited. If growth is high, then state managers will have more discretion over the ways in which they can deploy resources to shore-up support. In this sense, hegemonic projects are embedded within what Gramsci termed the 'decisive nucleus of economic activity' (Gramsci, 1971: 491). However, the relation between growth models and legitimation strategies does not run in only one direction. The pursuit of a particular legitimation strategy may in turn reshape the dynamics of the underlying growth model. For example, if the state channels 'excessive' resources to the social base, this can lead to inflationary pressures which undermine accumulation over time. In the 1970s, attempts to transfer income to organised trade unions led to growing inflation and ultimately to the transition to a distinct regime of financialised accumulation (Krippner, 2011). Similarly, redistribution of the surplus can flank and support a given growth model, in the sense that redistributive measures can enhance employment and living standards amongst sections of the population who might otherwise be excluded. The key point is that although legitimation strategies and growth models mutually condition one another, they are not reducible to a singular logic. As such, it is important to distinguish analytically between the two.

The state's capacity to pursue 'accumulation' and 'legitimation' strategies is also a decisive factor in stabilising capitalist development. The 'formal' separation of the capitalist state from the economic sphere means that the state is uniquely well placed to act as a stabilising force in capitalist societies (Jessop, 1990: 160). Other institutional complexes and interest groups within civil society are ill-suited to perform this task. Private corporations, for example, are unlikely to be able (or willing) to redistribute their profits to the population in the name of securing social stability. Competitive market pressures and the structural pressures which drive firms to prioritise shareholder value ensure that private capital is typically not in a position to redistribute the requisite level of funds to the social base. As such, essential public goods and services cannot be delivered through private sector economic activity alone. However, private capital invariably relies on these public goods—large-scale infrastructure projects, a relatively stable investment environment, a well-trained and educated labour force—if it is to function effectively at all (Gough, 1985).

It is in the 'general' interest of capital for these publically backed resources to be in place. However, left to their own devices, 'particular' capitals are unlikely to be able to provide these basic requirements. The state's relative autonomy from capital means that it is able to impose policies—for example tax increases or social policy initiatives—which might otherwise be resisted by dominant fractions of business. It is important, however, not to read the state's 'stabilising' interventions in a functionalist manner. Often, state interventions of this form are driven by alternative strategic considerations. States often increase public expenditure or public investment in line with their attempts to secure the support of the general population. The unanticipated consequence of these interventions can be capitalist stabilisation. The production of capitalist stability, then, is not typically the result of policymakers consciously seeking to 'rise above' particular interests and secure the 'general' conditions of prosperity of all. Instead, stability is often secured through the *combination* of accumulation and legitimation strategies which give rise to distinctive regimes of development over time.

The Strategic Deployment of Ideas

In classical conceptions of hegemony, 'ideas' play a key role in attempts to secure 'consent' for a given governing programme. By cultivating 'common sense' views throughout society, elites can present 'particular' interests as in the national interest. The ability of state managers to strategically deploy ideas in this way forms the second key element of legitimation strategies. The debate on Thatcherism in the 1980s is again instructive here. In analysing the emergence and consolidation of Thatcherism, some scholars emphasised its roots in 'New Right' ideology or its 'authoritarian populist' origins (Hall, 1979; Hall & Jacques, 1983). Other scholars, advocating a 'statecraft' approach, emphasised the strategic positioning of the Thatcher governments and drew attention to Thatcherism's essentially pragmatic and adaptable character (Beer, 1982; Bulpitt, 1986). These contending interpretations revolved around a dichotomy between 'ideas' on the one hand and 'strategy' on the other.

However, as Jessop and Hay argued in a series of contributions, it is possible to transcend this duality by advancing an approach which *synthesises* these two positions (Hay, 1996b; Jessop et al., 1988).

Jessop and Hay argued that Thatcherism (and by implication other political projects) should be analysed in terms of the ways in which such projects *strategically deploy ideas in order to mobilise key sections of the population in support of distinctive programmes of social, economic and political restructuring* (Hay, 1996a, 1999; Jessop et al., 1988). Thus, Jessop identifies the way in which the 'ideas' associated with Thatcherism—its neo-Conservative vision of social order and its advocacy of 'popular capitalism'—were strategically connected to a specific accumulation strategy and state project (Jessop et al., 1988: 68–98). Ideas, on this understanding, are not just a 'frame' through which policymakers understand, select and subsequently justify their policies; they also have an active, creative potential insofar as they can reshape the expectations of citizens in ways which consolidate emergent political projects. Rather than viewing state intervention as a tactical response to perceived electoral imperatives—as is the case with the statecraft approach—Hay and Jessop's alternative reading draws attention to the ways in which ideas can be strategically deployed in order to *shape* social expectations and to actively build support for far-reaching programmes of action.

Hay's contribution focuses on the relation between moments of 'crisis' and state transformation (Hay, 1999). The core of Hay's argument is that crises should not be viewed as objective or 'external' features of a social and economic system. Rather, 'crises' have to be interpreted subjectively by social and political actors. For example, the economic breakdowns of the 1970s revealed a series of structural weaknesses and dysfunctions at the heart of the British economy. These were reflected in the various dysfunctions associated with the 'stagflation' of this period: low productivity rates, increased levels of unemployment and declining profitability. However, Hay's argument is that the interpretation of the *cause* of these dysfunctions—the 'diagnosis' of the crisis—is not predetermined by an 'objective' feature of the crisis itself. Rather, breakdowns in the economy and society have to be interpreted and 'narrated' by social and political actors. Thus, advancing a case study of the 'Winter of Discontent', Hay argues that the success of the New Right was based on its capacity to *narrate* the breakdowns of the 1970s as emblematic of an overloaded state at the mercy of militant trade unions (Hay, 1996a).

However, alternative diagnoses of the crisis were also available. For example, the comparative weakness of the British economy in this period could have equally been attributed to the absence of a 'developmental state' or to the archaic structure of the British political system and its industrial base (Hay, 1999). Each of these 'diagnoses' would have led to very different kinds of state intervention and hence different patterns of social, economic and political reform. The key role of ideas then is that they contribute to the crisis constructions which in turn sanction different kinds of state intervention and programmes of social and economic reform.

'One Nation' and 'Two Nation' Legitimation Strategies

Legitimation strategies attempt to secure a base of support in society for distinct political programmes. State managers can seek to secure legitimation in two distinct ways: they can *actively shape* distributional processes, redistributing the surplus from the dominant growth model to strategically significant social groups. Alternatively, state managers can seek to *discursively construct* underlying distributional shifts in such a way as to gain support from the population. Following Jessop, we can distinguish in ideal typical terms between two forms of legitimation strategy which are likely to emerge in advanced capitalist societies. The first can be characterised as a 'One Nation' legitimation strategy or hegemonic project. At root, 'One Nation' strategies attempt to build a broad-based coalition of support by redistributing significant portions of the economic surplus to a wide range of social groups (Lacher, 2013: 82). In addition, such projects will typically attempt to construct the leading social and economic programme as in the 'universal' or 'general' interest of the nation as a whole. As Jessop has put it, '"One Nation" strategies aim at an *expansive* hegemony in which the support of the entire population is mobilised through material concessions and symbolic rewards' (Jessop, 1990: 211).

The second form of legitimation strategy can be characterised as a 'Two Nations' hegemonic project. 'Two nations' hegemonic projects do not aspire to unify social groups. Instead, they seek to unify and advance the interests of a 'privileged' section of the population whilst marginalising subordinate social groups. In this sense, '"two nations" hegemonic projects aim at a more *limited* hegemony concerned to mobilise the support of *strategically significant sectors* of the population and to pass the costs of the project to other sectors' (Jessop, 1990: 211). Furthermore, these strategies do not rest upon quietly ignoring the interests of subordinate social groups. Rather, the state identifies the retrenchment of this group's supposed privileges as a crucial precondition of securing economic advancement and national renewal. In this way, 'two nations' hegemonic projects involve attempts to secure legitimacy through building a (limited) coalition of social interests which can be unified in opposition to a subordinate 'Other'.

A 'two nations' legitimation strategy therefore involves the construction and entrenchment of what we can term *moralised antagonisms* between different social groups. The classic example of this approach is that which was deployed by Thatcher in the 1980s. Thatcherism distinguished between different social fractions based on their (perceived) contribution to the British economy and to the national interest. Specifically, it identified and entrenched a series of moralised antagonisms—for example between the 'deserving and undeserving poor' and 'productive and parasitic' economic sectors—in order to mobilise a limited base of support for a radical programme of retrenchment and social restructuring (Gough, 1980: 7; Jessop et al., 1988: 87). The Thatcher governments were not particularly concerned with commanding the active consent of unionised workers, public sector bureaucracies or electoral groups concentrated in Labour's industrial heartlands. Rather, in line with its 'two nations' strategy, Thatcherism aspired to achieve a *limited* hegemony, commanding the support of strategically significant sections of the population and mobilising this social coalition against subordinate groups who stood against the 'national interest' (Bruff, 2013; Gamble, 1988; Hall & Jacques, 1983).

We are now in a position to relate the above reflections to the overall argument of the book. In the previous chapter, it was argued that the growth model perspective deploys a limited conception of the state. Advocates of the growth model perspective identify the ways in which the state supported Britain's pre-crisis growth model of privatised Keynesianism. In this way, they focus on the *accumulation strategy* which was deployed in the pre-crisis conjuncture. What is missing from the growth model perspective is an account of the *legitimation strategy* which policymakers also deployed in Britain before and after the crisis. Growth model theorists rightly argue that New Labour advanced a finance-led accumulation strategy which underpinned the emergence of privatised Keynesianism in Britain. But, as will be argued in the following chapter, New Labour also advanced a distinctive 'One Nation' hegemonic project which attempted to secure the popular support of a broad base of the population. The combination of these two strategies underpinned the phase of relative stability which British capitalism experienced in the pre-crisis conjuncture. The Coalition, as will be argued in subsequent chapters, continued with New Labour's finance-led accumulation strategy. But, in a radically reconstituted fiscal climate, it broke with New Labour's 'One Nation' legitimation strategy. In its place, the Coalition advanced a 'two nations' strategy designed to secure the support of a limited section of the population. This undermined the redistributive mechanisms which had underpinned New Labour's political economy and re-embedded a series of structural weaknesses within British capitalism.

The Regulation Approach

The growth model perspective correctly identifies how pre-crisis British capitalism was underpinned by an unsustainable dynamic of privatised Keynesianism. However, as was argued in the previous chapter, this cannot capture the ways in which capitalist *stability* was secured throughout this period. In the above section, it was argued that the combination of accumulation and legitimation strategies can give rise to relatively stable and coherent 'regimes of development' over time. These 'regimes' are shaped by state interventions but they also assume a relatively independent and constant character. In order to grasp this point, it is helpful to draw on a second tradition within the neo-Marxist theoretical canon which places questions of stability at its core. In this respect, the 'Regulation Approach' (RA), can be usefully drawn upon and developed.

The RA emerged in the late 1970s within Europe. It was originally associated with the 'Parisian School' of regulation theorists, which included Michel Aglietta, Alain Lipietz and Robert Boyer amongst others (Aglietta, 1976; Boyer, 1990; Lipietz, 1987). The RA originated as a critique of both neoclassical economics and of orthodox Marxist theories of capitalist development and crisis. Regulationists argue that both these approaches treat the 'economy' as an autonomous sphere of social activity with its own developmental dynamic. In contrast, the RA insists that phases of stable economic expansion are possible only insofar as accumulation is embedded within a broader institutional framework

(Bertramsen et al., 1991). Rather than focussing on the transhistorical features of capitalism 'in general', the RA develops a systematic framework for conceptualising *temporally and spatially specific* capitalist social relations across particular historical conjunctures (Becker & Jäger, 2012: 172). To this end, the RA introduces three intermediate concepts which help to account both for the instituted nature of economic action and for the mechanisms through which capitalist stability might be (temporarily) secured in different phases of its development (Bertramsen et al., 1991: 66; Jessop, 1997: 288).

First, it deploys the conception of an *accumulation system* (Peck & Tickell, 1995: 357). This is defined as a 'macro-economically coherent production-consumption-distribution relationship' (Peck & Tickell, 1994: 286). An accumulation system can be said to be in evidence when the macroeconomic elements of a given growth model align in such a way as to reproduce distinctive distributional regularities over time (Dunford, 1990: 305; Jessop, 2013). For example, under Atlantic Fordism, the expansion of real wages in line with productivity growth ensured that sufficient domestic demand was in place for newly produced economic output (Aglietta, 1976; Ruccio, 1989: 36). The institutionalisation of these economic relations produced the framework for a 'virtuous' cycle of sustained economic expansion throughout the immediate post-war period.

Second, the RA advances the conception of the *Mode of Social Regulation* (MSR). The MSR refers to the ensemble of 'extra-economic' institutional forms which can temporarily stabilise and accommodate the crisis tendencies of capitalist development within particular times and spaces (Boyer, 1990: 43; Kenny, 1999). By 'extra-economic' institutions regulationists mean those modes of social organisation which are not directly oriented towards intervening within the sphere of production, consumption or distribution but which nonetheless play a crucial role in conditioning and stabilising economic development. Regulationists have drawn attention to a wide range of social practices and institutional forms which together constitute the MSR. For example, the MSR has been defined by Jessop as that, 'ensemble of norms, institutions, organisational forms, social networks, and patterns of conduct that can temporarily stabilise an accumulation [system]… despite the conflictual and antagonistic character of capitalist social relations' (Jessop, 2013: 8).

Third, the RA advances the conception of *regimes of accumulation* (RoA). This refers to a situation in which the underlying accumulation system is effectively 'coupled' with a complementary MSR (Jones, 2002: 39; Tickell & Peck, 1995: 360). It is under these conditions, regulation theorists submit, that periods of stable capitalist expansion become possible (Jessop, 1997: 291). A functioning RoA can therefore be understood as a relatively coherent model of social and economic development which combines 'economic' processes with 'extra-economic' institutional forms and social practices so as to sustain accumulation over time (Howell, 2016; Jessop, 1997: 288). The core axiom of the regulationist paradigm is therefore that periods of relative stability should never be understood as the result of 'economic' processes alone. Rather, in examining such periods, scholars should focus on the institutional nexus which links together accumulation on the one hand with 'extra-economic' institutional forms on the other (Tickell & Peck, 1995: 360).

The original RA begins to take us beyond the limitations of the growth model perspective. The RA asks us to conceptualise the role that *'extra-economic' institutional forms* play in stabilising advanced capitalist development. From a regulationist perspective, Britain's finance-led growth model would be understood as equivalent to an *accumulation system* insofar as it identifies a particular relationship between distribution, consumption and private debt expansion throughout the pre-crisis conjuncture (Crouch, 2011; Streeck, 2014). However, the RA insists that if this accumulation system is to be reproduced over time it must be embedded within an 'extra-economic' institutional context which is not itself reducible to the overall 'reproduction requirements' of the dominant growth model. This takes us away from the kind of questions which are typically asked by advocates of the growth model perspective. As was argued in the previous chapter, insofar as Hay and Crouch attempt to explain how 'privatised Keynesianism' was stabilised, they tend to appeal to mechanisms which were *internal* to the 'finance-led' accumulation system itself. Crouch, for example, argues that the expansion of credit to low income households and to wealthy asset-holders saved privatised Keynesianism 'from the instability that would otherwise have been its fate' (Crouch, 2011: 114). However, this provides us with an incomplete explanation of how capitalist stability was secured throughout this period. The growth model perspective explains the stability of pre-crisis British by appealing to a narrow range of *economic* mechanisms. But this isolates only one feature of Britain's pre-crisis political economy. As Streeck and Thelen have argued, 'institutional frameworks that exist in any particular society are never completely coherent. Whilst some institutional arrangements may impose a dominant logic of action, these typically co-exist with other arrangements…that embody conflicting and even contradictory logics' (Streeck & Thelen, 2005: 19). Privatised Keynesianism was certainly a core dynamic of pre-crisis British capitalism. But it *co-existed* with other dynamics which helped to stabilise Britain's finance-led growth model. In regulationist parlance, Britain's pre-crisis growth model was complemented by a series of 'extra-economic' institutions which together generated a relatively stable 'regime' of capitalist development in Britain before the crisis. As will be argued in subsequent chapters, the state was crucial in generating complementary 'flanking mechanisms' which stabilised 'privatised Keynesianism' over time. Public expenditure increases, state-backed employment and (limited) fiscal transfers to working households, organised around New Labour's 'One Nation' hegemonic project, served to stabilise Britain's finance-led growth model in the pre-crisis conjuncture. The Coalition's political economy unravelled this aspect of New Labour's 'hybrid' political economy, re-embedding a series of destabilising dynamics in the process.

Regulationist Approaches to Neoliberalism

The RA emerged in the historical context of 'democratic capitalism'. At the international level, the Bretton Woods system of fixed but adjustable exchange rates helped to insulate national states from destabilising bouts of currency volatility. This framework gave rise to an 'embedded liberalism', whereby expansive welfare states and free collective bargaining enshrined a compact between capital and labour (Ruggie, 2009). Global trade and investment expanded rapidly in this period. But this was tempered by controls on speculative capital flows. Profitability remained the organising motive of production, but this took place against within a context where power was partially transferred to organised labour and other democratic institutions. Post-war capitalism was stabilised by a series of counter-veiling institutions which in turn gave rise to a relatively stable 'regime of accumulation' in this period.

The breakdown of the Bretton Woods order generated a new research problematique for the RA. The stabilising institutional nexus of post-war capitalism was unravelling. In its place a new regime was emerging. There is not space to review the gargantuan literature on neoliberalism here (see Duménil & Lévy, 2004; see Harvey, 2005; Mirowski, 2013). At its heart, neoliberalism sought to prioritise inflation control over full employment. In so doing, neoliberalism sought to displace the post-war compact and to extend the scope of the market across numerous social domains. Competitiveness would be restored through re-establishing managerial control over the labour process and by disciplining organised groups, such as trade unions and public sector bureaucracies, who stood in the way of market liberal reform. This project would provoke huge levels of social resistance. As a result, neoliberalism involved imposing market liberal rule through utilising the power of the 'strong state' (Gamble, 1988).

Regulation theorists sought to chart the shape of the new regime. For some regulation theorists, the rise of neoliberalism signalled the transition to a new post-Fordist regime of accumulation (Dunford, 1990). According to this perspective, the industrial structure of capitalism was moving towards a model of 'flexible specialisation', exemplified by new 'just-in-time' production systems and other 'post-Fordist' practices. Other regulation theorists struck a more pessimistic tone. The rise of neoliberalism displaced the extra-economic institutions which had stabilised post-war capitalism. But no international institutional 'fix' such as the Bretton Woods monetary system had emerged in its place (Tickell & Peck, 1995). As such, the neoliberal regime was not restrained by countervailing institutions. In the absence of an alternative 'mode of social regulation', neoliberal capitalism would be characterised by persistent financial instability, growing inequality and recurrent crisis (Peck & Tickell, 1992).

This branch of regulation theory emerged in the 1990s and 2000s and was associated in particular with a group of economic geographers, including Jamie Peck, Adam Tickell and Nik Theodore. This 'British School' of regulation theory led to the emergence of the 'neoliberalisation' approach (Green & Lavery, 2018). The starting point for the neoliberalisation approach was that neoliberal capitalism lacked an overriding mode of social regulation which could secure the stability of the new regime. Neoliberalism would therefore enter into frequent bouts of crisis. However, in seeking to overcome these crises, neoliberals would seek to extend 'market' solutions, thereby deepening the regime's tendency towards dysfunction and breakdown. For this reason, Peck referred to neoliberalisation as 'an open-ended and contradictory process of regulatory restructuring' (Peck, 2010). This approach sought to overcome the weaknesses of existing treatments of neoliberalism. It positions itself against three other approaches within the heterodox IPE literature: the 'Varieties of Capitalism' approach, neo-Gramscian IPE and post-structuralist approaches (Brenner, Peck, & Theodore, 2010). The problem with these alternative schemas is that each tends to privilege one scale of analysis, whether this be the transnational scale (as is the case with neo-Gramscian IPE), the national (VoC framework) or the local (post-structualist approaches). This means that each tends to wrongly conceive of neoliberalism either as a totalising logic which is imposed 'from above' or as a series of diffuse and localised social practices which take place independently of broader structural factors (Brenner et al., 2010: 184). The neoliberalisation approach's core argument is that each of these approaches therefore misses the 'variegated' or *systematically uneven* nature of neoliberal development (Brenner et al., 2010). The neoliberalisation approach therefore views *uneven development* as a systemic and constitutive feature of neoliberalisation. It therefore aims to capture how localised and context-specific experiments in market liberal rule are shaped by a broader structural logic without themselves being reducible to that logic. The neoliberalisation approach develops this insight through the deployment of a series of concepts relating to the nature of the state under conditions of neoliberal restructuring. Each of these concepts will be deployed to conceptualise the evolution of British capitalism under both New Labour and the Coalition in subsequent chapters.

1. *Neoliberalisation as a 'hybrid' form*

The first proposition of the neoliberalisation approach is that neoliberalism always exists in a *hybrid form* (Jessop, 2002a; Peck, 2010: 6; see also Schmidt & Thatcher, 2013: 24). The idealised end point of the neoliberal imagination is a situation in which 'the market' becomes consolidated as the dominant mechanism of resource allocation in society (Mirowski, 2013; Peck, 2010: 16). However, projects of this form are likely to encounter a range of social and political barriers within advanced capitalist states. Workers, for example, are likely to resist attempts on the part of capital and the state to treat their labour power simply as a 'commodity' whose price fluctuates in line with changes in market sentiment (Hyman, 2005: 11). Similarly, informal coalitions of social groups (for example pensioners with a high propensity to vote in elections) are likely to receive an array of state-facilitated transfer payments which cannot be reduced to the logic of 'market allocation'. The result is that neoliberalism, 'typically coexists with elements from other discourses, strategies, and organizational patterns', which place definite limits on the legitimate scope of the price mechanism (Jessop, 2002a: 453). A key issue for the neoliberalisation approach is therefore to examine the ways in which neoliberal programmes conflict with and/or incorporate elements of the 'extra-economic' institutional contexts within which these programmes are embedded.

Each phase of neoliberalisation will therefore display novel characteristics as state managers seek to negotiate complex institutional terrains which have been shaped by previous programmes of social and economic restructuring. This has important methodological implications. It means that researchers examining processes of market liberal restructuring cannot 'read-off' processes of institutional change from an overriding structural logic, for example the 'logic of capital accumulation' or 'globalisation'. Rather, a *conjunctural* mode of analysis is necessary which acknowledges the ways in which novel institutional configurations and political contexts can strongly shape emergent models of social and economic development (Jessop, 2002b; Peck, 2010). In turn, this has the implication that researchers deploying the neoliberalisation approach need to be attentive to the ways in which societies which incubate neoliberalising tendencies also typically sustain a range of *counter-tendencies* which can effectively limit—but which can also ultimately stabilise—the broader developmental trajectory of a given growth model.

This has important implications for the argument of this book. In particular, it allows us to go move beyond the tendency of the growth model perspective to explain the stability of finance-led growth in terms of those mechanisms which were *internal* to that dominant growth model. Instead, the neoliberalisation approach invites us to explicitly identify those counter-tendencies and 'flanking mechanisms' which help to stabilise a given mode of economic development, but which are not themselves reducible to the 'reproduction requirements' of the dominant growth model. As shall be argued in the following chapters, this has important implications for how we conceptualise Britain's model of capitalism under New Labour and the Coalition respectively. For example, in contrast to dominant interpretations of New Labour which seek to characterise the Party's programme as either 'social democratic' or 'neoliberal', Chapter Four argues that New Labour established a distinctive *hybrid* regime of development which consolidated the UK's finance-led growth model whilst simultaneously expanding the scope of the state in a variety of different ways.

2. *The State and 'Roll Back' neoliberalisation*

Neoliberalism's essential 'hybridity' has important implications for the theory of the state deployed by the neoliberalisation approach. Peck distinguishes analytically between two modes of neoliberal state intervention. First, he identifies what he terms 'roll back' neoliberalisation (Peck, 2010: 22). This involves a situation where state managers identify specific social or political barriers to the expansion of 'self-regulating' markets and then subsequently attempt to retrench or restructure these impediments along market liberal lines. Characteristically, this involves the identification of specific organisations and social forces—typically trade unions, recipients of particular kinds of state welfare, planning agencies or government bureaucracies—which are perceived to impede the effective functioning of the price mechanism. In the 'roll back' phase of the neoliberalisation process, these forces are tackled head-on. The tactics and tools available to state managers in the name of such programmes will of course vary according to the particular context within which they find themselves (Burnham, 1999). For example, in the early 1980s in Britain, rapid interest rate hikes were used as an indirect means of flushing-out uncompetitive industries and re-establishing managerial control over the workplace (Bulpitt, 1986: 37). In other contexts, more direct methods were used, for example with the strategic deployment of the police in order to break pickets in the 1984-5 miners' strike. In each case, however, it is important to note that the 'size' of the state need not be quantitatively diminished as a result of 'roll back' neoliberalisation. Rather, 'roll back' neoliberalisation involves the strategic *redeployment* of state power in order to tackle those social groups and institutional forms which are perceived to represent barriers to further market liberal expansion (Bonefeld, 2010; Gamble, 1988).

Throughout the empirical chapters of the book, this conception of 'roll back' neoliberalisation will be used at various points in order to explain processes of social and political change in the post-crisis conjuncture. For example, Osborne's attempt to reduce the size of the budget deficit through large public expenditure cuts—as outlined in Chapter Five—could be conceptualised as a programme of 'roll back' neoliberalisation. However, this programme encountered a range of social and political barriers which in turn shaped the evolution of the Coalition's economic strategy in office. The neoliberalisation approach allows us to capture the ways in which programmes of 'roll back' neoliberalisation typically encounter historically-specific institutional legacies and political barriers which can in turn reshape the trajectory of advanced capitalist development.

3. *The State and 'Roll Out' neoliberalisation*

The second form of neoliberal state intervention identified by Peck is referred to as *'roll out' neoliberalisation* (Peck, 2010). This characteristically develops in response to the initial shock therapy of 'roll back' neoliberalisation insofar as this tends to create—quite predictably—an array of social problems and governing difficulties for policymakers. Two distinct forms of 'roll out' neoliberalisation can be identified in particular. The first form involves the emergence of extra-economic 'flanking mechanisms' which have the capacity to stabilise market restructuring processes within particular periods of time (Graefe, 2006; Jessop, 2002b). For example, the large interest rate hikes of the early 1980s produced a rapid surge in unemployment throughout Britain. However, this forced up the cost of the welfare bill as legions of workers were forced onto the unemployment register. Whilst this helped to mitigate some of the social problems which might have otherwise emerged from the initial phase of 'roll back' neoliberalisation, expanded spending on unemployment benefit also acted as a permanent brake on attempts to reduce the size of public spending as a proportion of GDP throughout the 1980s (Smith, 2014). The attempt to re-establish market discipline through tight monetary policy therefore generated a *roll out* of government spending in areas which suddenly experienced high levels of unemployment and deindustrialisation.

The second form of 'roll out' neoliberalisation involves attempts on the part of policymakers to reconfigure the state apparatus in ways which are 'functional' to the perceived requirements of a globalising, open economy (Jessop, 2007: 287). In particular, this tends to involve attempts 'to promote innovation, competition and structural competitiveness…by intervening on the supply-side, promoting a flexible and highly skilled labour force through training and reskilling policies that subordinate welfare to the perceived requirements of economic policy' (Hay, 1996b: 171). Again, this form of 'roll out' neoliberalisation can be viewed partly as a response to the dysfunctions and failures associated with previous rounds of neoliberal restructuring. For example, whilst the first wave of Thatcherite reform boosted certain geographically concentrated sectors of the British economy, it also consolidated the low skill, low productivity nature of the British labour market across large swathes of the country (Coates, 2005: 184). In particular, this was reflected in the decline in the tradeable goods sector and in the low levels of investment in skills and infrastructure which occurred throughout the 1980s and 1990s. Crucially, the absence of an activist state which would intervene effectively on the 'supply-side' increasingly came to be perceived as a key barrier to the development of a 'knowledge-based economy' which could compete in a globalising world economy (Thompson, 1996). As such, throughout New Labour's second and third terms, we can identify a *rolling out* of state programmes which aimed to remedy the failures of Thatcherite economic policy. This was to be achieved through the implementation of new skills, training and workfare policies designed to boost the competiveness of the British workforce and economy in general (Hindmoor, 2004: 106). Again, on this understanding 'roll out' neoliberalisation does not involve a reduction in the size of the state. Rather, it involves the qualitative reorganisation of the state apparatus and the development of new modes of intervention in the economy in ways which (are perceived to) facilitate expanded economic growth and competiveness. As Peck writes, 'a neoliberal state is not necessarily a less interventionist state; rather it organises and rationalises its interventions in different ways' (Peck, 2001: 447).

This conception of 'roll out' neoliberalisation will also be drawn upon throughout the empirical chapters of this book. For example, Chapter Four argues that the expansion of public expenditure in New Labour's second and third terms, whilst driven by internal party political and electoral calculations, effectively served to stabilise and 'flank' Britain's finance-led growth model. In particular, it ensured that regions which might otherwise have been excluded from the growth dividend associated with privatised Keynesian growth were at least partially compensated through enhanced levels of public sector employment and increased levels of public expenditure.

4. *Neoliberalisation as an evolutionary and contradictory developmental programme*

The neoliberalisation approach also provides us with a useful framework through which to understand continuity and change in advanced capitalist societies. In one sense, the framework can be used to facilitate 'synchronic' analysis. This is where analysts take a 'snapshot' of social and political processes at a particular moment in time in order to examine the relation between different elements of a social system (Hay, 2002: 114; Ruccio, 1989: 36). The neoliberalisation approach facilitates analysis of this kind insofar as it allows us to distinguish analytically between different forms of state intervention which may be in evidence within a society in a given period of time but which are seemingly oriented towards securing contradictory social objectives. For example, a government may weaken labour protections whilst at the same time advancing redistributive policies which subsidise low pay employment. The 'roll back' and 'roll out' concepts advanced by the neoliberalisation approach allow us to make sense of these seemingly incongruous forms of state intervention and helps us to think through some of the tensions and contradictions which may be associated with such strategies. In another sense, however, the neoliberalisation approach allows us to engage in longer-term *diachronic* analysis. This is where analysts trace processes of social and economic change over a longer period of time (Hay, 2002: 148).

The neoliberalisation approach therefore contributes to an understanding of the *developmental trajectory* of advanced capitalism in a number of ways. First, it emphasises that a 'pure' form of neoliberalism has not been, and cannot be, consolidated as a self-regulating and self-stabilising social and economic system. The 'end-point' of the neoliberal imagination—the 'pristine clarity' of the free market (Peck, 2010: 7)—is an impossible destination to reach since markets are always dependent on 'extra-economic' inputs which are not reducible to the 'economic' sphere (Streeck, 2012). The implication of this is that neoliberalisation processes are characterised as 'rolling programmes' of (pro) market regulatory restructuring (Peck, Theodore, & Brenner, 2012: 267). The very impossibility of extending the price mechanism into all social spheres means that neoliberal development is driven to engage in a 'permanent revolution', where its self-expansion is frustrated by socio-political barriers which then must be circumvented by further rounds of market liberal regulatory reform (Peck, 2010: 7). Second, the neoliberalisation approach draws attention to the ways in which 'roll out' state interventions under neoliberalism often form the terrain for future rounds of market liberal restructuring and retrenchment. For example, a government may choose to implement subsidies for low-paid workers in order to mitigate the effects of 'flexible' labour markets and rising levels of income inequality. However, the growing reliance of the workforce on such subsidies can become a target for future retrenchment (particularly in a context of public expenditure reduction). As such, the 'flanking mechanisms' which stabilise neoliberalism in one phase of its development may come to be identified as barriers to market liberal expansion in a subsequent timeframe.

This conception of neoliberalisation as an evolutionary, contradictory and conflict-ridden process will inform the subsequent analysis of the political economy of New Labour and the Coalition respectively. For example, Chapter Four argues that New Labour's political economy embodied a 'hybrid' regime of social and economic development. This is because it rested on the combination of two analytically distinguishable modes of state intervention in the economy. On the one hand, the New Labour government attempted to entrench and expand a distinctive finance-led growth model by increasingly subordinating economic policy to the perceived preferences of the financial markets (Shaw, 2012). At the same time, the Blair and Brown governments substantially increased spending on public services and boosted state-led job creation, 'rolling out' a series of flanking mechanisms which (partially) compensated those social groups which might otherwise have been excluded from the dominant finance-led growth model. The three chapters which follow then examine how New Labour's 'hybrid' regime of development was reconstituted throughout the post-crisis conjuncture under the Coalition. For example, Chapter Five examines the ways in which the Coalition government sought to 'rebalance' the British economy through a programme of 'expansionary austerity'. This strategy aimed to rapidly reduce public spending in order to encourage increased levels of business investment and private sector activity. However, as we shall see this form of 'roll back' neoliberalisation—the attempt to extend the scope of the market through sustained public sector retrenchment—very quickly encountered a range of social, economic and political obstacles which frustrated and subsequently reshaped the development of the Coalition's economic strategy.

Conclusion

This chapter has outlined the conceptual framework which is to be deployed throughout this book. This draws upon a range of different theoretical currents found within the tradition of neo-Marxist state theory and regulationist political economy. This conceptual framework seeks to go beyond the limitations of the existing growth model perspective as outlined in Chapter Two. First, the growth model perspective advances a limited conception of the state which privileges analytically forms of state intervention which were 'functional' to Britain's finance-led growth model. But policymakers do not only seek to secure the conditions for continued accumulation over time. They are also driven to maintain popular support within society. In so doing, state managers deploy legitimation strategies or 'hegemonic projects' which seek to build a base of support in society. Policymakers can *actively shape* and *discursively construct* distributional processes in pursuit of this objective. Drawing upon this insight we can distinguish, in ideal typical terms, between 'One Nation' and 'Two Nations' hegemonic projects. Whilst the former seeks to build an expansive hegemony by channelling material concessions to the social base, the latter works by constructing 'moralised antagonisms' between distinct social groups. This distinction allows us to draw-out processes of continuity and change in post-crisis British capitalism.

The second limitation of the growth model perspective in its current form is that it struggles to explain how British capitalism was *stabilised* throughout the pre-crisis conjuncture. It appeals to a series of mechanisms which were *internal* to the finance-led growth model itself whilst neglecting how alternative patterns of state intervention served to stabilise pre-crisis British capitalism. As will be argued in the following chapter, increased levels of public expenditure and the 'rolling out' of a (limited) redistributive social programme under New Labour played a key role in stabilising British capitalism before the crisis. New Labour deployed a *hybrid* political economy which combined a finance-led accumulation strategy with a 'One Nation' hegemonic project. The *combination* of these alternative developmental logics helps to explain how British capitalism was (temporarily) stabilised and reproduced throughout the pre-crisis conjuncture.

This provides us with a lens through which to conceptualise continuity and change in Britain in the pre- and post-crisis conjunctures. The extent to which institutional or policy change can be identified depends, of course, on which policy area or institutional complex one isolates in one's analysis (Marsh, 2010: 228). The conceptual framework advanced above suggests one way in which we can interrogate processes of continuity and change within post-crisis British capitalism. Specifically, we can distinguish between the *accumulation strategies* deployed by policymakers on the one hand from the *legitimation strategies* or 'hegemonic projects' they deploy on the other. To anticipate the argument of the subsequent chapters, whilst the Coalition effectively continued with New Labour's accumulation strategy and thereby re-established the conditions for a renewed wave of finance-led growth, it effectively broke with the legitimation strategy which New Labour had advanced in office. Whilst New Labour pursued an (incomplete and limited) 'One Nation' hegemonic project which sought to secure broad-based support through enhanced redistribution and state-led employment creation, the Coalition pursued a distinctive 'Two Nations' project which sought to secure a *limited* base of support amongst strategically significant sections of the social base. In order to advance these arguments, it is necessary to move away from conceptual considerations of this chapter towards an empirical analysis of the evolving political and economic programmes of New Labour and the Coalition in government.

References

Aglietta, M. (1976). *A Theory of Capitalist Regulation: The US Experience.* London: Verso.

Becker, J., & Jäger, J. (2012). Integration in Crisis: A Regulationist Perspective on the Interaction of European Varieties of Capitalism. *Competition & Change, 16*(3), 169–187.

Beer, S. H. (1982). *Britain Against Itself: The Political Contradictions of Collectivism.* London: Faber and Faber.

Bertramsen, R. B., Thomsen, J. P. F., & Torfing, J. (1991). *State, Economy, and Society.* London: Unwin Hyman.

Block, F. (1981). Beyond Relative Autonomy: State Managers as Historical Subjects. *New Political Science, 2*(3), 33–49.

Bonefeld, W. (2010). Free Economy and the Strong State: Some Notes on the State. *Capital & Class, 34*(1), 15–24.

Boyer, R. (1990). *The Regulation School: A Critical Introduction.* New York: Columbia University Press.

Brenner, N., Peck, J., & Theodore, N. (2010). Variegated Neoliberalization: Geographies, Modalities, Pathways. *Global Networks, 10*(2), 182–222.

Bruff, I. (2013). The Rise of Authoritarian Neoliberalism. *Rethinking Marxism, 26*(1), 113–129.

Bulpitt, J. (1986). The Discipline of the New Democracy: Mrs Thatcher's Domestic Statecraft. *Political Studies, 34*(1), 19–39.

Burnham, P. (1999). The Politics of Economic Management in the 1990s. *New Political Economy, 4*(1), 37–54.

Coates, D. (2005). *Prolonged Labour: The Slow Birth of New Labour in Britain.* Basingstoke: Palgrave Macmillan.

Crouch, C. (2011). *The Strange Non-death of Neoliberalism.* Cambridge: Polity Press.

Duménil, G., & Lévy, D. (2004). Neoliberal Income Trends: Wealth, Class and Ownership in the USA. *New Left Review, 30,* 105–133.

Dunford, M. (1990). Theories of Regulation. *Environment and Planning D: Society and Space, 8*(3), 297–321.

Femia, J. (1975). Hegemony and Consciousness in the Thought of Antonio Gramsci. *Political Studies, 23*(1), 29–48.

Gamble, A. (1988). *The Free Economy and the Strong State: The Politics of Thatcherism.* Durnham: Duke University Press.

Gough, I. (1980). Thatcherism and the Welfare State. *Marxism Today,* 7–12.

Gough, I. (1985). *The Political Economy of the Welfare State.* Basingstoke: Palgrave Macmillan.

Graefe, P. (2006). The Social Economy and the American Model Relating New Social Policy Directions to the Old. *Global Social Policy, 6*(2), 197–219.

Gramsci, A. (1971). *Prison Notebooks.* London: Lawrence and Wishart.

Green, J., & Lavery, S. (2018). After Neoliberalisation? Monetary Indiscipline, Crisis and the State. *Transactions of the Institute of British Geographers, 43*(1), 79–94.

Habermas, J. (1975). *Legitimation Crisis.* Boston: Beacon Press.

Hall, S. (1979, January). The Great Moving Right Show. *Marxism Today,* 14–20.

Hall, S., & Jaques, M. (1983). *The Politics of Thatcherism.* London: Lawrence and Wishart.

Harvey, D. (2005). *A Brief History of Neoliberalism.* Oxford: Oxford University Press.

Hay, C. (1996a). Narrating Crisis: The Discursive Construction of the 'Winter of Discontent'. *Sociology, 30*(2), 253–277.

Hay, C. (1996b). *Re-stating Social and Political Change.* Milton Keynes: Open University Press.

Hay, C. (1999). Crisis and the Structural Transformation of the State: Interrogating the Process of Change. *The British Journal of Politics and International Relations, 1*(3), 317–344.

Hay, C. (2002). *Political Analysis: A Critical Introduction.* Basingstoke: Palgrave Macmillan.

Hindmoor, A. (2004). *New Labour at the Centre: Constructing Political Space.* Oxford: Oxford University Press.
Howell, C. (2016). Regulating Class in the Neoliberal Era: The Role of the State in the Restructuring of Work and Employment Relations. *Work, Employment & Society, 30*(4), 573–589.
Hyman, R. (2005). Trade Unions and the Politics of the European Social Model. *Economic and Industrial Democracy, 26*(1), 9–40.
Jessop, B. (1983). Accumulation Strategies, State Forms, and Hegemonic Projects. *Kapitalstat, 10,* 89–111.
Jessop, B. (1990). *State Theory: Putting the Capitalist State in Its Place.* Cambridge: Polity Press.
Jessop, B. (1997). The Regulation Approach. *Journal of Political Philosophy, 5*(3), 287–326.
Jessop, B. (2002a). Liberalism, Neoliberalism, and Urban Governance: A State-Theoretical Perspective. *Antipode, 34*(3), 452–472.
Jessop, B. (2002b). *The Future of the Capitalist State.* Cambridge: Polity Press.
Jessop, B. (2007). New Labour or the Normalization of Neo-Liberalism. *British Politics, 2*(2), 282–288.
Jessop, B. (2013). Revisiting the Regulation Approach: Critical Reflections on the Contradictions, Dilemmas, Fixes and Crisis Dynamics of Growth Regimes. *Capital & Class, 37*(1), 5–24.
Jessop, B., Bonnett, K., Bromley, S., & Ling, T. (1988). *Thatcherism: A Tale of Two Nations.* Cambridge: Polity Press.
Jessop, B., & Sum, N.-L. (2006). *Beyond the Regulation Approach.* Cheltenham: Edward Elgar.
Jones, M. (2002). *New Institutional Spaces: Training and Enterprise Councils and the Remaking of Economic Governance.* London: Taylor & Francis.
Joseph, J. (2000). A Realist Theory of Hegemony. *Journal for the Theory of Social Behaviour, 30*(2), 179–202.
Kenny, M. (1999). Regulation Theory. In D. Marsh, A. Gamble, & T. Tant (Eds.), *Marxism and Social Science* (pp. 35–60). Chicago: University of Illinois Press.
Krippner, G. (2011). *Capitalizing on Crisis.* Cambridge: Harvard University Press.
Lacher, H. (2013). History, Structure and World Orders: On the (Cross-) Purposes of Neo-Gramscian Theory. In A. J. Ayers (Ed.), *Gramsci, Political Economy, and International Relations Theory: Modern Princes and Naked Emperors* (pp. 75–99). Basignstoke: Palgrave Macmillan.
Lipietz, A. (1987). *Mirages and Miracles: The Crisis in Global Fordism.* London: Verso.
Marsh, D., & Stoker, G. (2010). *Theory and Methods in Political Science.* Basingstoke: Palgrave Macmillan.
Mirowski, P. (2013). *Never Let a Serious Crisis Go to Waste: How Neoliberalism Survived the Financial Meltdown.* London: Verso.

O'Connor, J. (1973). *The Fiscal Crisis of the State*. New York: St. Martin's Press.
Offe, C. (1984). *Contradictions of the Welfare State*. Cambridge: MIT Press.
Peck, J. (2001). Neoliberalizing States: Thin Policies/Hard Outcomes. *Progress in Human Geography, 25*(3), 445–455.
Peck, J. (2010). *Constructions of Neoliberal Reason*. Oxford: Oxford University Press.
Peck, J., Theodore, N., & Brenner, N. (2012). Neoliberalism Resurgent? Market Rule After the Great Recession. *South Atlantic Quarterly, 111*(2), 265–288.
Peck, J., & Tickell, A. (1992). Local Modes of Social Regulation? Regulation Theory, Thatcherism and Uneven Development. *Geoforum, 23*(3), 347–363.
Peck, J., & Tickell, A. (1994). Searching for a New Institutional Fix: The After-Fordist Crisis and the Global-Local Disorder. In A. Amin (Ed.), *Post-Fordism* (pp. 280–315). Oxford: Blackwell Publishers.
Peck, J., & Tickell, A. (1995). The Social Regulation of Uneven Development: "Regulatory Deficit", England's South East, and the Collapse of Thatcherism. *Environment and Planning A, 27*(1), 15–40.
Poulantzas, N. (2014). *State, Power, Socialism*. London: Verso.
Ruccio, D. F. (1989). Fordism on a World Scale: International Dimensions of Regulation. *Review of Radical Political Economics, 21*(4), 33–53.
Ruggie, J. G. (2009). International Regimes, Transactions, and Change: Embedded Liberalism in the Postwar Economic Order. *International Organization, 36*(02), 379.
Schmidt, V., & Thatcher, M. (2013). *Resilient Liberalism in Europe's Political Economy*. Cambridge: Cambridge University Press.
Shaw, E. (2012). New Labour's Faustian Pact? *British Politics, 7*(3), 224–249.
Smith, M. (2014). Globalisation and the Resilience of Social Democracy: Reassessing New Labour's Political Economy. *The British Journal of Politics & International Relations, 16*(4), 597–623.
Streeck, W. (2012). How to Study Contemporary Capitalism? *European Journal of Sociology, 53*(1), 1–28.
Streeck, W. (2014). *Buying Time: The Delayed Crisis of Democratic Capitalism*. London: Verso.
Streeck, W. and Thelen, K. (2005). *Beyond Continuity: Institutional Change in Advanced Political Economies*. Oxford: Oxford Univesity Press.
Thompson, N. (1996). Supply Side Socialism: The Political Economy of New Labour. *The Socialist Register, 216*, 37–54.
Tickell, A., & Peck, J. (1995). Social Regulation After Fordism: Regulation Theory, Neo-Liberalism and the Global-Local Nexus. *Economy and Society, 24*(3), 357–386.
Williams, G. A. (1960). The Concept of "Egemonia" in the Thought of Antonio Gramsci: Some Notes on Interpretation. *Journal of the History of Ideas, 21*(4), 586–599.

CHAPTER 4

New Labour's 'Hybrid' Political Economy

New Labour came to power in May 1997. For the following decade, the Party presided over a period of consistent growth, low inflation and sustained economic stability. However, this expansionary period collapsed with the 2008 financial crisis and the Great Recession which followed. This chapter advances an assessment of New Labour's political economy. The first section assesses a body of literature which argues that New Labour's political economy was essentially neoliberal in character. The chapter examines New Labour policy across a range of policy areas, including its fiscal, monetary, labour market, welfare and financial regulation policy. Across these policy spheres, New Labour largely extended the neoliberalisation of the British economy which had begun under the Thatcher government. The second section examines counterarguments that New Labour pursued a 'social democratic' political economy. Particularly in its second and third terms, New Labour substantially increased spending on public services and implemented a range of redistributive social policies. The third section goes beyond these binary framings and argues instead that New Labour established a '*hybrid*' regime of social and economic development in the pre-crisis conjuncture. New Labour advanced a finance-led accumulation strategy but this was paralleled by a distinctive 'One Nation' hegemonic project. Whilst the former advanced the neoliberalisation of the British economy throughout the pre-crisis conjuncture, the latter was oriented towards securing broad-based support through channelling material concessions and symbolic

S. Lavery, *British Capitalism After the Crisis*, Building a Sustainable Political Economy: SPERI Research & Policy, https://doi.org/10.1007/978-3-030-04046-8_4

rewards to the social base. New Labour's 'hybrid' political economy stabilised British capitalism before the crisis. This provides a benchmark against which to assess the Coalition's government's political economy in the following chapters.

New Labour and Neoliberalism

New Labour has been widely characterised as advancing a neoliberal political economy (Coates, 2013; Hall, 2005; Hay, 2002; Heffernan, 2000). Neoliberal programmes typically seek to deploy the power of the state in order to defend and extend the market as the leading distributive mechanism within society. Neoliberal projects of course vary across different national states. Nonetheless, it is possible to identify six tendencies which neoliberal programmes will tend to exhibit. These include liberalisation, deregulation, re-commodification, privatisation, internationalisation and reduced direct taxes (Jessop, 2007: 283). The following subsections assess New Labour's economic policy across these five domains. In each case, it is argued that New Labour's accumulation strategy consolidated and deepened the 'neoliberalisation' of the British economy throughout the pre-crisis conjuncture.

Fiscal and Monetary Policy

In assessing New Labour's political economy, it is important to bear in mind that the Party's primary objective was to return a Labour majority government after eighteen years of Conservative rule. Its second objective was to retain power once it got into office. New Labour's economic policy was deeply conditioned by these considerations. Understanding New Labour's statecraft—'the art of winning elections and [of] achieving a necessary degree of governing competence in office'—is therefore an essential component of any analysis of its political-economic strategy (Bulpitt, 1986). The Party's electoral strategy in the run-up to the 1997 general election and after was underpinned by two complementary objectives in this regard. On the one hand, it sought to dispel any fears that a Labour government would be reckless with the public finances (Shaw, 2007). New Labour strategists were convinced the Party's enduring status as a 'high tax' political outfit had lost it the 1992 election (Panitch & Leys, 2001: 251). New Labour aimed to shed this image and to reassure the electorate that it could be trusted to run the economy efficiently without implementing punitive tax increases or engaging in reckless borrowing. In addition, both Brown and Blair were convinced that winning the active support of business—and in particular the confidence of the City of London—was a crucial pre-condition of establishing economic and political credibility (Andersson, Kelly, Shaw, & Wickham-Jones, 2011: 115). Previous Labour governments had regularly experienced a loss in market confidence upon entering office, resulting in capital flight and increased interest rates as the City took fright at the prospect of higher inflation and increased public spending (McAnulla, 2006: 122). New Labour's strategy was to anticipate these fears and to placate them before financial actors crippled them in government (Coates, 2001). The second element of New Labour's political strategy was to ruthlessly capitalise on the perception that John Major's government was economically incompetent. Ever since the forced devaluation of Sterling after 'Black Wednesday', the economic credibility of the Major government had been profoundly compromised (Driver & Martell, 2006: 69). The symbolic significance of this was central to Brown's strategic thinking as he sought to entrench Labour's new-found advantage on economic credibility New Labour's strategy was therefore to define itself against both the perceived imprudence of past 'Old' Labour governments as well as against the perceived incompetence of the Conservatives.

This goal of securing governing competence in the eyes of the electorate and credibility with international creditor institutions was the guiding principle of New Labour's macroeconomic policy both in opposition and in government (Burnham, 2001: 128). It is important, however, to be clear about what New Labour strategists meant by this term. In essence, 'credibility' was about ensuring price stability and protecting 'the solidity of the vital measure of value – money' (Shaw, 2007: 161). Other measures of economic performance—such as increased employment or rising real incomes—were presented primarily as the outcomes of a stable and 'prudent' monetary and fiscal framework. Labour's move to prioritise inflation control had already been set in place in the period following the Policy Review. However under Brown—in close coordination with his economic advisor, Ed Balls—Labour's counter-inflationary credentials were consolidated further (Kitson & Wilkinson, 2007: 806). Price stability and business 'confidence', they argued, rested on two fundamental preconditions: the government's capacity to control public expenditure and borrowing on the one hand and the effectiveness of its monetary policy regime on the other. New Labour's macroeconomic strategy in the pre-crisis conjuncture rested fundamentally upon establishing these two objectives (Keegan, 2003).

In terms of public spending, Brown famously developed what he termed two 'fiscal rules'. Originally outlined in a speech in May 1995, these rules stated that:

> First, Labour will be committed to meeting the golden rule of borrowing – over the economic cycle, government will only borrow to finance public investment and not to fund public consumption. Second… we will keep the ratio of government debt to GDP stable on average over the economic cycle at a prudent and stable level. (Brown, 1995, cited in Keegan, 2003: 145)

The first of these—the 'golden rule'—was intended to reassure business and the electorate that increased current spending would only be funded out of tax revenues generated through economic growth. Any additional borrowing would be utilised only to fuel capital investment. This was intended to neutralise Conservative claims that Labour would increase borrowing to fuel day-to-day spending in areas such as education, healthcare and transport, whilst establishing some 'wriggle room' for increased investment in infrastructure. The second of the fiscal rules sought to place Britain's public debt at a 'prudent' level, which Brown later defined as securing a debt-to-GDP ratio of 40% (Fielding, 2003). These rules were subsequently incorporated into the Party's manifesto for the 1997 general election, *New Labour: New Hope for Britain* and formed a core aspect of Brown's first budget in July 1997 (Brown, 1997). The fiscal rules were broadly adhered to until 2008, when they were 'quietly abandoned' by Alistair Darling in the midst of the financial crisis (Hodson & Mabbett, 2009: 1053).

In addition to developing this 'rule-based' fiscal framework, Brown aimed to consolidate Labour's position as being 'tough' on public spending by committing to Conservative spending plans for the first two years of government. As Chancellor, Brown successfully followed through on this policy: public spending fell from 41% of GDP in 1997 to 37.7% in 2000 (Driver & Martell, 2006: 75). As a result, over Labour's first term, public spending fell to a lower level than it had been throughout Major's premiership. These constraints on public spending and on borrowing were complemented by a second aspect of New Labour's fiscal policy: its position on taxation. Again, New Labour's policies here were designed to distance the Party from its supposedly profligate 'Old' Labour past. In this regard, New Labour symbolically ruled out an increase in the top rate of income tax. This position remained intact under New Labour throughout the pre-crisis conjuncture, with the 50p rate only being re-established in the March 2008 budget in the midst of the financial crisis (Diamond, 2013: 98). With respect to securing 'credibility' with business, Labour committed to *inter alia* maintaining low levels of corporation tax, cutting the rate from 33% in 1997 to 28% a decade later (Murphy, 2007). The result was that 'receipts from corporation tax fell from £34.3 billion for 1999/2000 to £28.8 billion in 2002/2003, [during] a period of increasing corporate profits' (Shaw, 2007). As a result, by 2005 corporate tax payments accounted for the smallest ever share of national income. By 2009, Britain had the second lowest rate of corporation taxation of the G7 economies (Toynbee & Walker, 2011: 71). In a further attempt to secure the confidence of business and of middle-class sections of the electorate, Labour also cut capital gains tax on business assets from 40 to 10% over a period of four years (ibid.: 81).

In addition to New Labour's 'constrained' approach to fiscal policy, the Party also sought to establish credibility through adopting a novel framework for monetary policy. In the past, the City had traditionally not trusted Labour to effectively protect the integrity of Sterling. Traders often feared that Labour would yield to pressures to lower interest rates in order to temporarily boost growth and employment, particularly in periods immediately before a general election (Coates & Hay, 2001: 458). This loosening of monetary policy would lead to periodic increases in inflation and a corresponding loss of counter-inflationary credibility. From the late 1980s onwards, leading Labour figures indicated that in order to achieve a regime of 'sound money' a new approach was needed.

On May 6, 1997—less than a week after the general election—Brown ceded 'operational independence' to the Bank of England. This move had been carefully devised since 1994 by Brown in concert with Ed Balls (Peston, 2005: 115). Operational independence handed the responsibility of setting interest rates—traditionally one of the core competencies of the Chancellor—to the newly created Monetary Policy Committee (MPC). This nominally independent body—chaired by the Governor of the Bank of England and composed of bank executives and technocrats—was charged with hitting an 'inflation target', initially set at a rate of 2.5%. In addition, the Bank was required to continue to provide quarterly inflation reports to the

Treasury and, in the event of missing the target, the Governor would be obliged to write a report to the Chancellor outlining the reasons for his or her failure and the action he/she would take to remedy the situation.

The development of this distinctive monetary policy framework was of considerable political utility to the Chancellor. First, it was a move of key symbolic importance in securing Labour's 'credibility' with the financial markets early on in Brown's Chancellorship. In this regard, the policy was successful. As a subsequent submission from the Bank of England to the Treasury Select Committee put it, 'the delegation of the operational responsibility for setting interest rates to the MPC in 1997 was… associated with an immediate credibility gain, with long-term inflation expectations falling sharply to around the new point target'. Second, it allowed the government to distance itself from any negative backlash which might have occurred if interest rates did in fact increase (Flinders & Buller, 2006: 296). Balls had acknowledged this point explicitly in a speech in 1995, when he said that ceding independence to the Bank would 'bring substantial benefits as well as a credibility boost. It would allow a Labour government the political freedom to criticise or express doubts about interest rate increases even when there is clearly little option but to raise them… independence means there is someone [other than the government] to blame' (Balls, 1995, cited in Peston, 2005: 125). Third, whilst the Bank now had 'operational' independence, the Treasury in practice retained crucial levers of control over the MPC. For example, the Chancellor set the overall inflation target, retained the right to appoint the Governor of the Bank as well as external members of the MPC, and the Bank remained accountable to the Commons through the Treasury Select Committee. In this way, whilst the government benefited from the 'distancing effect' associated with operational independence, it retained considerable control over the broad framework for monetary policy implementation. Fourth, the Bank's independence (in combination with Brown's 'fiscal rules') empowered the Treasury relative to other departments. Since there was now no question of the Treasury backing down on interest rate commitments or of reneging on public spending targets, Brown's position was bolstered relative to other departments and, significantly, relative to the Office of the Prime Minister (Peston, 2005: 76). For all the fanfare about this institutional change, however, important continuities remained in place. In particular, the objective of securing price stability endured as the principal goal of macroeconomic policy. Although

Brown's macroeconomic policy was driven primarily by a series of political considerations, its effect was to effectively consolidate a macroeconomic regime which contributed to the ongoing neoliberalisation of the British economy throughout the pre-crisis conjuncture. Price stability became encoded as the principle objective of macroeconomic policy, over and above full employment.

Labour Market and Welfare Policy

New Labour's drive to establish fiscal discipline and price stability was flanked by a series of policies designed to enhance the competitiveness of Britain's labour market (Balls, 1998). In opposition, Labour had criticised the Conservatives for the rise in low pay jobs and the various 'opt-outs' from European directives on labour rights which they had secured when in office (Panitch & Leys, 2001: 276). In its 1997 manifesto, the Party underlined its objective to reverse the low pay character of Britain's labour market, stating that 'low pay and low skills go together… there is no future for Britain as a low wage economy: we cannot compete on wages with countries paying a tenth or a hundredth of British wages' (The Labour Party, 1997). By 2007, however, New Labour's professed goal to establish a 'high-wage, high-productivity' economy had not materialised. Instead, between 2003 and 2007, real wages did not grow at all for those on low to middle incomes, in spite of economic growth over this period of 11%. In addition, despite Brown's drive to increase labour productivity, the trend rate did not increase, meaning that the 'productivity gap' relative to other OECD countries remained in place (Keegan, 2003: 273; Shaw, 2007: 134). As Coates wrote in 2010, 'New Labour came into power in 1997 committed to the creation of a high-investment, high-productivity, high-wage domestic economy which it then failed to deliver' (Coates, 2013).

A number of structural factors had contributed to the growth of low pay, low-skill jobs in Britain throughout the 1980s and 1990s. The rapid loss of manufacturing jobs and the marked increase in low productivity service sector employment had contributed to a pay squeeze for low- and middle-income households. When New Labour came to power, it inherited 'a low-wage, long-hour, low-skill economy off the edge of a prosperous European market' (Coates, 2005: 184). However, between 1997 and 2007, the structural shift in the British labour market from manufacturing towards lower productivity service sector employment intensified. One of the key factors driving the decline in manufacturing output and employment had been a relative lack of investment in productive activities relative to other sectors. Whilst manufacturing investment as a percentage of total manufacturing output was at 'just over 13% as New Labour arrived in power…by 2003 that figure had dropped to a little over 9%'; as a proportion of GDP, manufacturing investment was 2.4% in 1998, but by 2002 it had fallen to 1.4% (Coates, 2005: 174). In addition to the relative lack of investment in manufacturing, the high value of Sterling—a result of New Labour's regime of 'sound money', relatively high interest rates and fiscal discipline—further undermined the competitiveness of tradeable goods relative to comparator economies. The result of this was that manufacturing declined more quickly under New Labour than it had during the Thatcher years. This decline in output was paralleled by a continuing fall in manufacturing employment under New Labour. Whereas 4.3 million workers worked in manufacturing in 1997, just over 2.5 million did so by the end of the Labour government. The long-established trend towards an increasingly dominant service sector therefore continued. As services and house prices boomed in Labour's first term, manufacturing entered recession. This dynamic continued throughout the pre-crisis conjuncture, with output in construction, estate agency and property rising from 12.6 to 16.2% between 1997 and 2007.

For the above reasons, it has been argued that, 'the most striking aspect of structural change under [New] Labour has been the continued decline of manufacturing against a background of rapid growth in the service sector' (Coutts, Glyn, & Rowthorn, 2007: 849). However, it is important to note that this shift was not just the result of underlying changes in the structural composition of the British economy. Distinctive forms of state-led intervention and politically driven bouts of labour market restructuring had sustained and guided this process throughout the 1980s and 1990s (Peck, 2001). Four distinctive features of the labour market regime established under the Thatcher governments can be identified. These are: de-industrialisation and the weakening of trade unions in associated sectors; the passing of restrictive anti-trade union legislation; the increasing 'flexibilisation' of labour market practices; and the emergence of 'welfare-to-work' strategies or 'active labour market policies' (Jessop, 2003: 11). New Labour's labour market policies represented to a large extent an accommodation with and indeed an extension of this basic neoliberal framework

(Smith & Morton, 2006: 402). Two developments were particularly significant in this regard: the ongoing flexibilisation of British labour markets and the development of welfare-to-work policies, both of which had the goal of improving the international 'competitiveness' and efficiency of the British economy (Hay, 2004: 47).

First, New Labour remained committed to maintaining Britain's position as the most flexible labour market in Europe. Its 1997 manifesto, for example, stated that 'key elements of the trade union legislation of the 1980s will stay – on ballots, picketing and industrial action', whilst in 2003 the Department of Trade and Industry (DTI) 'reaffirm[ed] its commitment to retain the essential features of the pre-1997 law on industrial action' (DTI, 2003: 67). In relation to the Party's proposed programme of labour market reform, Blair affirmed in the same year that 'the changes that we do propose would leave British law the most restrictive on trade unions in the Western world' (Panitch & Leys, 2001: 254). Thus, under New Labour's Employment Relations Act (1999), for example, 'solidarity action [was] banned, legally permissible industrial action defined very narrowly and balloting procedures required for such action [were] extraordinarily complex and demanding' (Shaw, 2007: 131). Labour market flexibility and restrictive labour laws were regularly touted as a key comparative advantage of the British economy by New Labour. For example, a government document boasted that 'total wages in the UK are amongst the lowest in Europe…UK law does not oblige employers to provide a written employment contract…[and] the law governing conduct of employment agencies is less restrictive in the UK' (Shaw, 2007: 134)

The strategic centrality which the Blair government attached to labour market flexibility can be seen if we briefly consider the character of the employment relations legislation which was introduced in Labour's first and second terms. The term 'flexibilisation' refers to the 'capacity of employers to hire and fire employees at will, and to use part-time, temporary and short term contracts to match production to shifting market demands' (Shaw, 2007: 124). Under Thatcher, industrial legislation was radically reworked to enhance the control of management over the labour process and to reduce the capacity of organised labour to secure inflationary wage increases (Smith & Morton, 2006: 402). The result was that 'employers had been able to sack union members almost at will' (Fielding, 2003: 166). In its first and second terms, Labour passed landmark legislation—the Employment Relations Acts (1999 and 2004)—which had the ostensible aim of (partially) re-regulating the labour market and expanding the scope of employee rights in the workplace. This legislation was paralleled by the enactment of other policies—including the Part Time Workers Regulations and Working Times Directives—which were required by EU law and which in principle had the goal of expanding statutory protections to 'atypical' workers and limiting the length of the working week.

However, in practice these labour market policies were strongly diluted when they were implemented by the Blair government. A 'minimalist' approach was adopted so as to ensure that the reforms were compatible with the overriding objective of securing labour market flexibility (Smith & Morton, 2006). For example, the EU's Working Time Directive set an upper limit of 48 hours on the amount of time a worker could be expected to work in any given week. Since British employees worked substantially longer hours than their European counterparts, this could have been utilised to restructure the British labour market and to lessen the length of the working week for relatively overburdened British workers (Shaw, 2007: 128). Under pressure from the CBI, New Labour diluted the legislation substantially, through exempting a range of sectors and occupations and through allowing for an extensive 'opt-out' clause, meaning that employees could choose to waive their right to an upper limit on working hours (Deakin & Wilkinson, 2005: 340). However, 'the effect of the opt-out clause has been that many of the lowest paid have been more or less obliged to sign the 'voluntary' declaration as a condition of obtaining work' (Barnard, 2003: 247; Shaw, 2007: 128). Notably, other European countries did not qualify the legislation to nearly the same extent. As a result, the 'long hours' nature of the British labour market relative to other European economies was not reversed: by 2008 over 3.3 million workers worked over and above the 48 hours maximum established by the WTD (TUC, 2008).

Maintaining labour market 'flexibility' would remain the dominant organising principle of the British labour market. As a Treasury document put it at the time, labour market policy was designed to ensure that employers retained the power to 'adjust total pay, including overtime and bonuses, as well as employment numbers quickly and flexibly in response to changes in market conditions' (HM Treasury, 2002: 8). The allocative efficiency of markets and managerial control of the labour process therefore remained guiding principles of New Labour's labour market regime when in government. Second, New Labour consolidated and expanded the 'welfare-to-work' policies which had been tentatively put in place under the previous Conservative governments (Fielding, 2003: 198; Peck, 2001: 332). Workfare programmes—which 'involve the imposition of a range of compulsory programs and mandatory requirements for welfare recipients with a view to enforcing work while residualizing welfare' (Peck, 2001: 10)—had initially been piloted under Thatcher with the 1986 'Restart Program'. The Social Security Act 1988 represented a shift to 'harder' workfare and this trajectory was further consolidated under Major with the Jobseekers Allowance (JSA) of 1996, under which 'eligibility for benefits was narrowed and means testing expanded' (Jessop, 2003: 11; Peck, 2001: 282). In the light of strong public support for the JSA—polling suggested that two-thirds of the electorate supported it—the Labour leadership pledged to retain the framework in spite of opposition from within the Shadow Cabinet (Peck, 2001: 291). In addition to accepting the JSA, when New Labour came to power it set about developing its own extensive welfare-to-work programme through Brown's flagship 'New Deal' policy. This programme—funded out of an (electorally palatable) £3.6 billion 'windfall tax' on the private utilities—was designed to incentivise re-entry into the labour market for welfare recipients (Gamble & Kelly, 2001: 176; Ludlam, 2000). Under the New Deal, after six months of unemployment individuals would be required to sign up to a programme which would offer them employability support. After four months, if subsidised work was still not forthcoming, individuals could choose between entering a voluntary programme, or entering into an education or training programme (McAnulla, 2006: 127). Importantly, there would be 'no fifth option': if claimants refused to adopt any of the options, they could lose their benefit for between two to four weeks (Fielding, 2003: 198).

The New Deal has been described as a 'typical neo-liberal programme… designed to eliminate welfare dependency' (Jessop, 2003: 13). 'Welfare-to-work' policies redefine unemployment as a supply-side phenomenon relating to the 'job-readiness' and 'employability' of individuals rather than as a structural feature of the market economy which can in principle be responded to through demand management. In this sense, New Labour's 'welfare-to-work' programmes represented a continuation of the Thatcherite approach to labour markets. However, New Labour's approach was different in the sense that it sought to institute and deploy a more heavily centralised, more comprehensive 'dirigiste workfare state' (Marquand, 1998)—overseen by an empowered Treasury under Brown—which would actively seek to instil a work ethic in the citizenry and re-integrate the young and long-term unemployed into the labour market (Watson, 2013: 11). As one government document put it, 'our ambition is nothing less than a change of culture among benefit claimants' (Deacon, 2002: 106). The failures of Thatcherite market liberalisation—the creation of regional pockets of long-term unemployment and the creation of a 'surplus' population lacking basic skills—would be corrected through sustained political intervention. In this sense, New Labour's programme represented an example of 'roll out' neoliberalisation *par excellence*. Markets, including labour markets, are not just 'given' or naturally occurring entities: they must be actively instituted through sustained political intervention and through successive rounds of welfare reform.

Importantly, as well as seeking to institute new patterns of behaviour amongst the new long-term unemployed, welfare-to-work policies were informed by a second logic which sought to directly constrain real wage growth across the economy. As Mandelson and Liddle, two key New Labour strategists, put it:

> By focusing on those presently excluded from the labour market, the government can help to tip the balance in favour of the labour-market outsiders against the insiders and *thereby increase the general pressure for responsibility in pay levels.* (Mandelson & Liddle, 1996: 101, emphasis added)

Glyn and Wood have summarised this aspect of New Labour's logic as follows: since 'the long-term unemployed in particular exert little downward pressure on wage bargaining as they are semi-detached from the labour market…if they can be cajoled or enticed back into searching for work… then the extra competition they inject into the labour market will bring downward pressure on wages' (Glyn & Wood, 2001: 52). In this way, New Labour's welfare-to-work policies were designed not only to reduce levels of state expenditure on unemployment benefit; they also sought to consolidate the international competitiveness of the economy through undermining workers' capacity to secure potentially inflationary wage settlements (particularly in 'low pay' sectors). Again, the deployment of state power under New Labour's welfare-to-work policies was utilised not to counteract 'market forces' but rather to reinforce them. The Conservatives' implementation of 'active' labour market policies of this nature had only been partial. Under Blair, however, 'Britain's truncated workfare debate began to exhibit the features of a comprehensive and internally coherent programme of transformative action… piecemeal experimentation with workfare under the Conservatives led to a fully-fledged adoption of workfare principles by the New Labour government (Peck, 2001: 332). Rather than 'rolling-back' the labour market regime which it had inherited, New Labour extended it in line with the objective of securing wage constraint, reductions in the welfare bill and increases in international competitiveness.

The City of London

The City of London has long occupied a position of crucial importance in the British economy as a commercial 'entrepot' for international creditor institutions, insurance firms and commercial activity (Ingham, 1984). However, from the late 1980s onwards, the position of the City as an international financial hub and as a key strategic sector in the British economy grew further still in importance. The high-interest regime of the early 1980s combined with an increasingly lax regulatory system to attract huge inflows of international capital (Jessop, Bonnett, Bromley, & Ling, 1988: 171). As Britain's manufacturing capacity rapidly contracted and Sterling appreciated, the British economy recorded its first trade deficit in visibles in 1983. As a result, the British economy became increasingly reliant on the City to attract foreign investment and to contribute to the balance of payments through the export of financial services. In 1986, the so-called Big Bang—which involved a rapid deregulation of financial markets in Britain—secured the position of the City as a key international financial centre within the global political economy.

New Labour's approach to the City of London again followed the basic strategy that had been employed under the Thatcher and Major governments (Gamble, 2010: 648). First, New Labour's macroeconomic policy, as outlined above, was explicitly premised on securing a regime of 'sound money'. Tight restrictions on public spending in Labour's first term and the granting of operational independence to the Bank of England underlined the privileged position of international creditor institutions relative to industrial capital (Coates & Hay, 2001). Second, whereas previous Labour governments had attempted to rein in the power of the Treasury to foster industrial development, under Brown the Treasury was hugely empowered. This meant that 'rather than challenge the "City-Bank-Treasury" nexus, New Labour…sought to work with and reassure it' (McAnulla, 2006: 123). Third, New Labour further consolidated Britain's regime of low corporate taxation and limited regulation in order to secure the City's competitiveness relative to other international financial centres (Baker, 2010). For example, the Financial Services Authority—created in 2001—had the explicit remit of promoting the financial sector's competitiveness through a regime of 'light touch' regulation. The FSA identified its 'hands-off' approach to regulation as a key guiding principle in the pre-crisis period. When in 2005 Blair expressed concern about the City potentially losing its competitive advantage through new regulations, 'FSA Chairman Callum McCarthy was happy to reassure him "that the FSA applied to the supervision of its largest banks only a fraction of the resource applied by US regulators to banks of equivalent size and importance"' (Shaw, 2012: 233). The 'light touch' approach of the FSA complemented New Labour's general approach to the City which was to nurture and protect its status as a premier financial centre. As one government spokesman put it, 'we won't do anything that harms the City of London' (Shaw, 2007: 55).

New Labour therefore displayed a 'double dependence' on the City of London (Smith, 2014). On the one hand, committed as it was to the 'fiscal rules', Brown's Treasury relied on cheap credit from the City to help fuel modest increases in borrowing (ibid.). On the other hand, financial services grew in importance as a key strategic sector under New Labour, underpinning Britain's financialised growth model and contributing substantially to Treasury revenues throughout the pre-crisis conjuncture. Over the New Labour period, 'finance's share of GDP in the UK economy rose from 5.3% in 2001 to 9.1% on the eve of the recession. Finance generated foreign earnings and contributed 35% of all corporation tax in 2001… then there was housing stamp duty, inheritance and capital gains tax…in 2002–2003 these receipts were together equivalent to 3% of GDP. By 2007–2008 this had risen to 4.25%, and that growth accounted for half the increase in total receipts over these years'. Financial exports continued to grow in systemic importance under New Labour: the City's trade surplus rose from £8.7 billion to £25.1 billion between 1996 and 2006 (Shaw, 2012: 231). As a result of the rapidly growing size of the financial services sector, by the end of the New Labour period the UK had the highest private debt as a proportion of GDP of the G7 economies (Thompson, 2013: 477).

In addition, as we saw in the previous chapter, the financial services sector also played a crucial systemic role in sustaining pre-crisis British capitalism. Low commercial interest rates and increased lending helped to fuel rapid growth in the housing market and consumption in the pre-crisis conjuncture, with two-thirds of bank lending being channelled into commercial and residential property.

New Labour and Social Democracy

So far the analysis has focused on those features of New Labour's political economy which suggest that the Blair and Brown governments were essentially 'neoliberal' in orientation. However, as was acknowledged previously, a number of scholars would reject this characterisation. In line with those who originally advanced the 'modernisation' thesis, an alternative body of literature argues that despite its reformed policy platform, the core of the New Labour programme remained essentially social democratic in orientation (Driver & Martell, 2006: 3). Two policy areas are generally identified to make this argument: New Labour's record on public spending (particularly after the Comprehensive Spending Review of 2000) and the mixture of redistributive social policies which New Labour advanced throughout the pre-crisis conjuncture. These arguments are surveyed below before an alternative interpretation of New Labour's political economy is advanced in the following section which goes beyond the 'neoliberal' versus 'social democratic' dualism which characterises the existing literature.

Public Spending Increases

As outlined above, a key element of New Labour's electoral strategy in the run-up to the 1997 general election was to commit to Conservative spending plans for its first two years in government. From 1997 to 1999, Brown doggedly pursued this strategy: public spending fell from 41% of GDP in 1997 to 37.7% in 2000 (Driver & Martell, 2006: 75). This period represented what has been termed the 'safety first' or 'reassurance' phase of the New Labour project (Hindmoor, 2004: 106). What Brown was trying to do in this period was to reverse the pattern which had traditionally crippled Labour governments. Rather than splurging on public spending early on and then having to enact deflationary policies in response to market pressures, Brown sought to gain 'credibility' with the financial markets first so that he could subsequently increase public spending without being penalised by international creditors. As such, the first two years of fiscal constraint—combined with steady economic growth, increased tax revenues and falling social security payments due to declining unemployment—boosted Treasury revenues such that by 2000 Britain was recording a budget surplus of £20 billion (Driver & Martell, 2006: 75).

Starting from plans first announced in 1999, however, Labour began to shift its approach to public spending (Gamble, 2010: 649). The Comprehensive Spending Review (2000) put government spending firmly back on the public agenda, committing the government to increase expenditure by £68 billion over the next three years (Driver & Martell, 2006). This recalibrated position was confirmed in the 2000 Budget, when Brown promised to enact a 'net doubling of public investment as a percentage of GDP by 2004 – from 0.9% to 1.8%' (Coates, 2005: 65). This translated into what one commentator referred to an increase of 25% in departmental spending over the following four-year period. The 2000 CSR represented a deliberate shift in Labour's strategic orientation in the run-up to the 2001 general election. Rather than resisting public spending increases, New Labour now presented itself as the Party best placed to boost public sector investment and to correct years of neglect under the Conservatives (Fielding, 2003: 213). For example, in his November pre-Budget report Brown stated that 'the public sector had suffered from decades of under-investment' (Fielding, 2003: 215). Only increased public expenditure (working alongside public sector 'reform') could remedy the situation. As such, 'by the time of the 2001 general election, the Conservatives had committed themselves to significant tax cuts and New Labour reinvented itself as the party of higher public expenditure' (Hindmoor, 2004: 152). The issue of public spending became one of the crucial issues of the election campaign, characterised by Labour as a choice between public sector 'investment' under Blair or cuts to public services under William Hague and the Tories (Geddes & Tonge, 2002: 7).

The electorate opted for the former. Labour won another landslide in the 2001 election and proceeded apace with its programme of expanding public expenditure. The transition from the 'safety first' approach of the first two years of the New Labour government to a phase of increased public spending on services was now in full swing.

Over this period, public expenditure increases were substantial. The majority of the spending increases were concentrated across three departments: health, education and transport. From April 1997 to March 2008, spending on the NHS went up by 6.3% and spending on education increased by 4.3% year-on-year in real terms (Smith, 2014: 605). If we exclude the initial phase of fiscal constraint, the size of the expansion in spending on public services is even greater: between 2000 and 2005 the party increased spending by 8.1% per year on the NHS and 6.1% per year on education (Tomlinson, 2012b: 210). This meant that 'by 2008 the resources available to the NHS had more than doubled and as a percentage of GDP [had risen] from 6% to over 9%' (Gamble, 2010: 649).

These increases in public expenditure clearly differentiated the New Labour government from the Conservative administrations which had preceded it. For example, under Thatcher and Major, annualised spending increases on the NHS had been 3.2% whereas education had seen an annualised average increase of 1.5%. The average total increase in public expenditure in New Labour's second term was 4.5% per year; this compared to an average of 1.2% under Thatcher and 2.6% under Major. As Tomlinson highlights, New Labour's record on public expenditure did not only compare favourably relative to previous Conservative governments: rather, throughout the 2000s Labour's increased investment in public services was 'the largest expansion of public spending of any peacetime government' including past 'Old' Labour governments (Tomlinson, 2012b: 210).

New Labour's record in securing these large increases in public expenditure was hugely significant. Indeed, it suggests that some of the early interpretations of New Labour as representing a simple 'accommodation' with Thatcherism were premature. For example, in Heffernan's early characterisation of the Party, he wrote that 'Labour now accepts that traditional social democracy is a thing of the past, acknowledging its replacement by a new orthodoxy informed by neoliberalism where…an expanded public sector [is] an impossible fantasy' (Heffernan, 2000: 20). Labour's record in its second term suggests that such accounts over-stated the fiscal conservatism of New Labour and underplayed the extent to which its approach to public spending would differentiate Labour from the Conservatives.

Redistributive Social Policies

As well as highlighting the large increase in spending on public services in New Labour's second and third terms, those who argue that New Labour was essentially social democratic in orientation also typically highlight the range of 'redistributive' social policies which the Party pursued in government (Gamble, 2010; Shaw, 2007; Smith, 2014: 601). A wide range of policies are typically identified in this regard, including the implementation of the minimum wage, increases in child benefit, attempts to indirectly redistribute tax revenues to the working poor, the growth of Sure Start centres, and the growth of child, working family and pensioner tax credits (Chadwick & Heffernan, 2003: 17; Hindmoor, 2004: 202). These policies are commonly identified as embodying traditional social democratic commitments to redistribution and poverty alleviation. For example, as Gamble and Kelly have written, 'far from turning its back on redistribution it could be argued that New Labour has sought to redistribute incrementally by every means possible except direct taxation. It is redistributing through tax credits, changing expenditure priorities, and [initiating] shifts in the National Insurance system. It is, however a very particular type of redistribution, because it has targeted specific groups: those with children, low-income pensioners and the working poor' (Gamble & Kelly, 2001: 183).

The full array of New Labour's redistributive social policies need not concern us here. However, it is worthwhile to outline one policy area which is typically identified by those who advance the argument that New Labour was 'social democratic' in orientation: the issue of child poverty. In 1999, Blair announced that the Party would aim to 'eradicate' child poverty by 2020. Brown announced at the Labour Party conference in 2008 that the Party would formally enshrine this objective into law, a commitment which was realised in 2010 with the passing of the Child Poverty Act (2010) (Kennedy, 2010). Crucially, New Labour's commitment was to reduce *relative* child poverty, where poverty was defined as those children dwelling in a household with an income of less than 60% of the national median (Shaw, 2007: 49). In other words, the policy sought to do more than just secure a basic 'floor' for child living standards. Instead, the commitment was made to ensure that the poorest household incomes rose in line with the national average. In the light of this basic commitment to equity, many have argued that New Labour's child poverty alleviation strategy embodied a classic redistributive social democratic programme (ibid.).

A number of specific policies were oriented towards meeting the child poverty reduction targets, including maternity grants, child tax credits and working families' tax credits. These programmes aimed to incentivise work by ensuring that being in employment would always pay more than remaining on the unemployment register. For example, the WFTC aimed to guarantee a minimum income of £225 a week in 2001 for all in-work households (Coates, 2005: 78). However, as well as incentivising work, Brown's programme of tax credits played a particularly important role in targeting child poverty (Shaw, 2007: 50). For example, WFTC and childcare tax credit together substantially increased the incomes of low-wage families, with the latter tax credit meeting up to 70% of childcare costs for working families on low wages (Fielding, 2003: 188; Sefton, Hills, & Stewart, 2009: 43). These interventions strongly differentiated the New Labour government from their Conservative predecessors. As Sefton and his collaborators have noted, 'we estimate that overall poverty in 2008–2009 would have been up to six percentage points higher and child poverty in 2008–2009 would have been up to 13 percentage points higher under a continuation of the previous government's tax and benefit policies' (Sefton et al., 2009: 44)

New Labour's child poverty reduction strategy enjoyed a considerable degree of success. Throughout the pre-crisis conjuncture, Britain experienced the largest drop in child poverty in decades and experienced the largest decline in child poverty within the EU member states (Toynbee & Walker, 2011: 211). The array of tax credits which were targeted at low-income households with children meant that the incomes of some low-wage families nearly doubled (Fielding, 2003: 188). By 2010 considerable progress had been made on relative child poverty reduction; whilst 3.4 million children had this status in 1998/1999, by 2010 the figure had dropped to 2.3 million (DWP, 2010). Those who characterise New Labour as essentially social democratic typically point to such evidence in their arguments. For example, Shaw writes that, 'if the performance of the Blair Government is compared with the performance of previous Labour governments in the 1960s and 1970s – and not their rhetoric – then there is a strong argument to be made that it enjoyed greater success in implementing the key social democratic value of poverty relief' (Shaw, 2007: 53).

New Labour's 'Hybrid' Political Economy

Two dominant interpretations of New Labour's political economy have been critically evaluated so far in this chapter. On the one hand, one body of literature argued that New Labour's economic and social programme was essentially 'neoliberal' in orientation and represented a basic continuity with Thatcherism (Hall, 2005; Hay, 2002; Watkins, 2003). The above review of New Labour's macroeconomic, labour market, welfare and financial regulation policies suggests there is considerable evidence to confirm this view. On the other hand, a second body of literature argued that the core of the New Labour programme was 'social democratic' insofar as it sought to couple expanded public spending, mild redistribution and poverty alleviation with a dynamic market economy (Gamble, 2010; Shaw, 2007; Smith, 2014). The evidence suggests that there is considerable merit in this interpretation as well; in its second and third terms New Labour implemented very large increases in spending on public services and enacted an array of social policies which generated a (limited) degree of redistribution to low-income households.

However, this binary framing of New Labour's political economy as either 'neoliberal' or 'social democratic' is in fact highly limited. Both characterisations fail to adequately conceive of the way in which New Labour's political economy embodied a *hybrid* regime of development which combined distinct patterns of state intervention oriented to achieving distinct social and economic objectives. In Chapter 3, it was argued that neo-Marxist state theory provides us with a range of concepts which can help us to understand the ways in which advanced capitalist states are typically oriented towards securing a range of divergent social objectives. In particular, it was argued that a useful distinction can be drawn between the accumulation strategies deployed by state managers on the one hand and the legitimation strategies or 'hegemonic projects' which they typically advance to build up a broad base of support on the other (Jessop, 1990: 216). Introducing this analytical distinction can help us to move beyond the crude 'neoliberal/social democratic' dualism which dominates the existing literature on New Labour.

An accumulation strategy refers to those forms of state intervention which are oriented towards privileging certain economic sectors, developmental logics and economic subjectivities over others. Characterisations of New Labour as 'neoliberal' tend to emphasise the government's accumulation strategy whilst downplaying the ways in which the government simultaneously sought to reconcile this strategy with continued support from the social base. The literature tends to focus on the ways in which New Labour's social and economic policies were driven by an attempt to secure 'credibility' with international creditor institutions and the business community more broadly (Ryner, 2010). For example, the ceding of operational independence to the Bank of England, the enshrinement of tight fiscal rules and the ongoing deregulation of financial markets are regularly cited as evidence of New Labour's 'neoliberal' character. Whilst these characterisations of New Labour do correctly identify one dimension of government policy in this period, they tend to understate the ways in which government policy was also oriented towards securing a range of other social and political objectives. For example, whilst these characterisations do at times acknowledge that New Labour increased public expenditure and pursued (limited) forms of redistribution, they also tend to view these trends as 'noise' around a more basic neoliberalising dynamic (Hay, 2013a: 12). This—it is submitted here—is a mistake. Downplaying the significance of New Labour's programme of enhanced public expenditure and (limited) patterns of redistribution compromises the capacity of such accounts to explain the *stability* of British capitalism throughout the pre-crisis conjuncture. It also limits the capacity of such accounts to adequately conceptualise how Britain's political economy was restructured subsequently in the post-crisis conjuncture. In order to better conceptualise these trends, then, it is instructive to acknowledge that New Labour's finance-led accumulation strategy operated alongside a qualitatively distinct legitimation strategy or 'hegemonic project'. New Labour did not only deploy state power in order to extend its preferred finance-led accumulation strategy. Rather, through expanding public expenditure and through implementing (limited) forms of redistribution, New Labour sought to secure and build upon its popular base of support in society. It did this through channelling material concessions to social groups which might otherwise have been excluded from the dominant finance-led growth model (Jessop, 2003).

We can identify a number of trends which suggest that New Labour pursued a distinctive legitimation strategy or hegemonic project throughout the pre-crisis conjuncture. It is here where the arguments of those who characterise New Labour as 'social democratic' in orientation are important. The shift in New Labour's approach to public spending in the lead-up to the 2001 general election campaign is of considerable significance in this regard. As Keegan has written, 'the fact of the matter was that by the time the first Blair government faced the electorate in May 2001 very little of the "purpose" of the 2000 budget and Spending Review had become apparent on the ground' (Keegan, 2003: 291). The tight fiscal constraint of Labour's first two years had further depleted the public services such that between 1997 and 2001, 'public sector net investment as a proportion of GDP was lower by far than in any previous four-year period since the cutbacks began with the Callaghan government of 1976-9' (ibid.: 282). The danger was that Brown's 'safety first' approach to public spending in New Labour's first term would undermine its electoral support and frustrate the Party's chances of winning a second election. With this in mind, New Labour developed its approach to expanding public spending in order to secure its position as the dominant force in British politics.

Three strategic considerations informed this re-calibration of policy. First, as early as 2001, there was a growing awareness amongst New Labour strategists that support for the project was rapidly declining in its traditional 'heartland' constituencies. As Philip Gould put it, there was a serious danger that amongst its electoral base the New Labour 'brand' had been contaminated (Fielding, 2003: 106). Conscious of haemorrhaging large chunks of its core support in working-class communities and with public sector workers, the Labour Party began to change its position (Shaw, 2007: 197). Second, internal party pressures added to the clamour for increased public spending. Key sections of the Parliamentary Labour Party—no doubt with a nervous eye on their own seats—were becoming increasingly impatient with the lack of progress in increasing public spending throughout Labour's first term (Keegan, 2003: 291). This growing impatience was symbolised by Peter Kilfoyle's resignation from the cabinet in 2000, when he cited disillusionment with the leadership's failure to adequately support Labour's heartland constituencies as a key motivation for his departure (Hall, 2005). Third—and perhaps most importantly—there was a growing recognition that voters in key marginal constituencies were also seeking to see improvements in public services and enhanced investment in infrastructure. Indeed, 73% of the electorate cited the desire for improved health care and 62% improved education as a crucial factor in how they would vote in the 2001 election. As such, the Labour Manifesto for 2001 had one major theme—'Public Services: Investment and Reform'.

New Labour therefore pursued a distinctive legitimation strategy in its second and third terms which sought to *extend* the scope of the state in the name of securing broad-based electoral support and internal party cohesion. Crucially, the pursuit of electoral dominance led the Party to engage in patterns of state intervention which were not reducible to the 'requirements' of the dominant finance-led growth model. Rather, New Labour's programme of enhanced public spending was driven by an alternative, underlying objective: that of securing governing legitimacy and of expanding its base of support within society.

The pursuit of this legitimation strategy had important distributional implications throughout the pre-crisis conjuncture. In particular, large increases in spending on public services effectively redirected resources to regions and sections of the population which might otherwise have been excluded from the surplus generated by the dominant finance-led growth dynamic. This is reflected in the changing composition of the UK's labour market throughout the pre-crisis conjuncture. For example, public sector employment increased markedly—by over 700,000—under New Labour (Cribb, Disney, & Sibieta, 2014: 7). At the same time, 57% of net job creation was concentrated in sectors which were in large part or wholly dependent upon public funding in some way (Buchanan, Froud, Johal, Leaver, & Williams, 2009: 16). This form of 'para-state' work became increasingly important in the ex-industrial regions, where private sector job creation was particularly weak (Tomlinson, 2012a, 2012b). For example, in the North East of England, 73.1% of net job creation was in the state or para-state sector, whilst in the West Midlands the figure was 179% as autonomous private sector job creation effectively contracted (Ertürk et al., 2011: 11). Britain's pre-crisis growth model was not therefore simply sustained in line with a market liberal 'disposition' on the part of policymakers (Hay, 2013a: 73). Rather, it was simultaneously stabilised through an increase of state intervention in ex-industrial labour markets and in the emergence of state-led 'flanking mechanisms' within the ex-industrial regions. Crucially, these stabilising mechanisms did not emerge due to the 'reproduction requirements' of the dominant growth model. Nor were they the result of a conscious 'accumulation strategy' pursued by policymakers. Rather, they were the product of New Labour's attempt to secure broad-based support through the pursuit of a distinctive legitimation strategy. This legitimation strategy can be usefully characterised as embodying a 'One Nation' hegemonic project (Jessop, 2007). By increasing public expenditure and extending state-facilitated support to low-income households, New Labour effectively incorporated social groups who might otherwise have been excluded from the dominant finance-led growth dynamic.

Those who emphasise the 'social democratic' orientation of New Labour's policy platform rightly highlight the ways in which it pursued a series of social objectives through enhanced public expenditure. However, 'social democratic' characterisations themselves suffer from a second, distinct weakness. They deploy an inadequate definition of neoliberalism and thereby generally overstate the significance of New Labour's public spending programme and its redistributive social policies. As such, they tend to erroneously conclude that these interventions reveal that New Labour was 'non-neoliberal' in character. For example, Tomlinson has outlined how growing public expenditure fuelled a substantial increase in public sector jobs particularly in the ex-industrial regions under the Blair and Brown governments (Tomlinson, 2012b). This, he argues, undermines the argument that New Labour pursued a neoliberal economic strategy. Tomlinson concludes that 'we need to talk less about the "triumph" of neo-liberalism, and more about how and why, and with what political consequences, the state plays such an enormous role in sustaining current employment levels' (Tomlinson, 2012b: 221). Similarly, on the grounds that New Labour increased spending on public services relative to previous post-war governments, Smith concludes that the party was 'certainly not neo-liberal' (Smith 2014: 618). The problem with these arguments is that they rest on a simplistic understanding of neoliberalism which views it essentially as a 'free market' project concerned with establishing a limited, nightwatchman state. Expanded public expenditure and public sector job creation are better conceptualised as elements of a distinctive legitimation strategy—New Labour's 'One Nation' hegemonic project—which operated in parallel with the consolidation of finance-led growth dynamic throughout the pre-crisis conjuncture.

In contrast to the above 'neoliberal' and 'social democratic' conceptualisations, then, New Labour's political economy is conceived here as embodying a 'hybrid' regime of social and economic development. It rested upon two analytically distinguishable modes of state intervention which operated in distinctive ways throughout the pre-crisis conjuncture.

On the one hand, New Labour's approach was underpinned by a finance-led accumulation strategy which simultaneously relied upon and deepened the neoliberalisation of the British economy. On the other hand, New Labour's political economy was organised around a distinctive legitimation strategy or 'One Nation' hegemonic project through which it channelled material concessions and symbolic rewards to the social base. In accordance with this political orientation, New Labour substantially boosted spending on public services—in particular on health and education—which resulted in substantially increased levels of public sector and state-supported employment particularly across the ex-industrial regions (Tomlinson, 2012b). Additionally, this dynamic was flanked by a series of (often covertly employed) redistributive social policies which channelled resources to low- to middle-income households. These policies played a key role in reducing relative poverty, constraining the growth of income inequality and mitigating the uneven development of 'Anglo-liberal' capitalism in the pre-crisis conjuncture (Hay, 2013b; Joyce & Sibieta, 2013). As such, whilst under New Labour the neoliberalisation of the British economy continued apace, this dynamic was complemented and sustained by an *expansion* of state intervention in key areas of social life and a *rolling-out* of state capacities at a variety of different spatial scales.

The 'hybridity' of the New Labour project has been acknowledged elsewhere in the literature (Driver & Martell, 2006: 28; Hall, 2005). However, these conceptualisations typically conceive of the 'hybridity' or 'composite' nature of New Labour in terms of the myriad *ideological* strains and influences which it contained. The conception of 'hybridity' as it is advanced here goes beyond these ideational characterisations. Rather, in line with the reformulated regulationist conceptual framework advanced in Chapter 3, the argument is that New Labour's pursuit of a finance-led accumulation strategy and a 'One Nation' legitimation strategy gave rise to a temporary but nonetheless relatively durable *regime of development* throughout the pre-crisis conjuncture. This hybrid regime of development was crucial to stabilising British capitalism throughout this period. First, it ensured that social groups who might otherwise have been excluded from Britain's finance-led growth model were—at least to a limited extent—incorporated into the dominant regime of development. Second, this helped to underpin the legitimacy of Britain's growth model. Third, this helped to contain and mitigate the uneven development of British capitalism throughout the pre-crisis conjuncture, as resources and jobs were redistributed to Britain's ex-industrial regions that may have otherwise been excluded from Britain's finance-led growth model.

Conclusion

In the spheres of fiscal, monetary, labour market, welfare and financial regulation policy, New Labour effectively consolidated and extended the neoliberalisation of British capitalism. This neoliberalising dynamic was the dominant trend under New Labour in the pre-crisis conjuncture. However, a number of 'countervailing' developments were also in place throughout this period. New Labour's programme of expanding public spending from 2000 onwards and its (limited) redistributive social policies distinguished the Blair and Brown governments from their Conservative predecessors. New Labour's political economy is therefore best viewed as advancing a 'hybrid' regime of social and economic development. On the one hand, New Labour's approach was strongly informed by a finance-led accumulation strategy which sought to subordinate social policy to the perceived preferences of internationally mobile capital. However at the same time, New Labour advanced a distinctive legitimation strategy or 'One Nation' hegemonic project which was oriented towards securing broad-based support within society. This was achieved through expanding spending on the public sector and through the development of an array of redistributive social policies. This hybrid regime of development produced a relatively coherent framework which, for a period of time, secured stable accumulation and continued legitimation throughout the pre-crisis conjuncture.

This conception of New Labour's 'hybrid' regime of development provides us with a useful benchmark against which to analyse continuity and change within Britain after the 2008 crisis. The following chapters assess the Coalition's political economy by tracing the ways in which it represented a rupture with or a continuation of New Labour's hybrid regime of development. As we shall see, whilst the Coalition effectively re-established the conditions for a renewed wave of finance-led growth in Britain, it effectively broke with New Labour's 'One Nation' legitimation strategy or hegemonic project. This re-embedded a series of structural weaknesses within British capitalism which are likely to shape its development in the future.

References

Andersson, J., Kelly, J., Shaw, E., & Wickham-Jones, M. (2011). Understanding New Labour: A Symposium on Eric Shaw's "Losing Labour's Soul?". *British Politics, 6*(1), 101–125.

Baker, A. (2010). Restraining Regulatory Capture? Anglo-America, Crisis Politics and Trajectories of Change in Global Financial Governance. *International Affairs, 86*(3), 647–663.

Balls, E. (1998). Open Macroeconomics in an Open Economy Scottish Economic Society/Royal Bank of Scotland Annual Lecture, 1997. *Scottish Journal of Political Economy, 45*(2), 113–132.

Barnard, C. (2003). Opting Out of the 48-Hour Week: Employer Necessity or Individual Choice? An Empirical Study of the Operation of Article 18(1)(b) of the Working Time Directive in the UK. *Industrial Law Journal, 32*(4), 223–252.

Brown, G. (1997, July). Budget Speech. *PR Newswire*. Retrieved September 4, 2015, from http://www.prnewswire.co.uk/news-releases/gordon-browns-july-1997-budget-speech-156180625.html.

Buchanan, J., Froud, J., Johal, S., Leaver, A., & Williams, K. (2009). *Undisclosed and Unsustainable: Problems of the UK National Business Model* (CRESC Working Paper Series No. 75).

Bulpitt, J. (1986). The Discipline of the New Democracy: Mrs Thatcher's Domestic Statecraft. *Political Studies, 34*(1), 19–39.

Burnham, P. (2001). New Labour and the Politics of Depoliticisation. *British Journal of Politics & International Relations, 3*, 127 149.

Chadwick, A., & Heffernan, R. (2003). *The New Labour Reader*. London: Polity Press.

Coates, D. (2001). Capitalist Models and Social Democracy: The Case of New Labour. *The British Journal of Politics and International Relations, 3*(3), 284–307.

Coates, D. (2005). *Prolonged Labour: The Slow Birth of New Labour in Britain*. Basingstoke: Palgrave Macmillan.

Coates, D. (2013). Labour After New Labour: Escaping the Debt. *British Journal of Politics and International Relations, 15*(1), 38–52.

Coates, D., & Hay, C. (2001). The Internal and External Face of New Labour's Political Economy. *Government and Opposition, 36*(4), 447–471.

Coutts, K., Glyn, A., & Rowthorn, B. (2007). Structural Change Under New Labour. *Cambridge Journal of Economics, 31*(6), 845–861.

Cribb, J., Disney, R., & Sibieta, L. (2014). *The Public Sector Workforce: Past, Present and Future* (IFS Briefing Note BN145). London: Institute for Fiscal Studies.

Deacon, A. (2002). *Perspectives on Welfare: Ideas, Ideologies and Policy Debates.* Milton Keynes: Open University Press.
Deakin, S. F., & Wilkinson, F. (2005). *The Law of the Labour Market: Industrialization, Employment, and Legal Evolution.* Oxford: Oxford University Press.
Diamond, P. (2013). The Progressive Dilemmas of British Social Democracy: Political Economy After New Labour. *The British Journal of Politics & International Relations, 15*(1), 89–106.
Driver, S., & Martell, L. (2006). *New Labour.* Cambridge: Polity Press.
DTI. (2003). *Review of the Employment Relations Act.* London: Department of Trade and Industry.
DWP. (2010). *Child Poverty in the UK: The Report on the 2010 Target.* London: Department of Work and Pensions.
Ertürk, I., Froud, J., Johal, S., Leaver, A., Moran, M., & Williams, K. (2011). *City State Against National Settlement UK Economic Policy and Politics After the Financial Crisis* (CRESC Working Paper Series No. 44).
Fielding, S. (2003). *The Labour Party: Continuity and Change in the Making of "New" Labour.* Basingstoke: Palgrave Macmillan.
Flinders, M., & Buller, J. (2006). Depoliticisation: Principles, Tactics and Tools. *British Politics, 1,* 293–318.
Gamble, A. (2010). New Labour and Political Change. *Parliamentary Affairs, 63*(4), 639–652.
Gamble, A., & Kelly, G. (2001). Labour's New Economics. *New Labour in Government* (pp. 167–183). Basingstoke: Macmillan.
Geddes, A., & Tonge, J. (2002). *Labour's Second Landslide: The British General Election 2001.* Manchester: Manchester University Press.
Glyn, A., & Wood, S. (2001). Economic Policy Under New Labour: How Social Democratic Is the Blair Government? *The Political Quarterly, 72*(1), 50–66.
Hall, S. (2005). New Labour's Double-Shuffle. *Review of Education, Pedagogy, and Cultural Studies, 27*(4), 319–335.
Hay, C. (2002). The Political Economy of New Labour: Labouring Under False Pretences? *Capital & Class, 26*(2), 149–152.
Hay, C. (2004). Credibility, Competitiveness and the Business Cycle in "Third Way" Political Economy: A Critical Evaluation of Economic Policy in Britain Since 1997. *New Political Economy, 9*(1), 39–56.
Hay, C. (2013a). The British Economy: A Crisis of Anglo-Liberal Capitalism? *Renewal, 21*(2), 3.
Hay, C. (2013b). *The Failure of Anglo-Liberal Capitalism.* Basingstoke: Palgrave Macmillan.
Heffernan, R. (2000). *New Labour and Thatcherism: Political Change in Britain.* Basingstoke: Palgrave Macmillan.

Hindmoor, A. (2004). *New Labour at the Centre: Constructing Political Space.* Oxford: Oxford University Press.
HM Treasury. (2002). *Full and Fulfilling Employment: Creating the Labour Market for the Future.* London: HM Treasury.
Hodson, D., & Mabbett, D. (2009). UK Economic Policy and the Global Financial Crisis: Paradigm Lost? *Journal of Common Market Studies, 47*(5), 1041–1061.
Ingham, G. K. (1984). *Capitalism Divided? The City and Industry in British Social Development.* Basingstoke: Palgrave Macmillan.
Jessop, B. (1990). *State Theory: Putting the Capitalist State in Its Place.* Cambridge: Polity Press.
Jessop, B. (2003). From Thatcherism to New Labour: Neoliberalism, Work-Farism and Labour-Market Regulation. In H. Overbeek (Ed.), *The Political Economy of European Employment: European Integration and the Transnationalization of the (Un)Employment Question* (pp. 137–153). London and New York: Routledge.
Jessop, B. (2007). New Labour or the Normalization of Neo-Liberalism. *British Politics, 2*(2), 282–288.
Jessop, B., Bonnett, K., Bromley, S., & Ling, T. (1988). *Thatcherism: A Tale of Two Nations.* Cambridge: Polity Press.
Joyce, R., & Sibieta, L. (2013). An Assessment of Labour's Record on Income Inequality and Poverty. *Oxford Review of Economic Policy, 29*(1), 178–202.
Keegan, W. (2003). *The Prudence of Mr. Gordon Brown.* Chichester: Wiley.
Kennedy, S. (2010). *Child Poverty Act 2010: A Short Guide* (House of Commons Library Briefing Paper).
Kitson, M., & Wilkinson, F. (2007). The Economics of New Labour: Policy and Performance. *Cambridge Journal of Economics, 31*(6), 805–816.
Ludlam, S. (2000). New Labour: What's Published Is What Counts. *British Journal of Politics and International Relations, 2*(2), 264–276.
Mandelson, P., & Liddle, R. (1996). *The Blair Revolution: Can New Labour Deliver?* London: Faber & Faber.
Marquand, D. (1998). The Blair Paradox. *Prospect,* 19–24.
McAnulla, S. (2006). *British Politics: A Critical Introduction.* London: Bloomsbury Academic.
Murphy, R. (2007). *Brown's Decade: Was It Taxing? Tax Research UK.* Retrieved September 4, 2015, from http://www.taxresearch.org.uk/Blog/2007/06/14/brown%E2%80%99s-decade-was-it-taxing/.
Panitch, L., & Leys, C. (2001). *The End of Parliamentary Socialism: From New Left to New Labour.* London: Verso.
Peck, J. (2001). *Workfare States.* New York: Guilford Press.
Peston, R. (2005). *Brown's Britain.* London: Short Books.

Ryner, M. (2010). An Obituary for the Third Way: The Financial Crisis and Social Democracy in Europe. *The Political Quarterly, 81*(4), 554–563.

Sefton, T., Hills, J., & Stewart, K. (2009). Poverty, Inequality and Redistribution. In J. Hills, T. Sefton, & K. Stewart (Eds.), *Towards a More Equal Society? Poverty, Inequality and Policy Since 1997* (pp. 21–46). Bristol: Policy Press.

Shaw, E. (2007). *Losing Labour's Soul? New Labour and the Blair Government 1997–2007*. Abingdon, Oxon: Routledge.

Shaw, E. (2012). New Labour's Faustian Pact? *British Politics, 7*(3), 224–249.

Smith, M. (2014). Globalisation and the Resilience of Social Democracy: Reassessing New Labour's Political Economy. *The British Journal of Politics & International Relations, 16*(4), 597–623.

Smith, P., & Morton, G. (2006). Nine Years of New Labour: Neoliberalism and Workers' Rights. *British Journal of Industrial Relations, 44*(3), 401–420.

The Labour Party. (1997). *New Labour: Because Britain Deserves Better*. Labour Party Manifesto, General Election 1997. Retrieved September 9, 2015, from http://www.politicsresources.net/area/uk/man/lab97.htm.

Thompson, H. (2013). UK Debt in Comparative Perspective: The Pernicious Legacy of Financial Sector Debt. *British Journal of Politics and International Relations, 15*(3), 476–492.

Tomlinson, J. (2012a). De-globalization and Its Significance: From the Particular to the General. *Contemporary British History, 26*(2), 213–230.

Tomlinson, J. (2012b). From "Distribution of Industry" to "Local Keynesianism": The Growth of Public Sector Employment in Britain. *British Politics, 7*(3), 204–223.

Toynbee, P., & Walker, D. (2011). *Verdict: Did Labour Change Britain?* London: Granta Publications.

TUC. (2008). *People Working Over 48 Hours a Week Increases to 3.3 Million*. Trade Union Congress (TUC). Retrieved September 10, 2015, from https://www.tuc.org.uk/workplace-issues/chemicals-and-dust/welfare-and-benefits/people-working-over-48-hours-week-increas-0.

Watkins, S. (2003). A Weightless Hegemony. *New Left Review, 25*, 5–33.

Watson, M. (2013). New Labour's "Paradox of Responsibility" and the Unravelling of Its Macroeconomic Policy. *British Journal of Politics and International Relations, 15*(1), 6–22.

CHAPTER 5

The Coalition's Accumulation Strategy

The 2008 financial crisis ended the long upswing of the pre-crisis conjuncture. Lending dried up, economic output fell and the public finances deteriorated. New Labour's 'hybrid' political economy began to unravel. The following chapters examine the 'post-crisis conjuncture'. This refers to the decade which followed the 2008 financial crisis. During this period, a Coalition government, led by the Conservative Party in partnership with the Liberal Democrats, came to power in Britain. Under the Coalition, the British economy moved from a prolonged and deep economic stagnation to one of putative economic recovery. This chapter examines the *accumulation strategy* which the Coalition deployed in office and identifies five distinct 'phases' in its development. The Coalition's accumulation strategy rested upon two ostensible economic policy objectives: the goal of eliminating the budget deficit through reducing public expenditure and the goal of securing a sectoral and geographical rebalancing of British capitalism. By 2015, the Coalition had failed to deliver on both counts. Britain returned to the model of 'privatised Keynesianism' which had dominated in the pre-crisis conjuncture, albeit in a modified form.

The Conservatives' Economic Policy in Opposition

Since the UK's ejection from the ERM, the Conservatives had consistently been trusted less with the public finances than Labour. From the 2001 general election onwards, Labour had ruthlessly portrayed the Conservatives as a grievous threat to 'investment' in public services as

S. Lavery, *British Capitalism After the Crisis*, Building a Sustainable Political Economy: SPERI Research & Policy,
https://doi.org/10.1007/978-3-030-04046-8_5

well as a threat to economic stability (Hindmoor, 2004: 152). In order to unseat this impression, in the years immediately before and after the financial crisis, the Conservatives deployed two distinctive strategies to reclaim the mantle of economic 'credibility' and governing competence from the Labour Party.

The Conservatives' first approach, adopted broadly between 2005 and 2008, involved a *strategic emulation* of key aspects of New Labour's social and economic programme. In May 2005, the Conservatives suffered their third successive election defeat. Subsequently, David Cameron was elected party leader on a 'modernising' platform, positioning himself as a centrist candidate who would reform Conservative Party policy in order to 'de-toxify' the Tories in the eyes of the electorate (Evans, 2008). From 2005 to 2007, this 'modernisation' process was at its most palpable: Cameron attempted to move his party away from its 'traditional policy emphasis on issues such as Europe, taxation, immigration and welfare, [and] drew attention to the environment… the NHS, flexible working and international aid' (Dommett, 2015: 256). Drawing lessons from the Blair premiership, Cameron ostensibly sought to position his Party on the 'centre ground' of British politics, focusing on winning back voters in key marginal constituencies and appealing to social groups who had not previously supported the Conservatives (Quinn, 2011: 404).

Cameron's 'modernisation' project was pursued through two tactical manoeuvres. First, the Conservative leadership pursued a strategy of 'triangulation' through which it sought to mimic and ultimately take ownership of key aspects of New Labour's approach to social policy (Dorey, 2009: 260; Gamble, 2012: 62). For example, in 2006 Cameron acknowledged the importance of 'relative' poverty as well as 'absolute' deprivation and stated that reducing it would be one of his key goals in government (Cameron, 2006). This implied that income inequality would no longer be viewed as a 'natural' market outcome, as had been the case under the Thatcher governments, but rather was presented as a phenomenon which could in principle be effectively tackled through government policy (Page, 2010). Second, and relatedly, Cameron sought to distance his Party from certain aspects of its Thatcherite inheritance (Dorey & Garnett, 2012). In particular, Cameron criticised Thatcherism for its excessive emphasis on individualism and argued that the Conservatives should instead seek to nurture the 'Big Society'—one in which a communitarian as opposed to individualist ethos would become a central organising principle of government policy (McAnulla, 2010: 290).

This broad shift in the Conservatives' rhetorical positioning was paralleled by a significant reorientation of the Party's economic policy. Specifically, the Conservative leadership aimed to consolidate its move into the 'centre ground' of British politics by accepting key aspects of the political-economic paradigm which had been put in place by New Labour. For instance, the then-Shadow Chancellor George Osborne aimed to neutralise the claim that the Conservatives would recklessly cut taxes in a way that might damage public services and undermine economic stability (Ganesh, 2012: 186). In a speech to the Cass Business School in January 2006, Osborne outlined how securing tax cuts would no longer be a principal macroeconomic policy goal for the Conservatives. Rather, 'investment in hospitals and schools [would have] the same priority for the Tories as tax reduction' (Blitz, 2006). This position was consolidated at the Conservative Party conference later that year, when Osborne confronted tax-cutting agitators on the right of the Party, insisting that 'we must win the argument on the economy. We will never do that if people believe our tax policy comes at the expense of their public services … to those who still want us to make upfront tax cuts now, we say: we will not back down' (Osborne, 2006). In line with this new approach, in September 2007 Osborne committed to match Labour's spending plans for the next three years. The politics underlying this commitment were clear: as Osborne put it, 'the charge from our opponents that we will cut services [now] becomes transparently false' (BBC News, 2007). The Conservative leadership was seeking to reassure the electorate that the NHS and other vital public services would be safe in Tory hands (Gamble, 2012: 62).

Cameron and Osborne's early emulation of New Labour's social and economic programme yielded considerable political benefits. By the end of 2006, the Conservatives were as trusted as Labour to run the economy; eighteen months earlier they had trailed by 13 percentage points (Ganesh, 2012: 168). However, the financial crash of 2007–2008 led the Conservatives to fundamentally reassess their political-economic strategy. Initially, the Conservative response to the crisis was hesitant, as the opposition firstly condemned the Brown government for its indecisiveness and then proceeded to attack it for its interventions in the banking system (Dorey, 2009: 263). However, by the end of 2008, the Conservatives had begun to develop a more coherent—and ultimately more effective—economic policy narrative. Specifically, the Party moved from a strategy of *policy emulation* to one of *differentiation* from Labour and its newly tarnished macroeconomic policy record. The goal was to create 'clear blue water' between Cameron's Conservatives and the embattled Labour government (Dorey, 2009: 266). In the summer of 2008, 'economists close to the Osborne team were warning them to expect a budget deficit of at least £100 billion the following year' (Ganesh, 2012: 196). Osborne sensed that this deterioration of the public finances presented a political opportunity to the Conservatives insofar as this would undermine Brown's reputation for prudent economic management. The shadow Chancellor's goal was to capitalise on this loss of credibility and to recover the Conservatives' reputation as the most competent custodian of the public finances.

It was this political calculation more than anything else which underpinned the Conservatives' new statecraft and its second economic strategy in opposition: that of blaming the crisis on Labour's 'over-spending', defining the crisis as one of 'debt' and then advocating a strategy of fiscal retrenchment to remedy the situation (The Conservative Party, 2009; Hay, 2011). In line with this discursive shift, the Conservatives opposed Brown's 2008 'Keynesian' fiscal stimulus package on the grounds that it would add to the public debt and deficit (McAnulla, 2010: 291). This strategy of differentiation—of prioritising a reduction of Britain's burgeoning budget deficit and tackling 'Labour's debt crisis'—would subsequently become the key organising principle of the Conservatives' governing strategy in office.

In February 2010, three months before the general election, Osborne outlined the core tenets of the Conservatives' emergent economic strategy in the annual Mais Lecture (Osborne, 2010a). This was a significant intervention because it outlined explicitly for the first time the intellectual rationale for the austerity programme which the Conservatives would subsequently pursue in government (Dellepiane-Avellaneda, 2015: 411). Two core themes underpinned this new approach: the objective of reducing the budget deficit immediately through public spending cuts and the goal of 'rebalancing' Britain's debt-laden economic model (Osborne, 2010a). In emphasising the need to reduce the budget deficit—which stood at 11.2% of GDP in 2009–2010—Osborne was at one with Alistair Darling's Treasury and the Liberal Democrats (Toynbee & Walker, 2015: 84). However, deficit reduction can be achieved through a variety of different channels, including through cutting spending, reducing borrowing or raising tax revenues. The key political question in the pre-election period concerned the timing of and the appropriate balance between these three options. Whilst Labour aimed to half the budget deficit by 2014, it sought to 'support the economy through the recession and then to cut the deficit once growth was established' (Dellepiane-Avellaneda, 2015: 411). Osborne, on the other hand, signalled that he would proceed with fiscal tightening upon taking office and would seek 'to eliminate the bulk of the structural current budget deficit over [one] Parliament' (Osborne, 2010b). In addition, whereas Labour planned to hold off on fiscal consolidation until 2011 in order to protect the fragile economic recovery, Osborne made the case for initiating immediate public spending cuts within the first year of the next parliament (Watt & Mulholland, 2010). The Conservatives' strategy of 'differentiation'—focusing in particular on the timing and the scale of deficit reduction—subsequently 'became a key dividing line in the election between the Tories and the other two main parties' (Quinn, Bara, & Bartle, 2011).

The Evolution of the Coalition's Accumulation Strategy

In spite of the deep recession, Labour's lagging position in the polls and Brown's low approval ratings, the Conservatives failed to win a parliamentary majority in the May 2010 election. This was at least partly due to the economic policy narrative which the Party had employed since the beginning of the global financial crisis. Whilst the charge that the crisis had been caused by Labour's 'over-spending' had gained popular traction, the Conservatives' proposed solution—of implementing rapid public expenditure cuts and reducing the size of the state—was regarded with suspicion by key sections of the electorate, particularly by public sector workers (Hay, 2010: 395). In response to private polling which revealed the Party's vulnerability in key marginal constituencies, the Conservatives reined in their austerity narrative in the immediate pre-election period (ibid.). Rather than specifying precisely where the axe would fall, they instead 'appealed for a general mandate to bring down the deficit' (Gamble, 2012: 64).

However, sections of the electorate remained unconvinced and feared the implications of a Conservative-led austerity programme. This meant that whilst the Conservatives enjoyed an average three per cent poll lead over Labour on the economy, this was far lower than might have been expected given the wider political and economic context (Dorey, 2010: 413).

The Conservatives' political strategy was therefore a double-edged sword: whilst the 'debt' narrative successfully reinforced the perception that Gordon Brown was responsible for wrecking the public finances, this narrative also contributed to 'considerable concern about the severity or speed of the cuts that might be imposed by a Conservative government' (Dorey, 2010: 414). Partly as a result of this perception, the Conservatives fell twenty seats short of a majority at the general election (Dorey, 2010: 430; Quinn et al., 2011).

In the absence of a parliamentary majority, on 7 May the Conservatives invited the Liberal Democrats to become junior partners in a coalition government. This arrangement was ratified on 12 May with the publication of the 'Coalition Agreement' and subsequently formalised on 20 May with the publication of *The Coalition: Our Programme for Government* (Cabinet Office, 2010). Two distinctive objectives underpinned the Coalition's economic programme from the outset. Both clearly bore the stamp of the economic strategy and political narrative which Osborne had developed in opposition. The first was a commitment to a programme of *deficit reduction*. This framing narrative set the government the objective of securing a balanced structural budget and a falling debt-to-GDP ratio primarily through spending cuts as opposed to tax increases. The second objective aimed to bring about a *rebalancing* of the British economy between sectors and the regions by building a 'new economic model' based on saving and investment rather than consumption and debt (Berry & Hay, 2016). In the following sections, the initial framing, implementation and evolution of the Coalition's economic strategy will be analysed with these two objectives in mind.

Phase I: Strategic Positioning (May 2010–October 2010)

On 20 May 2010, Cameron and Clegg outlined the core principles which would underpin their economic policy in *The Coalition: Our Programme for Government* (Cabinet Office, 2010). There is some evidence that the policy content of the Coalition agreement was closer to the Liberal Democrats' election manifesto than to the Conservatives' (Quinn et al., 2011: 302). Whilst this might suggest that the junior partners did 'better' out of the coalition negotiations than their senior partners, on the question of economic management and specifically on the question of the timing, scale and nature of the anticipated public spending cuts, the Conservatives' preferred approach to economic policy clearly prevailed (Gamble, 2012: 64). In the coalition negotiations, the issue of implementing public spending cuts had been one of Cameron's 'red lines' which he would not cross (Quinn et al., 2011: 306). Thus, whilst the Conservatives did grant some minor policy concessions to the Liberals, they did not concede any ground on the fundamentals of their proposed economic strategy (Bale, 2011: 6). For example, in the foreword to the *Programme for Government*, it was stated that 'the most urgent task facing this coalition is to tackle our record debts, because without sound finances, none of our ambitions will be deliverable' (Cabinet Office, 2010: 7). To place the Coalition's central economic objective beyond any doubt, the final page of the *Coalition Agreement* underlined in an embossed, stand-alone box that:

> The deficit reduction programme takes precedence over any of the other measures in this agreement, and the speed of implementation of any measures that have a cost to the public finances will depend on decisions to be made in the Comprehensive Spending Review. (Cabinet Office, 2010: 35)

As well as prioritising deficit reduction, the document stated that 'the main burden of deficit reduction [will be] borne by reduced spending rather than increased taxes' (Cabinet Office, 2010: 15). These commitments were consistent with Conservative policy in the pre-election period and served to consolidate Osborne's control over the Coalition's central economic agenda (Hayton, 2013: 7). Thus, whilst prior to the election the Liberals had argued that implementing immediate spending cuts would 'undermine the much-needed recovery', they were now compelled to support and defend these measures in government (Watt, 2010). As such, 'the Liberal Democrats were co-opted into an agenda of shrinking the size of the state which they would be forced to defend in principle, even if they fought for specific concessions and exemptions within the overall framework' (Hayton, 2013: 7). The principal goal of the Coalition's *Programme for Government* was therefore not primarily economic but political in two respects. First, it consolidated the Conservatives' deficit reduction strategy as the core organising principle of the Coalition's economic programme and rendered the Liberals 'prisoners of the austerity narrative which was about to unfold'. Second, it helped to cement the internal stability and unity of the Coalition government by identifying a common enemy and therefore a common cause around which the new governing partners could coalesce—the project of 'clearing-up Labour's mess' in line with a particular conception of the 'national interest' (Atkins, 2015. As such, whilst the Coalition's *Programme for Government* clearly signalled the Coalition's commitment to pursue a strategy of fiscal austerity, the specific details of where the cuts would fall would not be outlined until later in the year with the June Emergency Budget and the October Spending Review (Gamble, 2012: 65; Taylor-Gooby & Stoker, 2011: 5).

The 'Emergency Budget', published on 22 June 2010, was a crucial staging post in the Coalition's approach and a 'grand strategic budget', driven primarily by Osborne. Whereas Osborne had previously suggested that he would seek to eliminate approximately half the budget deficit over one parliament, his political 'masterstroke' in the June 2010 Budget was to announce that the Coalition government would aim to eradicate the entirety of the budget deficit in a single parliament (Gamble, 2014: 47). Specifically, the Conservative-led government would now aim to reduce cyclically adjusted net borrowing from 8.7% of GDP in 2009–2010 to 0.3% in 2015–2016 (Grimshaw, 2013: 1). The Budget also set a target for debt to be falling as a percentage of GDP by the same year (Osborne, 2010b). These moves were designed to entrench the dividing line between a fiscally 'responsible' Conservative-led Coalition and the Labour opposition. A broad prospectus of where the burden of deficit reduction would fall was also provided: spending cuts as opposed to tax increases would account for 77% of total fiscal planned consolidation (HM Treasury, 2010a: 15). In order to achieve this, the Budget stated that public spending would be cut by £83 billion between 2010 and 2015, which translated into an average cut of 25% for 'non-protected' government departments. In terms of specific tax and benefit measures, the Budget increased VAT from 17.5 to 20%, which 'constituted a £12 billion tax rise per annum, the equivalent of almost 1% of GDP' (Keegan, 2014: 47). This represented a reversal of the expansionary cut to VAT which the Brown government had implemented as part of its initial response to the economic crisis. This was flanked by 'in-year' spending cuts of £6.2 billion, with £4.8 billion of this secured from reduced central government spending on public services and their administration (Watt, 2010). Whilst in the pre-election period the Conservatives had been unwilling to specify where the cuts would fall, in the June Budget Osborne 'significantly hardened his fiscal stance'. The transition from Labour's two years of moderately expansionary fiscal policy to the politics of austerity and public sector retrenchment had begun to take shape.

However, the June Budget only gave a 'taster' of the cuts which were to come. The full details of the deficit reduction programme were announced in the Spending Review of 20 October 2010. This outlined where the majority of the cuts would fall for the following four years starting from April 2011 (Ferry & Eckersley, 2012; Sowels, 2014). Additional savings from the welfare budget allowed Osborne to announce a fiscal consolidation programme which at first appeared to be less harsh than the cutbacks which had been anticipated in the June Budget (Ganesh, 2012: 265). Rather than the projected 25% average cut, non-protected departmental budgets would instead be slashed by 19% over four years in order to save £81 billion (Ferry & Eckersley, 2012: 17). Nevertheless, the Spending Review still 'envisaged the tightest squeeze on overall public expenditure since 1945; the tightest settlement for spending on public services [since the mid-1970s]... and the tightest squeeze on NHS spending since the period from April 1951–1956'. As such, 'the plans set out by the government in the October 2010 Spending Review...[implied] public service spending [would decline] rapidly as a share of national income, falling from 31.7% in 2009–10 back to 25.6% of national income in 2014–15' (Crawford, Emmerson, Phillips, & Tetlow, 2011: 135). Local government funding was to be hit hardest, with a 27% cut amounting to £5.5 billion in real terms between 2010–2011 and 2014–2015. The Spending Review also anticipated that as a result of the spending cuts, 490,000 jobs would be lost in the public sector (HM Treasury, 2010b: 38). Again, it was confirmed that the burden of deficit reduction would be borne by public spending cuts rather than tax increases, with 80% of fiscal tightening focused on the former (Emmerson & Tetlow, 2015: 21).

The Coalition's first six months in power can therefore be characterised as a phase of ***strategic positioning*** in the sense that the government's principal objective in this period was primarily political as opposed to economic. As the above paragraphs suggest, three strategic goals in particular underpinned the early positioning of the Conservative-led Coalition: (i) reinforcing the unity and stability of the Coalition government, (ii) securing Conservative control over the Coalition's central economic agenda, and (iii) entrenching the narrative that the crisis was caused by Labour's 'profligacy' and that only a programme of rapid expenditure cuts as opposed to tax increases could repair the nation's finances. As this implies, the Coalition's austerity programme should not be viewed simply as an economic policy platform designed to bring about budgetary balance. From the beginning, the Coalition's fiscal consolidation strategy was underpinned by highly political considerations. It embodied a distinctive post-crisis statecraft which outwardly concentrated on the issue of the budget deficit but which in practice sought to entrench a new dividing line in British politics between a 'credible' Conservative-led government and an 'irresponsible' Labour Party which was in a state of 'deficit denial' (Wickham-Jones, 2013: 41).

Phase II: 'Expansionary Austerity' and Policy Failure (October 2010–December 2012)

Whilst the early strategic positioning of the Conservatives within the Coalition entrenched the central economic narrative of the new government and consolidated its political position, the commitment to securing immediate spending cuts represented a high-risk economic strategy in a context of low growth and fragile economic recovery. Although a nascent recovery had begun to emerge under Darling's chancellorship between the fourth quarter of 2009 and the second quarter of 2010, unemployment remained high at 2.5 million, demand remained weak and business confidence remained low (Keegan, 2014: 42). It is worth noting that the Coalition's total fiscal consolidation package advanced in the October CSR was equivalent to 7% of national income (Emmerson & Tetlow, 2015: 20). However, as the IMF warned at the time, fiscal consolidation equivalent to 1% of GDP typically reduces output by 0.5% and impacts negatively on domestic demand (IMF, 2010: 96; Sawyer, 2012: 208). The danger was that pursuing a potentially deflationary programme whilst output and confidence remained low risked pitching the British economy into a 'double dip' recession (TUC, 2010).

The Coalition's accumulation strategy and its public rationale for austerity rested upon a critique of deficit-financing and upon the articulation of a positive vision of how austerity could actually facilitate an economic recovery. Between 2010 and 2012, Osborne rationalised and defended his approach through an appeal to the idea of 'expansionary austerity'. This is the principle that enacting deficit reduction through spending cuts during a recession can lead to lower commercial interest rates, increased business confidence and ultimately to a private sector-led recovery. This conception therefore offered a critique of Keynesian deficit-financing as well as a positive vision of how austerity could facilitate private sector expansion and economic recovery. In making this argument, Osborne drew on a series of economic ideas associated with the 'Bocconi School' of neoclassical economics and specifically on the theory of 'expansionary fiscal contractions' as advanced by Alberto Alesina and his collaborators (Dellepiane-Avellaneda, 2015; Giavazzi & Pagano, 1990).

The 'expansionary fiscal contraction' thesis makes two key empirical claims: (i) that rapid fiscal consolidation during an economic downturn can successfully reduce debt-to-GDP ratios without undermining economic growth and (ii) that such programmes are more likely to be successful if they place the burden of deficit reduction on spending cuts as opposed to tax increases (Alesina, 2010; Dellepiane-Avellaneda, 2015: 400). The approach therefore explicitly rejects the Keynesian argument that cutting public expenditure in an economic downturn is likely to deepen the slump. Indeed, it inverts this logic and makes the argument that fiscal consolidation during a recession can actually prove to be expansionary, boosting business investment and employment levels. The key mechanism which underpins this conception of 'expansionary austerity' is what is termed an 'expectations channel' (Blyth, 2013: 172). According to this argument, private firms and households recognise that deficit-financing must ultimately be paid for out of future taxation. As a result, if governments run large deficits, private actors will rationally withhold investment and consumption as they anticipate future hikes in taxation. The policy prescription—advanced in a series of contributions by Alesina and others—was that if governments commit themselves to a 'credible' programme of deficit reduction focused on spending cuts this would signal to market actors that they could expect tax reductions in the future as interest payments on the national debt would subsequently decline (Alesina, 2010; Ardagna & Alesina, 1998). As a result, cutting public expenditure in a recession could, *pace* the Keynesian proposition, have a 'benign impact on expectations' and fuel economic growth (Dellepiane-Avellaneda, 2015: 393).

This conception of expansionary austerity became a key point of reference in the Conservatives' economic strategy and in Osborne's public rationale for austerity in the first two years of the parliament (Henry, 2014). Indeed, as Baker has argued, the conception of 'expansionary fiscal contractions' is 'as close as we get to an intellectual underpinning for the coalition's policies' (Baker, 2011). For example, in his Mais Lecture Osborne had claimed that if governments did not reduce their budget deficits rapidly, firms and households would anticipate future tax increases which in turn would lead them to hold back on current investment and expenditure (Osborne, 2010a). In the same year, Osborne argued that 'there are many well-studied examples of "negative fiscal multipliers", in which credible fiscal retrenchments in fact stimulated the economy, via greater consumer and investor outlays, by reducing borrowing costs and spurring confidence' (Osborne & Sachs, 2010). These arguments for expansionary austerity were echoed by Osborne's Chief of Staff, Matthew Hancock, when he approvingly cited 'research into dozens of past fiscal tightenings [showing] that, more often than not, growth doesn't fall but accelerates', adding that, 'the second lesson from the research is that consolidation helps growth when it's mostly done through spending cuts, not tax rises' (Hancock, 2010). Similarly, Osborne argued in the same year:

> A credible fiscal consolidation plan will have a positive impact through greater certainty and confidence about the future. Businesses can expand safer in the knowledge that an out of control budget is not going to lead to ever higher taxes. Consumers can spend safer in the knowledge that mortgage rates will remain lower for longer. (Osborne, 2010a)

This argument for 'expansionary austerity' was complemented by two further justifications for implementing immediate spending cuts. First, the Coalition argued that excessive public expenditure 'crowds out' private sector activity. Specifically, this argument claims that if the government sustains a large deficit this will increase demand for credit which in turn increases borrowing costs for private firms and households (Baker, 2011). Government spending—including in the midst of a recession—therefore discourages private investment and compounds economic stagnation. Conversely, if the government commits to a reduction in its own borrowing, this will translate into lower commercial interest rates for the private sector which in turn will create the conditions for increased business investment. In the June Budget, Osborne confirmed this line of reasoning when he stated that, 'it is my deeply held belief that a genuine and long-lasting economic recovery must have its foundations in the private sector'. For that to happen, he argued, it was crucial that the state was not 'crowding out private endeavour' (Osborne, 2010b). This was complemented by a second line of argument which emphasised the non-negotiable nature of implementing an immediate austerity package.

Specifically, Osborne argued that if the government did not implement austerity on its own terms, it would be forced to do so by international financial markets subsequently. He invoked the example of Greece to argue that failing to constrain public spending would lead to capital flight and punitive bond yields. Drawing on this line of argument at the 2010 Conservative Party conference, Osborne said: 'so, why do we have to sort out the public finances? Quite simply because we have to. Because any other road leads to ruin' (Cheesman, 2014: 6).

Three related arguments were therefore deployed in defence of the Coalition's austerity programme: (i) a positive case for fiscal consolidation couched in terms of 'expansionary austerity'; (ii) a critique of public spending and deficit-financing as 'crowding out' private investment; and (iii) an identification of the exogenous constraints imposed on the government's room for manoeuvre given the nature of international creditor institutions. This vision quite clearly promoted the idea that only the private sector could effectively lead the British economy out of the downturn and into a phase of recovery. Indeed, since the Coalition's spending plans were set to substantially reduce the size of the public sector, the government relied on increased private investment and exports to fill the 'demand gap' left by the programme of fiscal austerity (Sargent, 2014: 394). The key mechanism through which this was expected to take place was through an increase in private sector investment as lenders—buoyed by loose monetary policy, lower commercial interest rates and renewed confidence in the government's fiscal position—expanded their economic activities (Dellepiane-Avellaneda, 2015: 411). However, this approach was not without its risks. As one commentator put it, 'Osborne was laying a colossal bet on the future - that the private sector would rebound as the state pulled back' (Ganesh, 2012: xiii). Between the period of 'strategic positioning' in 2010 and the middle of 2013, this gamble on 'expansionary austerity' backfired.

First, business investment did not only fail to 'fill the gap' created by the public expenditure cuts; it actually *fell* for the first three years of the Coalition government (Keegan, 2014). The Coalition's original plans had assumed a 'crowding in' of investment and growth by the private sector equivalent to 9% of GDP (Lee, 2011: 63). However, 'real private investment, which had been forecast to grow by 33.7% from the first quarter of 2010 to the end of the second quarter of 2013, had actually fallen by 10.5%' (Lee, 2015: 23). Far from unleashing the 'animal spirits' of private investors, rapid fiscal consolidation was accompanied by a sharp decline in business confidence between 2010 and 2012. One report, for example, found that 'the Coalition had experienced the weakest spell of business confidence in two decades' (Roland, 2012). This absence of private investment was compounded by huge cuts to the government's capital budget. The Treasury had made the calculation that reductions to the capital budget would be less politically harmful than current expenditure cuts as the effects of reducing the former would not be felt immediately by the electorate. As such, in their first two years the government cut investment spending rapidly from 3.3 to 1.9% of national income, a cut of around 40% (Van Reenen, 2015: 3). This added to the absence of overall investment and compounded the weak growth figures which stalked the Coalition's first three years in office. Indeed, the OBR—which had consistently assumed that an increase in both investment and net trade would accompany the Coalition's austerity programme—acknowledged in its 2013 Forecast Evaluation Report that the anticipated increase in investment had not materialised (Lee, 2015: 22; Sawyer, 2012).

Second, the Coalition's objective of facilitating an export-led recovery also failed to materialise. Partly as a result of QE and a historically low base rate, Sterling had depreciated by 25.4 and 15.4% in 2008 against the dollar and the euro respectively (Berry, 2013: 3). Usually—as in the devaluations of the 1976 and 1992—currency depreciation on this scale would lead to an increase in exports and a decrease in imports as the cost competitiveness of tradeable goods increases relative to other currencies. However, the annual trade balance between 2009 and 2012 declined by an average of 8% (Berry, 2013: 3). Indeed, between 2009 and 2013, industrial production fell substantially in Britain (ONS, 2013: 1). Whilst in the 2011 Budget Osborne had promised a 'march of the makers' and a resurgence of Britain's industrial base, by January 2013, manufacturing had contracted by 0.4% and the construction sector by 9% (Inman, 2013).

Falling levels of private investment and weak exports meant that in the first half of the parliament, the anticipated economic recovery remained elusive (Lee, 2015). For example, between the third quarter of 2011 and the first quarter of 2013 output expanded by a meagre 0.4% (ONS, 2013: 1). It was clear that Osborne's vision of 'expansionary austerity' had not delivered the private sector-led resurgence which both he and the OBR had anticipated. As a result, whereas the OBR had forecast in October 2010 that by 2013 the UK would have achieved 7.7% growth, the actual figure turned out to be less than a third of that at 2.6%. Crucially, there is strong evidence that Osborne's programme of rapid fiscal consolidation was responsible in large part for weak growth in this period: the OBR itself estimated that fiscal contraction had reduced growth by 1% in both 2010–2011 and in 2011–2012, although other studies argued that this was a conservative estimate once 'fiscal multipliers'—i.e. the 'knock-on' effect that this contraction in output had on the wider economy—are taken into account (Jorda & Taylor, 2013). The long-term impact of this decline was that 'it took five and a half years for real GDP per quarter to attain the level of [the first quarter of] 2008' (Ellman, 2015). Fiscal contraction, *pace* Alesina and his fellow-travellers, had not proven to be expansionary; it had been contractionary, full stop.

The delayed and weak economic recovery significantly undermined the Coalition's deficit reduction targets. In order to deliver the £81 billion of savings which the 2010 *Spending Review* had outlined, the government needed growth rates to follow the OBR's predictions (Ferry & Eckersley, 2012: 21). As we have seen, this didn't happen. Deficit reduction was frustrated largely because the poor performance of the economy between 2010 and 2012 had a strongly negative impact on tax revenues (Emmerson & Tetlow, 2015). One of the key issues here was the changing composition of the labour market under the Coalition. Firstly, low pay work proliferated: 77% of net job creation between June 2010 and December 2012 was concentrated in 'low pay' sectors such as retail and residential care activities (TUC, 2013: 5). Since low pay employment typically generates lower tax revenues than well-remunerated work, this undermined the Coalition's deficit reduction targets. Secondly, the recession had been accompanied by a rapid decline in real wages which was unprecedented in modern times: in 2012 real wages remained 7.9% below their pre-crisis peak whilst 41% of workplaces had implemented wage-freeze or wage cut programmes (WERS, 2013: 7). This dynamic of real wage stagnation compared unfavourably with the recessions of the early 1980s and 1990s, where real median wages had both recovered within two years of each respective downturn (Green & Lavery, 2015: 15). As a result, stagnant real wage growth from 2010 to 2013 further undermined demand and constrained tax revenues accruing to the Treasury. The result of this was that whereas in June 2010 the OBR had forecast that public sector net borrowing would be £60 billion in 2013, the actual figure came in at £108 billion. As one report put it at the time, of this shortfall of £58 billion, 'more than half of [it] – over £30 billion – can be explained by weaker income tax receipts and national insurance contributions, with the continued weakness of earnings growth a key drag' (OBR, 2014b: 54). Whilst public employment declined the private sector did 'fill-in' in a sense—for example private sector employment increased by 4% between 2011 and 2012, bringing the figure above its pre-crisis peak—but the precarious, low pay nature of many of these jobs meant that the tax revenues generated were lower than anticipated and deficit reduction was therefore rendered more difficult.

By the end of 2012, the Conservative strategy of 'expansionary austerity' had failed to deliver the private sector-led recovery which the Coalition had anticipated in Phase I of its strategic positioning. Private investment and net trade remained unimpressive. Weak tax revenues and real wage stagnation were frustrating the Coalition's deficit reduction targets. Whilst Osborne had inherited a growth rate of 2.6% between 2009 and 2010, between September 2010 and April 2013 growth had registered at a paltry 0.8% *in total* (Blanchflower, 2013). However, despite this, the idea of 'expansionary austerity' remained a key discourse underpinning Osborne's economic strategy in Phase II of the Coalition period. As one scholar put it:

> The coalition's initial diagnostic and proposed solutions [of expansionary fiscal contraction] remained unchanged over time, even in the face of missed targets and policy failures. The proposed path has been insulated from policy learning. On the contrary, sticking to the course, the model of expansionary contraction, was the main theme of the 2011 and 2012 Budgets…no policy anomaly, the double-dip recession, the possibility of a triple-dip one, the downgrading of British public debt, was enough to shock the cognitive foundations of existing policy commitments. (Dellepiane-Avellaneda, 2015: 412)

However, despite retaining a rhetorical commitment to the original deficit reduction strategy, Osborne came under severe political pressure between the end of 2011 and the spring of 2013 to change course. As one commentator noted, 'when growth went sickly in 2010 and then stagnated for much of 2011 and 2012, one government figure recalls: "Osborne was shitting himself"' (Rawnsley, 2015). In March 2013, Osborne's personal approval ratings registered at negative 33 points—the lowest level recorded by any Chancellor since the recession of the early 1990s (Stacey, 2013). In the same year, 60% of voters perceived that the government was managing the economy 'badly' (May 2015, 2014). These perceptions were compounded by negative external evaluations of the Coalition's economic record. In January 2013, Olivier Blanchard of the IMF argued that Osborne needed to reassess his deficit reduction programme, whilst between February and April 2013 the ratings agencies Moody's and then Fitch downgraded the UK's credit rating for the first time since 1978 (BBC News, 2013). The Labour opposition, for its part, did its best to capitalise on Osborne's failure to deliver growth and deficit reduction according to the Coalition's own targets. For example, in his response to the 2012 Autumn Statement, Shadow Chancellor Ed Balls said that, 'the defining purpose of the Government, the cornerstone of the Coalition, the one test they set themselves – to balance the books and get the debt falling by 2015 – is now in tatters' (BBC, 2012).

The transition into 'Phase III' of the Coalition's economic strategy was underpinned by the goal of reversing these negative perceptions of the government's record and in particular of returning growth to the British economy before the 2015 election. Achieving this objective, however, would lead the Coalition to violate some of the key principles which it had set out in Phase I and II of its accumulation strategy.

Phase III: Policy Change and Discursive Continuity (December 2012–December 2014)

It is widely acknowledged that weak economic growth and the associated failure to keep to the planned programme of deficit reduction led the Coalition to modify its economic strategy in the first half of the parliament. However, there are two ambiguities in the literature which need to be dealt with. The first is that the specific timing of this shift in direction remains rather ambiguous. For example, Lee acknowledges that in the 'first two years of office [i.e. up to May 2012], fiscal contraction did not fuel the expected economic expansion', but then goes on to identify the OBR's October 2013 *Forecast Evaluation Report* as a key moment which symbolised that there had been a shift in the Coalition's economic strategy (Lee, 2015: 20–22). Similarly, Gamble states that 'in 2012, faced with the prospect of a double dip recession in the UK and with no recovery in sight, Osborne did adopt a Plan B, easing up on austerity, and postponing many of the cuts in public spending to the next parliament'. However the precise moment at which this change in direction took place remains unspecified. This ambiguity over the question of timing is perhaps unsurprising; in the complex world of economic policymaking there is rarely a single identifiable 'moment' at which a definite shift in strategy takes place. However, one contribution of this section will be to more clearly delineate the key moments when the Coalition's deficit reduction strategy began to shift. The second point of ambiguity in the literature is that it tends to not distinguish adequately between two closely related but nevertheless distinct aspects of the shift in the Coalition's economic strategy. The first change is the one noted above: the move to postpone the original timetable of deficit and debt reduction into the next parliament. The second change was the return of economic growth and the re-emergence of what some have termed 'privatised Keynesianism Mark II' (Hay, 2013a). The following sections distinguish analytically between these two shifts and relate these changes to the strategic priorities of the Coalition government. Let us now take each point of transition in turn.

The Postponement of Deficit Reduction

The first explicit acknowledgement that the original timetable for deficit reduction would not be met came as early as November 2011 in the Chancellor's Autumn Statement (Osborne, 2011). In its report accompanying the Autumn Statement, the OBR massively downgraded its growth forecasts: whereas it had previously predicted growth of 1.7% for 2011, this was downgraded to 0.9%, whilst its forecast for 2012 was downgraded from 2.5 to 0.7% (OBR, 2011). As a result, it was forecast that the structural deficit would remain until 2016–2017, two years later than initially anticipated. This was significant for two reasons. First, it frustrated the Chancellor's original plan of 'frontloading' the public spending cuts so that he could, in a context of rising growth, offer pre-election tax cuts in 2015 (Dolphin, 2011: 3). Second, it was the first time that the Chancellor conceded that his own original deficit and debt reduction targets would not be met (Osborne, 2011). As one commentator put it at the time, 'the landscape is fundamentally transformed. A government that promised to eliminate the budget deficit by the next election has admitted that it will fail. It now says it needs another two years to meet its deficit target' (Landale, 2011).

This represented a key moment of transition in the Coalition's economic strategy. As has been outlined above, the Coalition's self-proclaimed *raison d'etre* had been to eliminate the deficit in one parliament. Osborne now faced a choice. On the one hand, he could stick to his original deficit reduction targets. This, however, would require very large spending cuts and tax increases in addition to those which had already been put forward in 2010. Alternatively, he could broadly stick with his current spending plans but accept that borrowing would remain much higher than had been initially hoped for. The Chancellor opted for this latter option. As the IFS put it, increased borrowing in 2011–2012 was:

> Not matched by an announcement of further austerity for the current parliament on top of what the coalition government had already set in place during its first six months in office – instead the government responded by pencilling in more spending cuts for the first half of the forthcoming parliament. (Emmerson & Tetlow, 2015: 13)

A year later in the December 2012 Autumn Statement, Osborne confirmed that he would stick to this revised approach. As a result, borrowing was expected to still be running at 5.2% of national income by 2014–2015, almost three times the 1.9% that had been forecast in the November 2010 Spending Review (Emmerson & Tetlow, 2015: 22). Figure 5.1 compares the projected scale of deficit reduction as outlined

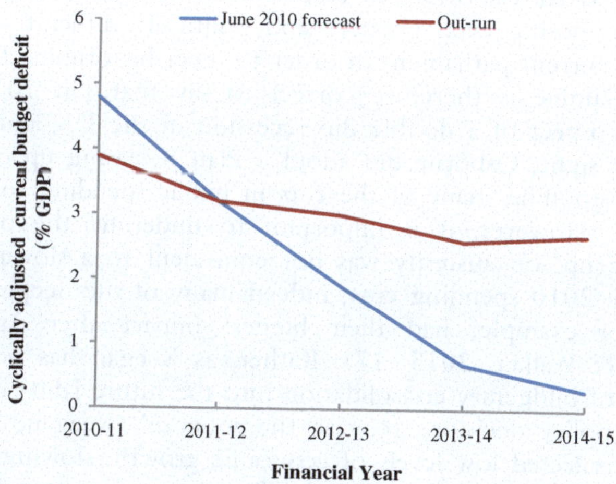

Fig. 5.1 Projected v. Actual Deficit Reduction (*Source* Adapted from: Van Reenen, 2015: 3)

in the June Budget to the 'out-run'—i.e. the level of deficit reduction which was actually achieved over the parliament. As the graph shows, in the financial year 2011–2012, the scale of fiscal consolidation failed to keep pace with the original deficit reduction plan and then levelled out between 2012 and 2014. As Lee has written, between '2010-11 fiscal tightening had amounted to 1.5 per cent of national income, followed by a further 2.3 per cent during 2011-12. However, the realisation that a further acceleration in fiscal tightening might drive the economy into recession persuaded Osborne to loosen fiscal policy, with the result that fiscal consolidation was planned to be only 0.7 per cent of GDP in 2014-15 and 0.6 per cent in 2015-16' (Lee, 2015: 21).

Between the Autumn Statements of 2011 and 2012, the Coalition did therefore adopt a 'Plan B' in the sense that it retreated from its original 2010 timetable of deficit reduction. However, it is important to note two points. First, the 'levelling out' of the deficit after 2011–2012 did not mean that Osborne had substantially reneged on the Coalition's original programme of spending cuts. Indeed, as the IFS pointed out, 'virtually no net additional measures have been announced since November 2010...instead the coalition government chose largely to stick to its originally planned pace of fiscal tightening and leave the additional cuts for after 2015' (Emmerson & Tetlow, 2015: 29). What Osborne *did* choose to do in 2011–2012 was to withstand imposing even greater—and politically difficult—spending cuts in the current parliament in order to meet his original fiscal programme. Gamble is therefore correct to say that, 'in 2012, faced with the prospect of a double dip recession in the UK and with no recovery in sight, Osborne did adopt a Plan B, easing up on austerity, and postponing many of the cuts in public spending to the next parliament'. However, it is important to underline the point that this 'easing up' on austerity was not equivalent to a slowing of the pace of the 2010 spending cuts; indeed many of the deepest cuts to welfare, for example, had their biggest impact after April 2013 (Toynbee & Walker, 2015: 17). Rather, as Keegan has noted, 'the stretching of budgetary consolidation into the future [did] not reflect deliberate policy decisions to ease the squeeze' (Keegan, 2014: 5). Instead it reflected low levels of economic growth, slowing tax revenues and a choice on the part of the Treasury to not introduce additional public spending cuts to meet the original 2010 targets. Similarly, as the IFS noted at the time:

> It is important to understand why the deficit hasn't fallen. It is emphatically not because the government has failed to impose the intended spending cuts. It is because the economy performed so poorly in the first half of the parliament, hitting revenues very hard. (IFS, 2014: 3)

However, this acceptance of sustaining higher borrowing presented a political dilemma for the Coalition. During the phase of 'strategic positioning' and throughout the first two years of the parliament, Osborne had persistently emphasised the need to eliminate the deficit within one parliament. Failing to do so had been presented as the mark of fiscal irresponsibility. Indeed, in 2010, Osborne had argued that Darling's plans for cutting borrowing were too slow and would provoke a lending strike from international creditors which would pitch the economy back into a severe economic crisis. However, by 2013, 'critics noted that [Osborne's] deficit reduction plan had ended up less ambitious than the one adopted by Alistair Darling'. Whereas Darling had originally planned to cut the deficit by 33.9% by 2013, the Chancellor had in fact secured a smaller reduction of 24.3% in the same time frame. Indeed, whereas 'in 2010 Osborne had predicted that net borrowing would be £37 billion in 2015-16, it was closer to £100 billon' (Toynbee & Walker, 2015: 87).

The key question for the Coalition was how it would now defend sustaining a large budget deficit given its previous narrative that this would lead to economic catastrophe. The answer was that in spite of retreating from its original targets, the Coalition retained a discursive commitment to austerity. The difference was that now the programme of further cuts was displaced into the next parliament, under the guise of a 'long term economic plan' (Lee, 2015: 23). The Coalition's strategy from 2013 onwards therefore sought to retain the focus on the importance of deficit reduction as the key dividing line between the Conservatives and the Labour Party. However, at the same time, the Coalition employed a range of discursive strategies to displace responsibility for the failure of Phase I and II of its economic programme. First, Osborne argued that the scale of the problem inherited from the previous Labour government was much larger than had initially been understood. For example, in a speech in September 2013 defending his government's record, Osborne stated that, 'the economic collapse was even worse than we thought. Repairing it will take even longer than we hoped. But we held our nerve when many told us to abandon our plan' (Osborne, 2013b). In this way, the Coalition sought to present its failure to match its original 2010 targets not as the fault of the government but rather as an example of the enduring legacy of Labour's mismanagement of the economy. Second, the Coalition redefined the criteria by which to judge its fiscal record. For example, in the March 2013 Budget, Osborne stated:

> The deficit continues to come down. We have taken many tough decisions to bring that deficit down and we will continue to do so. The deficit has fallen from 11.2 per cent of GDP in 2009-10, to a forecast of 7.4 per cent this year. That is a fall of a third. It then falls further to 6.8 per cent next year, 5.9 per cent in 2014-15. (Osborne, 2013a)

Rather than emphasising the non-negotiable imperative of eliminating the budget deficit in one parliament as he had done in the previous three years, the Chancellor now extolled the virtues of reducing it by half. Indeed, despite borrowing £100 billion more than had originally been anticipated in the 2010 Spending Review, the Chancellor presented his approach as embodying a 'tough and credible fiscal policy' (Emmerson & Tetlow, 2015: 23; Osborne, 2013a). Third, the Chancellor sought to present the failure to meet his debt and deficit targets as the result of external factors, specifically pointing to 'external inflation shocks, the Eurozone crisis and the ongoing impact of the financial crisis on financial conditions' (Osborne, 2013b). Fourth—and perhaps most importantly—the Coalition retained and indeed intensified its attack on Labour as 'deficit deniers'. For example, in his 2013 Budget, Osborne said:

> I've also had representations at this Budget for measures that would add £33bn a year extra to borrowing on top of the figures I've announced. It's from people who seem to think that the way to borrow less is to borrow more. That would pose a huge risk to the stability of the British economy, threaten a sharp rise in interest rates and leave the burden of debts to our children and grandchildren. I will not take that gamble with the future of this country. (Osborne, 2013a)

As these four elements of the Coalition's 'Phase III' strategy suggest, although the deficit reduction programme had been delayed in policy terms, as a *discursive strategy* it retained a central place within the

Conservative-led government's approach. For example, at the 2013 Conservative Party conference, Osborne announced a commitment to run a permanent budget surplus in the next parliament, a move which was confirmed in the March 2014 Budget. At a time when the Coalition was effectively abandoning its initial deficit reduction strategy in policy terms, discursively it was entrenching and embedding this narrative as the essential benchmark of economic competence. This is what Gamble means when he refers to 'austerity as statecraft'. The pattern and pace of deficit reduction is not simply the result of 'ideology'—for example the belief in a small state or a revitalised private sector—however strongly held these beliefs may or may not be held. Rather, the austerity programme provided the Conservatives with an effective narrative with which to undermine the Labour opposition and to entrench its own position as the most credible custodian of the public finances. It was for this reason that appearing to stick to 'Plan A' whilst in practice postponing further spending cuts into the future ('Plan B') was so essential to the Conservatives' strategy. Additionally, the failure of 'expansionary austerity' underlines the point that economic 'competence' and 'credibility' are not secured simply through the successful enactment of policy. Rather, 'credibility'—the benchmark of economic success—has to be constructed and defended through discursive mobilisation. In this respect, although the Conservative-led coalition failed on its own policy terms, in terms of its governing strategy it was highly successful.

The Failure of 'Rebalancing': The Return of Privatised Keynesianism?

From May 2010 onwards the Coalition's economic strategy had been underpinned by a second, subsidiary discourse: the goal of economic 'rebalancing'. It is important to distinguish analytically between this 'rebalancing' narrative and the Coalition's leading programme of deficit reduction because the 'rebalancing' discourse was underpinned by two distinct diagnoses of the structural weaknesses which underpinned the British economy. On the one hand, it advocated a 'rebalancing' of economic activity away from the public and towards the private sector (Pugalis & Bentley, 2013: 669). This was entirely compatible with and indeed complementary to the Coalition's austerity programme insofar as both discourses claimed that government spending 'crowds out' private economic activity and acts as a drag on economic growth.

However, there was also a second component of the rebalancing discourse which focused specifically on the need to secure a ***sectoral and geographical*** rebalancing of the British economy, away from financial services towards manufacturing and away from London and the South East and towards the ex-industrial regions (Berry & Hay, 2016: 2; Gamble, 2012: 71). For example, in his first speech on the economy as Prime Minister, Cameron said, 'our economy has become more and more unbalanced, with our fortunes hitched to a few industries in one corner of the country, while we let other sectors like manufacturing slide' (Cameron, 2010). The Conservatives framed their economic strategy partly as an attempt to rectify this state of affairs. In 2010, for example, Osborne argued that a 'recovery will only be sustainable if it is accompanied by an internal and external rebalancing of our economy: in other words a higher savings rate, more business investment, and rising net exports' (Osborne, 2010a). This objective was paralleled by a critique of New Labour's economic legacy which went beyond the charge that it had borrowed and spent too much in the pre-crisis period. For example, Osborne argued that 'Britain has been failed by the economic policy framework of the last decade. We have to move away from an economic model that was based on unsustainable private and public debt' (ibid.). In another speech, the Chancellor directly attributed blame for the 'imbalanced' state of the British economy to the previous Labour government by stating that the Conservatives would 'avoid the mistakes of the past…we cannot rely on consumers alone for our economic growth, as we did in previous decades, and we cannot put all our chips on the success of the City of London, as my predecessors did' (Osborne, 2010a).

The emergence of the 'rebalancing' agenda as an organising principle of the Coalition might have suggested that the new government was committed to affecting a qualitative transformation of British capitalism. There is clear documentary evidence that between 2010 and 2012, this 'rebalancing' discourse was incorporated into the Coalition's economic narrative and policy programme (Berry & Hay, 2016: 4; Craig, 2014: 118). However, as was argued with respect to the Coalition's deficit reduction strategy, it is important to distinguish analytically between the discursive commitment to a particular economic programme and the extent to which such a programme is in fact implemented in government. Insofar as the 'rebalancing' agenda did remain a policy narrative and explicit objective of the Coalition government, the evidence suggests that it was not achieved over the course of the parliament (Berry & Hay, 2015, 2016; Lee, 2015: 16).

This is evidenced by the composition of GDP growth in the Coalition period, in particular when a putative economic recovery began to take hold in spring 2013. In this year, growth picked up for the first time in three years and registered at 1.7% (Sargent, 2014: 395). This was followed by successive quarters of growth, such that by July 2014 the British economy had surpassed its pre-crisis level of output. However, if we look at the composition of growth over this period, it becomes clear that it was secured in a way that directly contravened key principles of the rebalancing agenda. First, rather than delivering growth through higher levels of saving and exports as Osborne had initially envisioned, Britain's economic recovery was largely based on higher consumer spending. As Sargent has noted, 'the annual rate of growth of consumption spending by households in real terms had begun to exceed 1 per cent during 2012. This became 2 per cent in the first half of 2013, and 2.5 per cent in the third quarter' (Sargent, 2014: 138). As a result, rising household consumption accounted for slightly more than half of the growth in this period (Sowels, 2014). The economic recovery became entrenched in 2014, 'with quarterly growth averaging 0.7 per cent through the year and 2.6 per cent for the year as a whole' (Goodwin & Beck, 2015: 74). However, consumer spending again remained the biggest contributor to GDP, registering 'an annual rise of 2.3 per cent [which] was the strongest since 2007' (ibid.). From 2013 onwards, the Coalition predictably welcomed this rise in economic activity and drew attention to increased growth as evidence that the 'long-term economic plan' was working. However, the fact that this was not being delivered through a 'rebalancing' of the economy away from consumption towards savings was quietly ignored.

Second, investment in housing re-emerged as a key driver of growth and consumer confidence from 2013 onwards. Indeed, taken alongside rising levels of consumption, increased household investment accounted for two-thirds of the increase in GDP in 2013 (Bean, 2014: 2). Specifically, throughout 2013 housing investment increased by 10% whilst house prices increased by 22% (Bean, 2014: 2; Toynbee & Walker, 2015). However, the rapid increase of house prices taken in the aggregate conceals the uneven nature of this growth across the UK's regions. For example, as Fig. 5.2 shows, whilst house prices in London had increased by 22% above their pre-crisis peak by March 2014, house prices across

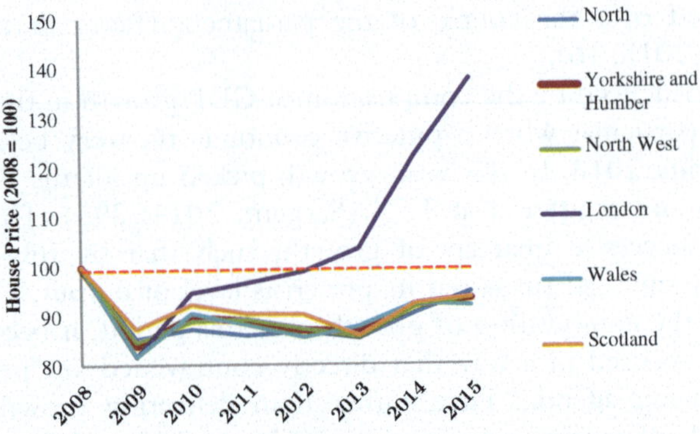

Fig. 5.2 Regional House Prices, 2008–2015 (*Source* Nationwide House Price Index)

the North of England, Scotland and Wales remained well below their 2008 levels. As one housing economist put it at the time, 'the gap between house prices in London and the rest of the UK is the widest it's ever been, both in cash and percentage terms' (Nationwide, 2014: 1). As such, the return of rapid house price inflation not only represented a failure to 'rebalance' the British economy away from the trajectory of asset-price inflation which had been in place in the pre-crisis period; it also exacerbated pre-existing regional differences and further entrenched the unevenness of the Coalition's economic recovery.

Third, this continuation of pre-crisis trends was also reflected in the sectoral composition of growth between 2010 and 2014. Whilst Osborne had initially anticipated an increase in net exports—i.e. an increase in the contribution of net trade to the composition of GDP—this was not delivered in office. Rather, the trade balance deteriorated throughout the parliament, with a total trade deficit of £34.8 billion recorded in 2014 (ONS, 2014). Since the trade balance forms the largest component of the current account, 'by the third quarter of 2014 the current account deficit registered at six per cent', which constituted 'the joint largest such deficit since ONS records began in 1955' (Lee, 2015: 26). This trend became increasingly pronounced from 2013 onwards as Sterling appreciated relative to other currencies.

One key factor behind the negative trade balance was that the manufacturing sector had not been revitalised under the Coalition as had been promised. This was significant from the perspective of the balance of payments because manufacturing typically contributes around half of British export earnings (Keegan, 2014: 91). However, by the end of 2014 the manufacturing sector represented a *smaller* component of overall output (at 9.7%) compared to when the Coalition had assumed office (Berry & Hay, 2016). As this suggests, Osborne's goal of driving GDP growth through an increase in net exports did not come to fruition. Rather, relative to 2008—and throughout the Coalition's time in office—industrial production failed to surpass pre-crisis levels of output. Instead, the recovery from 2013 onwards was led by the service sector, again underlining the point that Osborne's 'rebalancing' of the British economy had not been delivered. Based on the above evidence, we can conclude that although economic growth did increase from spring 2013 onwards, this was not delivered through a successful 'rebalancing' of the UK economy (Lee, 2015: 25). Growth remained heavily reliant upon consumption, Britain's long-standing trade deficit was not reduced but rather widened, and business investment—which had been forecast to contribute to 56% of GDP growth in 2015 but which was subsequently revised down to 39%—remained unimpressive (Weldon, 2013a).

On this basis, a number of observers have argued that from 2012 onwards, the Coalition effectively secured an economic recovery through resurrecting Britain's pre-crisis growth model of 'privatised Keynesianism'. For example, Gamble has written:

> When the recovery failed to arrive spontaneously in 2012 the Government reverted to…a version of privatised Keynesianism, reliant upon loading more and more debt upon citizens…the voters who had previously been told that everyone, including the state, should live within their means were now being urged to get their credit cards out again…although many were uneasy about the return of the previous growth model, no one had any very clear alternative.

Similarly, Hay wrote:

> The Coalition has found itself resorting to the pump priming of mortgage-debt. This, it need hardly be pointed out, is a most desperate and dangerous move – with lots of downstream risk and very little, if any, substantive gain to date or in prospect. This is privatised Keynesianism mark II. (Hay, 2013: 82)

There is much to commend in these analyses. The broad shape of the economic recovery from 2013 onwards certainly suggests that the Coalition had not successfully established a 'new economic model', but rather had reverted to facilitating old patterns of growth which had been in place in the pre-crisis conjuncture. This is attested to by a number of indicators. As mentioned above, real wages had undergone their longest sustained decline in modern history, with real median wages falling by between 8 and 10% between 2008 and 2014. Stagnant median wages had been one of the crucial preconditions of Britain's pre-crisis growth model, in particular from 2003 to 2007, as this created an incentive for low- to middle-income households to draw on credit to fuel current consumption (Berry & Hay, 2016: 3; Lansley, 2011). As such, the sustained decline in real wages between 2008 and 2013 represented a continuation and indeed an intensification of this wage-deflationary dynamic under the Coalition (Green & Lavery, 2015). However, as was outlined above, rising household consumption became a crucial driver of growth between 2012 and 2014. Indeed, between 2012 and 2013 household consumption rose by around £10.6 billon, but household incomes rose by less than £2.0 billion (Weldon, 2013b). If rising incomes didn't explain this rise in consumption, then what did?

At this point, those arguing that the Coalition re-established a variant of 'privatised Keynesianism' might argue that the same dynamic which had driven consumption growth throughout the pre-crisis period—namely rising private indebtedness fuelling consumption and economic growth—had re-emerged between 2013 and the end of 2014. However, this argument needs to be qualified somewhat in the light of three observations. First, as was outlined in Chapter 2, one of the key channels identified by the privatised Keynesian conception was the role of Mortgage Equity Withdrawal (MEW) in facilitating increases in consumer spending. As Berry and Hay put it, 'the housing market as a source of funds for private consumption' was central to the privatised Keynesian growth model perspective (Berry & Hay, 2016: 3). However, as the British economic recovery began to take hold from spring 2013 onwards, mortgage holders were not borrowing against their homes to fuel current consumption. Rather, in the middle of that year households injected £15.4 billion of equity *into* their properties as they took advantage of low interest rates to pay-off mortgage debt (Stewart, 2013). This dynamic of *negative* equity withdrawal continued through the economic recovery, such that by the first quarter of 2015 there had been

28 successive quarters of net injection of equity into houses, taking the total to £313bn since June 2008 (Collinson, 2015). What this suggests is that in contrast to the pre-crisis period, MEW was not fuelling current consumption to a significant extent under the Coalition; on the contrary in the aggregate households were withholding on current consumption in order to reduce their exposure to mortgage debt. One of the key drivers of 'privatised Keynesianism' Mark I was therefore not re-established during the economic recovery of 2013. Second, there was no surge in the household debt over this period: household debt-to-income ratios remained below their pre-crisis peak at approximately 140% of income between 2010 and 2015. Whilst this remained high relative to other advanced economies, the increase in growth in 2013 was not correlated with a sudden increase in household indebtedness. This suggests that another factor was behind consumption growth in this period. Third, in line with the above observations, data from the ONS shows that there was not a significant increase in net loan acquisitions between 2012 and 2014. Net loan acquisitions account for the value of new loans which are taken out by households (e.g. through mortgages) minus the value of loan repayments which households make in a given time frame. As can be seen from Fig. 5.3, whilst net loans-to-households were extremely

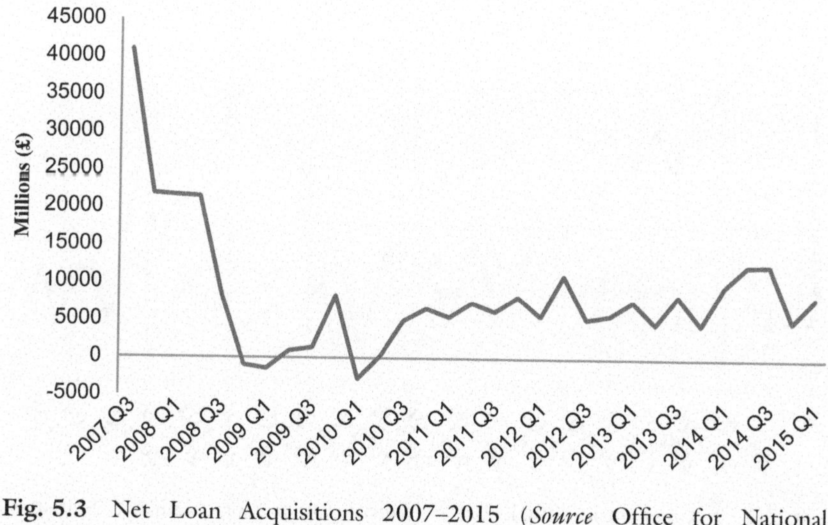

Fig. 5.3 Net Loan Acquisitions 2007–2015 (*Source* Office for National Statistics. National Accounts)

high immediately before the crisis, there was not a net lending spree concentrated on households during the 2013–2015 economic recovery. Rather, the volume of net loans taken out by households up to the end of 2014 did not significantly surpass its lowest ebb in this period.

What, then, explains the increase in household consumption at a time of real income stagnation? The answer lies partly with what is termed the 'savings ratio'. This is the proportion of disposable (after-tax) income that households save in the aggregate. As can be seen in Fig. 5.4, before the crisis of 2007–2008, the savings rate fell steadily as households took advantage of low commercial lending rates and increased their borrowing in order to gain access to the housing market. However, in the period of uncertainty which followed the 2008 financial crash, households rapidly 'deleveraged'—they paid down their debts in order to improve their net financial positions—with the result that from 2008 Q3 to 2010 Q3 the savings ratio increased rapidly, rising to 11.5% by 2010. This dynamic had of course been one of the key drivers of the recession, as increased savings by the household sector reduced consumption and temporarily constrained aggregate demand in a context of increased credit constraints and widespread uncertainty. As Sargent notes, households 'were stepping up their efforts to improve their financial position,

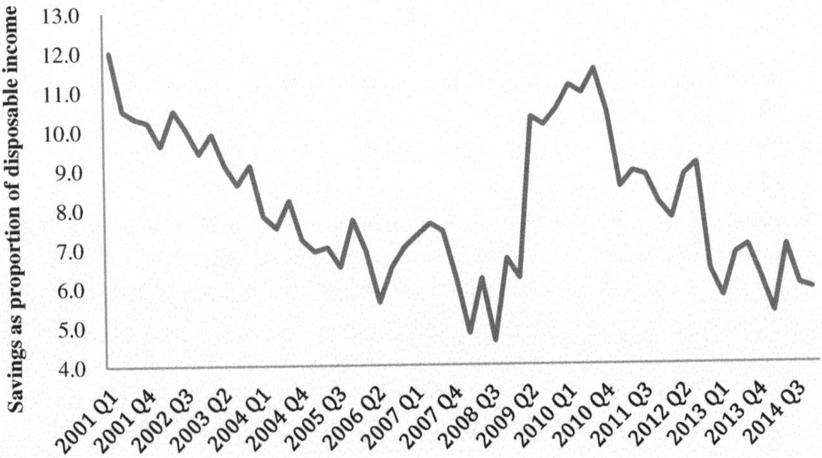

Fig. 5.4 Savings ratio 2001–2014 (*Source* Office for National Statistics. National Accounts)

by paying off debt or adding to their assets. The flow of savings directed towards these two financial objectives together rose from £20.7 billion in 2008 to £75.0 billion in 2012 in absolute terms' (Sargent, 2014: 395). The result was that by 2012–2013, households had significantly improved their net financial positions: household financial liabilities declined from 1.7 times disposable income in 2008 to 1.4 times in 2012 (ibid.). One result of this was that as the Coalition entered Phase III of its economic strategy, households were in a position to draw upon their savings—or at least could choose to save less of their disposable income—in order to increase their current consumption levels (Hardie & Wales, 2013: 2). As the graph shows, this was exactly what happened: the savings ratio declined between 2010 and 2014. It was this, rather than massively increased household borrowing, which underpinned consumption and boosted the economic recovery in the second half of the parliament.

What does this imply for the argument that the 2013 economic recovery was fuelled by a renewed phase of 'privatised Keynesianism'? Did the Coalition effectively re-establish the growth model which had been in place under New Labour throughout the pre-crisis conjuncture? On the one hand, as we have seen the Coalition certainly did not bring about a 'new economic model' as Osborne had envisioned in 2010. The recovery was consumption-led, business investment remained poor and Britain's net trade position deteriorated. In this sense, the basic structure of Britain's model of capitalism endured (Gamble, 2012: 23; Hay, 2013b). In addition, as will be shown below, for all the talk of 'rebalancing', the Coalition was in fact attempting to return the British economy to a situation where high loan-to-value ratios in the mortgage credit market would become once again a key driver of economic growth. However, the specific mechanisms which had been in place in the 2000s and which had underpinned the first phase of privatised Keynesianism were not fully re-established during the economic recovery either: MEW was not driving consumption, household debt-to-income ratios remained relatively flat and households had not increased their net borrowing substantially throughout the Coalition period. Instead, the increase in household consumption was fuelled largely through the decline in the savings ratio from 2010 to the end of the parliament.

Despite this, there are two reasons why the 'privatised Keynesianism' analogy remains a useful analytical tool for analysing the trajectory of the British economy in the post-crisis conjuncture. First, the running down of the savings ratio is not a dynamic which can continue indefinitely. As can be seen in Fig. 5.4, the savings rate had fallen by 2014 to 2006 levels, two years before the GFC first broke. This suggests that the 2013 recovery rested on weak foundations and that its basic trajectory emulated pre-crisis trends. Indeed, in this period the Bank of England increasingly recognised that the shape of the Coalition's economic recovery represented a potential threat to financial stability. For example, in February 2014 the Governor of the Bank argued that 'the recovery is neither balanced nor sustainable. A few quarters of above trend growth driven by household spending are a good start but they aren't sufficient for sustained momentum … wage growth remains weak, and the household savings rate is likely to fall further' (Carney, 2014: 4). The economy's capacity to drive consumption through collapsing household savings was all but exhausted by the end of the parliament. There were two possible pathways out of this scenario. The most optimistic assessment was that as the recovery became established, household income growth would increase to such an extent that consumption growth could continue apace whilst the savings ratio would not decline any further (as rising incomes would allow for increased expenditure without compromising savings). Clearly, predicting the trajectory of the British economy between 2015 and 2020 is beyond the scope of this book. As such, the figures cited below remain indicative. That said, detailed projections of income growth from 2015 to 2020/1 suggest that a surge in median income growth is highly unlikely in the near future. Rather, one substantial study produced by the Resolution Foundation noted that:

> A low income household in 2008-09 … had an income of £10,600 a year. By 2020-21, the forecasts predict that a similar household will have an income of just £9,000 a year (in 2008-09 prices), a real-terms decline of 15 per cent… median income falls from £22,900 per year in 2008-09 to £22,100 in 2020-21, a real-terms fall of 3 per cent. This would return median income to a level last seen in 2001, two decades earlier, again an unprecedented period of no income gain. (The Resolution Foundation, 2012: 76)

In a context of large welfare cuts, weak productivity growth and stagnant low to middle incomes, the prospect of producing a wage-led recovery looks to be an unlikely pathway out of the current conjuncture. This opens up the second potential pathway out of the low savings rate conundrum: a further increase in private indebtedness in order to fuel further consumption growth. This would represent a return to the classic model of 'privatised Keynesianism'. Again, the figures here are projections and so must be treated with caution. However, the OBR—the government's own fiscal watchdog—has predicted that by 2019 the household debt-to-income ratio will increase to 182% (OBR, 2014a: 76). This exceeds the household debt-to-income ratio of 169% which was established at the height of the credit boom in the pre-crisis conjuncture. In relation to income growth, one study demonstrated how on the OBR's own figures 'while wages are forecast to grow at 16 per cent over the period [from 2015–2019], total household debt is forecast to grow 2.7 times as fast at 42 per cent' (TUC, 2015). In addition, the same study predicted that unsecured debt was 'forecast to grow 4.5 times as fast as wages – by 70 per cent between 2015 and 2019...[reaching] an average of around £29,000 of unsecured debt per household by 2019' (ibid.). In other words, income growth is forecast to fall well behind rising levels of private indebtedness, suggesting that the savings ratio will either remain at its current low level or decline even further. On these forecasts, the second pathway out of the current conjuncture looks more likely.

Help to Buy: State Intervention and the Delayed Return of 'Privatised Keynesianism'

As the above analysis suggests, claims that the 2013 economic recovery was driven by a re-emergence of Britain's pre-crisis 'privatised Keynesianism' growth model were somewhat premature. These analyses miss some of the key differences which remained—particularly in the early stages of the economic recovery—between the pre- and post-crisis conjunctures. However, the evidence does suggest that after a brief interregnum under the Coalition, a renewed wave of 'privatised Keynesianism' is likely to re-emerge in the future. There is another sense, however, in which we can argue that the Coalition at least attempted to re-establish the conditions for a renewed wave of 'privatised Keynesian' growth in the post-crisis conjuncture. This is evidenced in the range of 'credit-easing' policies which emerged in this period. There is not sufficient space to overview all of these policies in detail here. However, a brief review of one such policy intervention—'Help to Buy'—serves to underline the way in which the Coalition actively sought to re-establish some of the key features of Britain's pre-crisis growth model in the post-crisis conjuncture.

The key objective of Help to Buy was to respond to the fact that lenders were reluctant to advance high loan-to-value mortgages to potentially risky (particularly first-time) buyers in the aftermath of the financial crisis. By 2013 mortgage lending had fallen 40% below its pre-crisis peak whilst the number of property transactions had dropped by 60%. High loan-to-value mortgages which had accounted for just short of 10% of all loans in Q2 2007 had dropped to below 2.5% in Q2 2009 and remained there until late 2013. In other words, in a context of increased economic uncertainty, mortgage lenders were demanding much larger deposits from potential borrowers. As a result, it would have taken nineteen years for someone on an average salary to afford the average first-time buyer deposit. This acted as a considerable barrier to entry for first-time homebuyers: indeed 62% reported that punishingly high deposit rates acted as the principal barrier to accessing mortgage finance (Alakeson, Fearn, & Cory, 2013).

Help to Buy was introduced in response to this perceived market failure. It involved two dimensions: the equity loan scheme and the mortgage guarantee scheme (HM Treasury, 2013). The equity loan scheme—introduced in 2013 and rolled-out until 2020 (Stacey, 2014)—required that borrowers advance 5% of the value of the mortgage in a deposit. This was far lower than the average 'market rate' which in July 2012 stood at 19% (BBC News, 2012). The government then provides a loan (interest free for the first five years) which covers up to 15% of the remaining deposit. The Mortgage Guarantee Scheme conversely represents an insurance policy for mortgage lenders. Whilst the borrower again is expected to advance a 5% deposit, the government guarantees up to 15% of the remaining deposit in case of default. The goal of these two mechanisms is to encourage mortgage lenders to advance higher loan-to-value ratios, thereby allowing greater access to mortgage credit for those who can afford monthly repayments but who could not afford high deposits.

Crucially, as articulated in George Osborne's correspondence with the Treasury Select Committee, the explicit goal of the policy is to return to a situation where median loan-to-value ratios are at the level which prevailed in the pre-crisis period (Osborne, 2014b: 2). In other words, although net lending to households and overall household debt remained below their pre-crisis peaks in 2013, the Coalition nonetheless pursued a range of policies which sought to counteract this trend by widening access to mortgage finance. Within twelve months, Help to Buy had had a considerable impact in both the mortgage and construction markets. In 2014, first-time buyers accessing mortgage finance had increased by 70% relative to 2008, with a significant proportion of these mortgages resulting from the Help to Buy policy (Barrett, 2015). Partly as a result of this, the average cost of a deposit fell by over 7% in 2014. In addition, the increased demand for new-build properties contributed to a boost to the construction industry, with 50,000 new homes calculated to have been built up to 2015 as a result of Whitehall support (Armitage, 2015).

The relative merits and risks embodied in Help to Buy need not concern us here. What is of significance is that the policy represents a clear instance of state intervention to widen access to mortgage credit and to therefore re-establish one of the key drivers of growth which had been in place throughout the pre-crisis conjuncture. However, as outlined in Chapters 2 and 4, the provision of mortgage credit had in this period been left to market actors in the sense that benign economic conditions—including a glut of credit and high levels of demand for mortgage finance—had generated high levels of credit expansion. This was reflected in rapid spikes in loan-to-earnings ratios, which increased from 3.14 in 1998 to 5.86 in 2007 (Chamberlin, 2009: 31). As a result, the provision of mortgage credit increased substantially throughout this period, to the extent that between 1997 and 2007 a record £1.2 trillion of new mortgage loans were made (Martin, 2010: 41).

With Help to Buy, the state now bears a considerable risk in guaranteeing new mortgage loans: £3.5 billion of the government's capital budget was set aside to cover equity loans over the first three years of the policy and £130 billion was made available to fund the mortgage guarantee scheme (HM Treasury, 2013). Whilst house prices continue their upward trajectory, the scheme will help to generate additional revenue for the government; however, in the event (which seems increasingly likely) that the housing market's upward price trajectory slows or even reverses, it will be taxpayers who ultimately bear the brunt of any defaults. This prospect reinforces the political incentive to secure increasing house prices, further entrenching the (now explicitly state-backed) logic of credit indiscipline so central to the UK's growth model.

In the light of the Help to Buy example and the above analysis of the Coalition's failed 'rebalancing' programme, we can draw four conclusions. First—contrary to the professed objective of Osborne to rebalance the UK economy away from debt and consumption and towards savings and exports—the Coalition did not initiate a radical transformation of

Britain's growth model in office. In this respect, those who have argued that the 2013 economic recovery resembled a return to the fundamentals of Britain's pre-crisis growth model are broadly correct. However, second, it is important to also note that the key mechanisms which had underpinned Britain's pre-crisis growth model—MEW, rising household debt-to-income ratios and increased net lending to households—were not key drivers of the economic recovery in the final two years of the Coalition's period in office. The *sui generis* nature of the economic crisis had precipitated a rush into liquidity for the household sector between 2008 and the end of 2010. In the early years of the economic recovery, this provided an alternative reservoir for consumption expenditure which households duly drew upon without relying upon increasing their personal debt levels. However, by 2014 this alternative source of consumption had been largely exhausted. Third, it is consequently better to view a 'privatised Keynesian' dynamic as *emergent* out of the framework which the Coalition had established in the post-crisis conjuncture rather than already established in this period. In other words, after a brief interregnum, of a renewed wave of 'privatised Keynesian' growth looked likely to take hold again in the 2015 to 2020 parliament. Fourth, despite the fact that the economic recovery was not driven in the first instance by enhanced household indebtedness, we can identify—in Help to Buy amongst other policies—deliberate attempts on the part of the government to re-establish the conditions for a second round of private debt-led expansion. As such, despite its professed commitment to 'rebalance' the British economy, the Coalition in fact effectively re-established the conditions for a renewed wave of 'privatised Keynesianism' and a return to the finance-led growth model which had been in place under New Labour.

Conclusion

The Coalition's accumulation strategy rested upon two distinct objectives. The first was to eliminate Britain's large budget deficit within one parliament through spending cuts. The second was to secure a sectoral and geographical rebalancing of the British economy. On both counts, the Coalition failed. The original 2010 fiscal consolidation targets were effectively abandoned from 2012 onwards. British capitalism remained deeply imbalanced. The Coalition's accumulation strategy evolved in response to these policy failures. Between May and October 2010, the Coalition pursued a policy of *strategic positioning* where it sought to entrench the narrative that the government was 'clearing up Labour's mess' by committing to an immediate and rapid programme of deficit reduction. By October 2010, the Coalition moved into a phase of *implementation* wherein departmental expenditure limits were cut and the austerity programme began to take effect. However, by December 2012 this phase had ran aground, as growth and tax revenues stagnated and deficit reduction was thwarted. As a result, between December 2012 and December 2014, the Coalition abandoned its commitment to 'expansionary austerity' and moved into a third phase of its strategy by effectively adopting a 'Plan B', giving up in the process the original deficit reduction targets by postponing further spending cuts into the future.

By the end of the Coalition period, a putative economic recovery had emerged across Britain. It appeared that Britain's 'privatised Keynesian' growth model had re-emerged. However, many of the key drivers of 'privatised Keynesianism' Mark I—high levels of equity withdrawal, rapidly increasing household indebtedness and high levels of net lending to households—were simply not in place during the initial stages of the economic recovery. Rather, the consumption-led recovery was largely due to the temporarily boosted 'savings ratio'—a legacy of the deep recession which had preceded the return to growth—the decline of which provided a temporary boost to consumption in the second half of the parliament. As such, the Coalition period is perhaps better viewed as an *interregnum* period between New Labour's pre-crisis model of privatised Keynesianism and a probable wave of renewed private debt-led growth in the future. Whilst being ostensibly committed to a 'rebalancing' of the British economy, the Coalition initiated a programme of sustained state intervention in the mortgage credit markets from 2013 onwards in the form of its Help to Buy policy. This suggests that in terms of its policy orientation the Coalition did very much actively seek to re-establish some of the key features of Britain's pre-crisis growth model in the form of high (now state-backed) loan-to-value ratios. The Coalition did effectively re-establish the conditions for a renewed wave of 'privatised Keynesian' growth in Britain, albeit after a significant time lag and with some minor modifications. By the end of the 2010–2015 parliament, the Coalition had therefore effectively re-established Britain's pre-crisis 'privatised Keynesian' growth model. Continuity with New Labour's accumulation strategy prevailed. However, important changes were also afoot in the Coalition era. The Coalition's austerity programme led to a decisive break with the second element of New Labour's 'hybrid' political economy, namely its 'One Nation' hegemonic project.

References

Alakeson, V., Fearn, H., & Cory, G. (2013). *One Foot on the Ladder: How Shared Ownership Can Bring Owning a Home into Reach*. Resolution Foundation. Retrieved from https://www.resolutionfoundation.org/publications/one-foot-ladder-shared-ownership-can-bring-owning-home-reach/.

Alesina, A. (2010). *Fiscal Adjustments: Lessons from Recent History*. Retrieved from https://scholar.harvard.edu/alesina/publications/fiscal-adjustments-lessons-recent-history.

Ardagna, S., & Alesina, A. (1998). *Tales of Fiscal Adjustment*. London: Wiley-Blackwell.

Armitage, J. (2015, August 11). Help to Buy and Other State Support Built These Housebuilders' Bonuses. *The Independent*.

Atkins, J. (2015). "Together in the National Interest": The Rhetoric of Unity and the Formation of the Cameron—Clegg Government. *The Political Quarterly, 86*(1), 85–92.

Baker, A. (2011). Austerity in the UK: Why It Is Not Common Sense but Politically Driven Nonsense. *Social Justice Review*. Retrieved from www.trademarkbelfast.com/wp-content/.../09/trademark-reveiw-stevie-edit-PRESS.pdf.

Bale, T. (2011). The Black Widow Effect: Why Britain's Conservative-Liberal Democrat Coalition Might Have an Unhappy Ending. *Parliamentary Affairs, 65*(2), 323–337.

Barrett, C. (2015, January 6). Number of First-Time UK Homebuyers Hits 7-Year High, Says Halifax. *The Financial Times*.

BBC. (2012). Ed Balls: Coalition's Economic Credibility in Tatters'. BBC News Website. Retrieved November 12, 2018, from https://www.bbc.co.uk/news/uk-politics-20613886.

BBC News. (2007). *Tories "To Match Labour Spending."* BBC News Website. Retrieved October 13, 2015, from http://news.bbc.co.uk/1/hi/uk_politics/6975536.stm.

BBC News. (2012, September 12). Mortgage Deposits Drop Below 20% for First-Time Buyers. BBC News Website.

BBC News. (2013). *UK Loses Top AAA Credit Rating for First Time Since 1978*. The BBC. Retrieved November 2, 2015, from http://www.bbc.co.uk/news/business-21554311.

Bean, C. (2014). *Sustaining the Recovery*. North East Chamber of Commerce President's Club Talk, Rockcliffe Hall Hotel, Darlingtons Club Talk, Rockcliffe Hall Hotel, Darlington. Retrieved November 5, 2015, from http://www.bankofengland.co.uk/publications/Documents/speeches/2014/speech710.pdf.

Berry, C. (2013). *Sterling Depreciation and the UK Trade Balance* (SPERI) Policy Briefing. Sheffield: Sheffield Political Economy Research Institute.

Berry, C., & Hay, C. (2015). Has the UK Economy Been "Rebalanced"? (SPERI Briefing No. 12). Sheffield.

Berry, C., & Hay, C. (2016). The Great British "Rebalancing" Act: The Construction and Implementation of an Economic Imperative for Exceptional Times. *The British Journal of Politics & International Relations, 18*(1), 3–25.

Blanchflower, D. (2013, April 4). George Osborne Called Us Deficit Deniers, but We Were Right. His Economic Era Is Over. *The Independent*.

Blitz, J. (2006, January 23). Stability Before Tax Cuts, Says Cameron. *The Financial Times*.

Blyth, M. (2013). *Austerity: The History of a Dangerous Idea*. Oxford: Oxford University Press.

Cabinet Office. (2010). *The Coalition: Our Programme for Government*.

Cameron, D. (2006). Scarman Lecture. Conservative Party Speeches. Retrieved October 6, 2015, from http://conservative-speeches.sayit.mysociety.org/speech/599937.

Cameron, D. (2010). *Transforming the British Economy: Coalition Strategy for Economic Growth*. Cabinet Office. Retrieved November 5, 2015, from https://www.gov.uk/government/speeches/transforming-the-british-economy-coalition-strategy-for-economic-growth.

Carney, M. (2014). *Inflation Report Press Conference—Governor's Opening Remarks* (Inflation Report). Press Conference. Retrieved November 9, 2015, from http://www.bankofengland.co.uk/publications/Documents/inflationreport/2014/irspnote140212.pdf.

Chamberlin, G. (2009). Recent Developments in the UK Housing Market. *Economic and Labour Market Review, 3*(8), 29–38.

Cheesman, H. (2014). Cameron's Tories: Talking Conservative, Acting Radical. *Revue LISA/LISA E-Journal, 7*(8).

Collinson, P. (2015, July 6). UK Households Paying Off Mortgages in Record Time, Says Bank of England. *The Guardian*.

Craig, M. (2014). Post-2008 British Industrial Policy and Constructivist Political Economy: New Directions and New Tensions. *New Political Economy, 20*(1), 107–125.

Crawford, R., Emmerson, C., Phillips, D., & Tetlow, G. (2011, February). Public Spending Cuts: Pain Shared? In *The IFS Green Budget* (pp. 130–162).

Dellepiane-Avellaneda, S. (2015). The Political Power of Economic Ideas: The Case of "Expansionary Fiscal Contractions". *The British Journal of Politics & International Relations, 17*(3), 391–418.

Dolphin, T. (2011). *Autumn Statement 2011: George Osborne Performs a U-Turn*. London: Institute for Public Policy Research.

Dommett, K. (2015). The Theory and Practice of Party Modernisation: The Conservative Party Under David Cameron, 2005–2015. *British Politics, 10*(2), 249–266.

Dorey, P. (2009). "Sharing the Proceeds of Growth": Conservative Economic Policy Under David Cameron. *The Political Quarterly, 80*(2), 259–269.
Dorey, P. (2010). Faltering Before the Finishing Line: The Conservative Party's Performance in the 2010 General Election. *British Politics, 5*(4), 402–435.
Dorey, P., & Garnett, M. (2012). No Such Thing as the "Big Society"? The Conservative Party's Unnecessary Search for "Narrative" in the 2010 General Election. *British Politics, 7*(4), 389–417.
Ellman, M. (2015). The UK's Coalition Government and Heterodox Economics. *Cambridge Journal of Economics, 39*(5), 1457–1464.
Emmerson, C., & Tetlow, G. (2015). *Public Finances Under the Coalition.* The Institute for Fiscal Studies (March 2008), 10–32.
Evans, S. (2008). Consigning Its Past to History? David Cameron and the Conservative Party. *Parliamentary Affairs, 61*(2), 291–314.
Ferry, L., & Eckersley, P. (2012). Budgeting and Governing for Deficit Reduction in the UK Public Sector: Act 2 "The Annual Budget". *Public Money & Management, 32*(2), 119–126.
Gamble, A. (2012). Economic Policy. In T. Heppell & D. Seawright (Eds.), *Cameron and the Conservatives: The Transition to Coalition Government* (pp. 59–73). Basingstoke: Palgrave Macmillan.
Gamble, A. (2014). Austerity as Statecraft. *Parliamentary Affairs, 68*(1), 42–57.
Ganesh, J. (2012). *George Osborne: The Austerity Chancellor.* London: Biteback Publishing.
Giavazzi, F., & Pagano, M. (1990). *Can Severe Fiscal Contractions Be Expansionary? Tales of Two Small European Countries* (NBER Macroeconomics Annual 5).
Goodwin, A., & Beck, M. (2015). The UK Economic Outlook. In *The IFS Green Budget.* London: IFS.
Green, J., & Lavery, S. (2015). The Regressive Recovery: Distribution, Inequality and State Power in Britain's Post-crisis Political Economy. *New Political Economy, 20*(6), 894–923.
Grimshaw, D. (2013). Austerity, Privatization and Levelling Down: Public Sector Reforms in the United Kingdom. In D. Vaughan-Whitehead (Ed.), *Public Sector Shock* (pp. 576–626). Geneva: Edward Elgar.
Hancock, M. (2010, September 22). Stick to Plan A and the Growth Will Follow. *The Times.*
Hardie, M., & Wales, P. (2013). *Economic Review 2013.* Office for National Statistics. London.
Hay, C. (2010). "Things Can Only Get Worse …": The Political and Economic Significance of 2010. *British Politics, 5*(4), 391–401.
Hay, C. (2011). Pathology Without Crisis? The Strange Demise of the Anglo-Liberal Growth Model. *Government and Opposition, 46*(1), 1–31.

Hay, C. (2013a). The British Economy: A Crisis of Anglo-Liberal Capitalism? *Renewal, 21*(2), 3.

Hay, C. (2013b). *The British Growth Crisis: A Crisis of and for Growth* (No. 1). Sheffield.

Hayton, R. (2013). Conservative Party Statecraft and the Politics of Coalition. *Parliamentary Affairs, 67*(1), 6–24.

Henry, S. G. (2014). The Coalition's Economic Strategy; Has It Made a Bad Thing Worse? *Economic Outlook, 38*(2), 14–20.

Hindmoor, A. (2004). *New Labour at the Centre: Constructing Political Space.* Oxford: Oxford University Press.

HM Treasury. (2010a). *Budget 2010.* London.

HM Treasury. (2010b). *Spending Review 2010.* London.

HM Treasury. (2013). *Budget 2013.* London.

IFS. (2014). *Autumn Statement Briefing, 2014.* Institute for Fiscal Studies.

IMF. (2010). *Recovery, Risk, and Rebalancing.* IMF World Economic Outlook (WEO). Retrieved October 14, 2015, from https://www.imf.org/external/pubs/ft/weo/2010/02/.

Inman, P. (2013). *Britain Halfway to Triple-Dip Recession as Manufacturing Sector Stalls.* London: The Guardian.

Jorda, O., & Taylor, A. M. (2013). *The Time for Austerity: Estimating the Average Treatment Effect of Fiscal Policy* (NBER Working Paper 19414). National Bureau of Economic Research Inc.

Keegan, W. (2014). *Mr Osborne's Economic Experiment.* London: Searching Finance Limited.

Landale, J. (2011). *Autumn Statement: Why Osborne Speech Changes Everything.* BBC News Website. Retrieved November 3, 2015, from http://www.bbc.co.uk/news/uk-politics-15952413.

Lansley, S. (2011). *The Cost of Inequality.* London: Gibson Square.

Lee, S. (2011). No Plan B: The Coalition Agenda for Cutting the Deficit and Rebalancing the Economy. In S. Lee & M. Beech (Eds.), *The Cameron-Clegg Government: Coalition Politics in an Age of Austerity* (pp. 59–74). Basingstoke: Palgrave Macmillan.

Lee, S. (2015). Indebted and Unbalanced: The Political Economy of the Coalition. In M. Beech & S. Lee (Eds.), *The Conservative-Liberal Coalition: Examining the Cameron-Clegg Government* (pp. 16–35). Basingstoke: Palgrave Macmillan.

Martin, R. (2010). Uneven Regional Growth: The Geographies of Boom and Bust Under New Labour. In N. Coe & A. Jones (Eds.), *The Economic Geography of the UK* (pp. 29–46). London: Sage.

May 2015. (2014). *GDP Figures May Be Misleading, but Osborne Is Benefiting.* May 2015: 2015 General Election Guide. Retrieved November 2, 2015, from

http://www.may2015.com/parties/gdp-figures-may-be-misleading-but-osborne-is-benefiting/.
McAnulla, S. (2010). Heirs to Blair's Third Way? David Cameron's Triangulating Conservatism. *British Politics, 5*(3), 286–314.
Nationwide. (2014). *House Price Growth Moderates in March*. London.
OBR. (2011, November). *Economic and Fiscal Outlook*. London.
OBR. (2014a, December). *Economic and Fiscal Outlook*. London.
OBR. (2014b, October). *Forecast Evaluation Report*. London.
ONS. (2013, May). *Economic Review*. London.
ONS. (2014). UK Trade, December 2014. *Statistical Bulletin*. Retrieved November 5, 2015, from http://www.ons.gov.uk/ons/dcp171778_391926.pdf.
Osborne, G. (2006). *Economic Policy for a New Generation*. Conservative Party Conference Speech 2006. Retrieved October 6, 2015, from http://conservative-speeches.sayit.mysociety.org/speech/599982.
Osborne, G. (2010a). *A New Economic Model*. Mais Lecture. Retrieved from http://www.totalpolitics.com/print/speeches/35193/george-osborne-mais-lecture-a-new-economic-model.thtml.
Osborne, G. (2010b). Budget 2010: Full Text of George Osborne's Statement. *The Telegraph*. Retrieved October 16, 2015, from http://www.telegraph.co.uk/finance/budget/7846849/Budget-2010-Full-text-of-George-Osbornes-statement.html.
Osborne, G. (2011). Autumn Statement 2011: George Osborne's Speech. *The Telegraph*. Retrieved November 3, 2015, from http://www.telegraph.co.uk/finance/budget/8923191/Autumn-Statement-2011-George-Osbornes-speech.html.
Osborne, G. (2013a). *Budget 2013: Chancellor's Statement*. HM Treasury. Retrieved November 4, 2015, from https://www.gov.uk/government/speeches/budget-2013-chancellors-statement.
Osborne, G. (2013b). *Chancellor Speech on the Economy*. HM Treasury. Retrieved November 4, 2015, from https://www.gov.uk/government/speeches/chancellor-speech-on-the-economy.
Osborne, G. (2014a). *Chancellor's Economy Speech in Hong Kong*. HM Treasury. Retrieved November 5, 2015, from https://www.gov.uk/government/speeches/chancellors-economy-speech-in-hong-kong.
Osborne, G. (2014b). *Letter from George Osborne to Andrew Tyrie*. HM Treasury.
Osborne, G., & Sachs, J. (2010). A Frugal Policy Is the Better Solution. *The Financial Times*.
Page, R. M. (2010). David Cameron's Modern Conservative Approach to Poverty and Social Justice: Towards One Nation or Two? *Journal of Poverty and Social Justice, 18*(2), 147–160.
Pugalis, L., & Bentley, G. (2013). Economic Development Under the Coalition Government. *Local Economy, 28*(7–8), 665–678.

Quinn, T. (2011). From New Labour to New Politics: The British General Election of 2010. *West European Politics, 34*(2), 403–411.
Quinn, T., Bara, J., & Bartle, J. (2011). The UK Coalition Agreement of 2010: Who Won? *Journal of Elections, Public Opinion & Parties, 21*(2), 295–312.
Rawnsley, A. (2015). So How Did George Osborne the Failure Become the People's Favourite? *The Guardian*. London.
Roland, D. (2012). Business Confidence Is Still Fragile. *The Telegraph*. London.
Sargent, J. R. (2014). Economic Recovery in a Time of Austerity. *Economic Affairs, 34*(3), 393–398.
Sawyer, M. (2012). The Tragedy of UK Fiscal Policy in the Aftermath of the Financial Crisis. *Cambridge Journal of Economics, 36*(1), 205–221.
Sowels, N. (2014). The Coalition's Economic Policy of Fiscal Austerity and Monetary Experimentation by the Bank of England. *Observatoire de La Société Britannique, 15,* 165–188.
Stacey, K. (2013). Just How Unpopular Is George Osborne? *The Financial Times*. London.
Stacey, K. (2014). George Osborne Extends Help to Buy Scheme to 2020. *The Financial Times*.
Stewart, H. (2013, October 2). Homeowners Inject Record £15.4bn of Equity into Housing Market. *The Guardian*. London.
Taylor-Gooby, P., & Stoker, G. (2011). The Coalition Programme: A New Vision for Britain or Politics as Usual? *The Political Quarterly, 82*(1), 4–15.
The Conservative Party. (2009). *Labour's Debt Crisis*. London.
The Resolution Foundation. (2012). *Gaining from Growth: The Final Report of the Commission on Living Standards*. Resolution Foundation. London.
Toynbee, P., & Walker, D. (2015). *Cameron's Coup: Anatomy of a Revolution*. London: Faber & Faber.
TUC. (2010). *TUC Congress to Launch Campaign Against the Cuts*. London.
TUC. (2013). *The UK's Low Pay Recovery*. Trade Union Congress (TUC). Retrieved November 2, 2015, from https://www.tuc.org.uk/sites/default/files/Lowpayreport.pdf.
TUC. (2015). *Trades Union Congress—Household Debt to Grow Nearly Three Times Faster Than Wages Under Osborne's Plans, Says TUC*. TUC Press Release. Retrieved November 9, 2015, from https://www.tuc.org.uk/node/122167.
Van Reenen, J. (2015). Austerity: Growth Costs and Post-Election Plans.
Watt, N. (2010). George Osborne Unveils £6.25bn Spending Cuts. *The Guardian*. London.
Watt, N., & Mulholland, H. (2010). UK Must Cut Fiscal Deficit Now, Warns George Osborne. *The Guardian*. London.

Weldon, D. (2013a). *Abandoning Rebalancing?* TUC Touchstone Blog. Retrieved November 5, 2015, from http://touchstoneblog.org.uk/2013/03/abandoning-rebalancing/.

Weldon, D. (2013b). *The Impact of the Falling Savings Ratio.* TUC Touchstone Blog. Retrieved November 9, 2015, from http://touchstoneblog.org.uk/2013/07/the-impact-of-the-falling-savings-ratio/.

WERS. (2013). *The 2011 Workplace Employment Relations Study: First Findings.* London.

Wickham-Jones, M. (2013). Labour's Austerity Problem. *Dissent, 60*(4), 38–42. https://doi.org/10.1353/dss.2013.0075.

CHAPTER 6

The Coalition's 'Two Nations' Hegemonic Project

As was argued in Chapter 3, it is useful to distinguish analytically between two modes of state intervention within advanced capitalist economies. On the one hand, state managers pursue *accumulation strategies* which systematically seek to privilege certain economic sectors and behavioural patterns over others. On the other hand, state managers are also driven to secure the conditions for continued legitimation over time. In so doing, they advance *legitimation strategies* or 'hegemonic projects' which are oriented to securing a popular base of support within society. Legitimation strategies are closely tied to distributional questions. On the one hand, state managers can seek to secure support by *actively shaping* distributional processes. Through tax cuts, public expenditure increases, or through subsides targeted at specific sectors or social groups, state managers can seek to secure a popular base of support. On the other hand, state managers can seek to *discursively construct* underlying distributional trends in order to secure popular support. This involves 'framing' redistributions of wealth and power in a way that maintains a sufficient degree of consent amongst the population at large. For these reasons, legitimation strategies are intimately tied to the underlying growth model within a given conjuncture, insofar as the latter produces a distributional opportunity structure through which state managers can seek to build and maintain support for their governing programmes.

The Coalition sought to entrench its position by advancing a far-reaching programme of fiscal austerity. This allowed it to claim the mantle of economic 'credibility' from Labour. But this strategy had

S. Lavery, *British Capitalism After the Crisis*, Building a Sustainable Political Economy: SPERI Research & Policy, https://doi.org/10.1007/978-3-030-04046-8_6

important implications for the legitimation strategy which the Coalition could pursue in office. In particular, its ability to actively secure support through channelling material concessions to strategic social groups became highly limited. New Labour's 'One Nation' strategy of increasing public expenditure, which Osborne had attempted to emulate in the early years of Cameron's leadership, was decisively abandoned after the 2008 crisis. The Coalition had to develop a new legitimation strategy for this hostile fiscal climate. In place of New Labour's 'One Nation' hegemonic project, the Coalition deployed a 'two nations' strategy oriented towards securing a limited but durable base of support in society. This strategy rested upon discursively framing underlying distributional shifts in a way that would secure support. The strategic deployment of ideas therefore became the central plank of the Coalition's legitimation strategy in office. As such, it is helpful to consider the character of the 'ideas' which the Coalition deployed in office.

The Coalition and the Strategic Deployment of Ideas

The literature on the ideological character of the Coalition is split between two apparently incompatible interpretations. The first interpretation emphasises the ideological *radicalism* of the Coalition (Cheesman, 2014; Hall, 2011) and draws attention to the ways in which its austerity programme flowed from an ideological commitment to a form of anti-statist liberalism (Atkins, 2015; Cheesman, 2014; Lakin, 2013: 488). One commentator referred to the Coalition government's programme as 'the best prepared, most wide-ranging, radical and ambitious' neoliberal project since the breakdown of the post-war settlement in the 1970s (Hall, 2011: 718). Another argued that the Coalition was mobilised by an 'ideological vision that seeks to radically reduce what is perceived to be an oversized and over-centralised public sector' (Grimshaw, 2013: 4). Others have argued that the Coalition's approach involved imposing a programme of public sector cuts which 'even Mrs Thatcher would have baulked at' (Cheesman, 2014: 2; Kerr, Byrne, & Foster, 2011: 196).

Considerable evidential support can be found for these characterisations of the Coalition programme. For example, as we saw in the previous chapter, the envisioned scale and speed of the Conservatives' austerity programme announced in the 2010 Spending Review was larger than any other programme of fiscal consolidation in modern British political history

(Ferry & Eckersley, 2012: 21; Lee, 2011b: 21). In the 2014 Autumn Statement, plans to run a budget surplus by 2019/2020 implied that the Conservatives were committed to reducing public spending to 35% of GDP, its lowest level since the 1930s (OBR, 2014). Even the NHS, which was protected relative to other departments, saw the tightest squeeze on its real terms budget since the 1950s (Lee, 2011a: 15). Within the space of three years, rapid cuts to public spending had reduced the size of the public sector workforce as a proportion of the employment total to its lowest level in at least forty years (Cribb, Emmerson, & Sibieta, 2014: 2). In the light of these observations, it is clear why many scholars have emphasised the *radicalism* of the Conservative-led government and have argued that the project was mobilised by an ideological commitment to shrink the size of the state (Atkins, 2015; Beech, 2011; Keegan, 2014: 64).

On the other hand, a number of commentators have emphasised the *pragmatic* character of Conservative statecraft in the post-crisis period (Gamble, 2011: 176; Hayton, 2013; Taylor-Gooby & Stoker, 2011: 12). These accounts emphasise the flexibility of the Conservatives' policy platform in general and of Osborne's political manoeuvrings in particular (Ganesh, 2012). Once in 10 Downing Street, Cameron did not develop a coherent or consistent governing philosophy (Lakin, 2013: 487). Indeed, in government the Conservatives changed course on a number of core policy issues on a number of occasions. For example, as we saw in Chapter 5, when it became apparent in 2011–2012 that the government would not meet its original deficit reduction targets, these were quietly abandoned despite considerable internal opposition from the Tory backbenches and from large sections of the business community. Similarly, the 'Big Society' concept—which had been the key ideational motif of Cameronism in the pre-election period—was largely abandoned in 2010 when it was not well received on the doorsteps or by focus groups (Dorey & Garnett, 2012; Ganesh, 2012: 236). Furthermore, the Coalition programme contained certain policy commitments, including its (partial) protection of the NHS and foreign aid budgets relative to other departments, which suggested that the government was willing to incorporate distinctly post-Thatcherite policies into its prospectus so long as these reaped a discernible political dividend. In short, characterisations of Cameron's government as essentially *pragmatic* argue that 'ideological' analyses of the Coalition underestimate the key role that electoral calculations and ad hoc manoeuvring played in the formation of the government's economic and social policy in the post-crisis conjuncture (Hayton, 2013).

We are left, then, with a seeming paradox: on the above evidence, we can characterise the Conservative-led government as simultaneously *radical* and *pragmatic*: as committed to a long-term, fundamental restructuring of the British state and economy whilst at the same time willing to abandon key aspects of this programme in the light of short-term political calculations (Cheesman, 2014). However, this dichotomy rests on a false distinction between 'ideology' and 'statecraft' (Griffiths, 2015). Previous debates on the character of Thatcherism are instructive here. In explaining the development of Thatcherism, some scholars emphasised its roots in 'New Right' ideology or its 'authoritarian populist' origins (Hall, 1979; Hall & Jacques, 1983). Others emphasised the strategic positioning of Thatcherism and its essentially pragmatic character (Bulpitt, 1986; Marsh & Rhodes, 1995). Thus, such interpretations revolved around a broad distinction between 'ideas' and 'strategy'. However, as Jessop and Hay argued, it is possible to transcend this dichotomy by advancing an approach which *synthesises* these two positions (Hay, 1996b; Jessop, Bonnett, Bromley, & Ling, 1988). Specifically, they argued that analysis should focus on the ways in which policymakers strategically deploy ideas in order to mobilise key sections of the population in support of their governing programmes (Hay, 1996a, 1999; Jessop et al., 1988). In this way, the framing of whether a Party's strategy is 'ideological' or 'pragmatic' is transcended. Rather, the emphasis turns to the ways in which ideas are themselves deployed in a strategic manner in order to advance longer-term political goals.

This has two implications for our analysis of the Coalition. First, it suggests that those who view the Coalition government as essentially 'pragmatic' and therefore 'non-ideological' in orientation underplay the extent to which the Cameron government strategically deployed ideas in order to realise specific social objectives. As we shall see in the following sections, the immediate post-crisis context generated a series of novel distributional trends. In particular, the incomes of welfare claimants and public sector workers were (temporarily) protected relative to other social groups due to the rapid downturn in private sector real wages in the aftermath of the 2008 crash. However, this distributional context did not of itself produce political outcomes. Rather, leading government officials within the Coalition actively sought to construct this reformulated distributional context in a particular way so as to secure support for a policy of far-reaching retrenchment. Second, an emphasis on the strategic deployment of ideas moves us away from the question of the Coalition's 'ideology' insofar as this is understood as a unified and fully formed worldview. Rather, it is more helpful to study the ways in which certain ideas and governing narratives—and in particular the cultivation of 'moralised antagonisms' between different social groupings—were deployed in specific policy areas in order to build support for the Coalition's restructuring programme. As Jessop has written, 'it is difficult to discuss hegemony... [or] hegemonic projects...without reference to specific examples and the substance of particular political, intellectual and moral discourses' (Jessop, 1990: 212). As such, analysis of the ideas which the Coalition strategically deployed should be understood in relation to the practical objectives which it sought to achieve in government.

The Coalition's 'Two Nations' Hegemonic Project

The Coalition's hegemonic project broke with the strategy which New Labour had advanced in the pre-crisis conjuncture. New Labour's 'One Nation' hegemonic project involved channelling revenues towards subordinate social groups in order to build and maintain its base of support. In the case of the Coalition, we can identify attempts to 'frame' its political programme as in line with a 'One Nation' governing narrative (Cheesman, 2014; McAnulla, 2010: 294). For example, upon signing the Coalition Agreement, Cameron and Clegg underlined their shared commitment to work together in the 'national interest' (Atkins, 2015; Crines, 2013). In particular, the newly formed government argued that its deficit reduction programme was designed to deliver 'a stronger society, a sound economy, an accountable state, and power and responsibility in the hands of every citizen' (Osborne, 2010). This programme was presented as benefiting the entire population and therefore as representing the 'national interest' (Atkins, 2015: 88). The Coalition's attempt to associate austerity with a 'One Nation' politics was perhaps at its clearest in Cameron's habitually deployed aphorism that 'we are all in this together' (Lee, 2011b). According to this narrative, the government accepted that austerity would involve painful sacrifices on the part of British citizens; however, the government emphasised that it would ensure that these losses were distributed 'equitably' across society (Evans, 2010: 337). For example, in Osborne's speech to parliament announcing the details of his 2010 *Spending Review*, he said that, 'on fairness, we are all in this together and all must make a contribution... across the entire deficit reduction plan, those with the broadest shoulders will bear the greatest burden' (Osborne, 2010).

This 'One Nation' discursive framing was bolstered by a limited range of policy commitments. For example, whilst the Conservatives proposed a public sector pay freeze, it simultaneously sought to abolish tax credits for families with an annual income of more than £50,000 (Evans, 2010: 337). Similarly, until February 2012, the government retained Labour's 50p tax rate in spite of business opposition, with government officials justifying this on the grounds that, 'in our efforts to reduce the deficit we need to demonstrate that we are doing that in a fair way' (Hope & Winnett, 2012). In this way, austerity was presented as a collective project of self-sacrifice which would deliver benefits in the future for all members of British society. This logic was epitomised in Cameron's 2010 Conference Speech, when he said, 'I promise you this: that if we pull together to deal with these debts today, just a few years down the line the rewards will be felt by everyone in our country' (Cameron, 2010).

There were clear limits to the Coalition's capacity to discursively frame its political programme as embodying 'One Nation' principles of equity and fairness. New Labour's 'One Nation' hegemonic project had been supported by concrete redistributive policies. Rising economic growth and enhanced tax revenues created a pool from which the Blair and Brown governments could draw to fuel mildly redistributive fiscal transfers. As such, to the extent that New Labour 'framed' its policies in line with a 'One Nation' discourse, it could partially back this up through enhanced redistribution to the social base. Its capacity to do this of course rested upon the success of its economic strategy and on the revenue base which was generated by the (temporary) success of Britain's finance-led growth model. When that growth model collapsed—and once the Coalition had committed to its austerity programme—the new government's ability to channel material concessions to the social base became severely constrained.

The Coalition had staked its economic credibility on 'clearing up Labour's mess' and on eliminating the budget deficit in one parliament. Since this was to be achieved primarily through spending cuts, this severely limited the extent to which the Coalition could incorporate subordinate social groups into its political programme through redistributive fiscal transfers and expanded state provision. In certain politically sensitive areas, the Coalition did maintain spending levels to a certain extent. In particular, it protected the incomes of pensioners and 'ring-fenced' the budgets of some government departments in relative terms (notably health and education) (Lupton et al., 2015: 3). However, this meant that very substantial cuts were necessary in 'non-protected' departments and in the welfare budget (ibid.). Indeed, the very rationale of austerity was to reduce these transfers and to retrench large sections of the public sector in order to put the government's finances onto a sounder footing. Thus, whilst the Coalition attempted to advance a 'One Nation' discursive framing of its political programme, this was compromised by its relative inability to back this up with complementary concrete policy interventions.

This rendered the Coalition's political programme and its 'One Nation' framing vulnerable on a number of fronts. We can see this if we briefly consider the distributional impact of the government's fiscal and monetary policy over the 2010–2015 parliament. On the fiscal side, consolidation was to be secured through large cuts to the budgets of unprotected government departments. However, households lower down the income scale characteristically rely more heavily on public services than those higher up the income distribution. As a result, taken as a whole, cuts to public services took 'just over twice the proportion of income from the poorest fifth of the population as from the richest fifth' (Taylor-Gooby & Stoker, 2011: 8). In line with this analysis, the IFS reported that the Coalition's 'tax and benefit changes…[were] *clearly regressive* as, on average, they hit the poorest households more than those in the upper-middle of the income distribution in cash, let alone percentage, terms' (IFS, 2010). Between 2010 and 2014, a household in the bottom tenth of the income distribution would lose approximately 5% of its income as a result of the Coalition's tax and benefit changes, compared to a household at the median which would lose 3% and a household in the 9th decile which would lose just under 2% (ibid.). Additionally, the composition of cuts to local authority budgets disproportionately impacted upon areas with highest levels of deprivation (Grimshaw, 2013). Indeed, one report showed that urban areas with high levels of poverty and unemployment lost almost 9% of their spending power as a result of the cuts, whereas less deprived districts lost less than 1% (Easton, 2011). As such, despite the Coalition's 'One Nation' rhetorical positioning, the distributional impact of its fiscal policy ensured that households lower down the income scale bore a greater proportionate burden of deficit reduction than those higher up.

At the same time, this ratcheting up of fiscal discipline was paralleled by a prolonged period of loose monetary policy. From March 2009, interest rates fell to a historic low and the Bank of England embarked upon a sustained programme of 'Quantitative Easing'. However, both of these policies tended to benefit households at the upper end of the income distribution. In particular, sustained low interest rates lowered mortgage servicing costs, such that housing costs for owner occupiers fell by 37% between 2007–2008 and 2012–2013 (IFS, 2014b: 51). This primarily benefited households in the upper half of the income distribution where the vast majority of homeowners are concentrated (ibid.: 56). At the same time, the Bank of England conceded that QE had a regressive distributional impact, primarily benefiting the top five per cent of wealthiest households (Bank of England, 2012: 254). As such, despite its 'One Nation' rhetoric, the Coalition's period in office was underpinned by a dynamic of *regressive redistribution*—a process of state-led restructuring which combined real wage stagnation with sustained asset-price inflation (Green & Lavery, 2015). Rather than expanding the base of social wealth and incorporating subaltern social groups through redistributive transfers, the Coalition's austerity programme deepened the structural shift towards inequality in Britain (SPERI, 2015). The distributional dynamics which underpinned the Coalition's political economy undermined the government's attempts to frame its policies as working towards a 'common' or 'national-popular' interest.

This underlying dynamic of regressive redistribution posed a series of political risks for the Conservative-led government. For example, throughout the post-crisis conjuncture, two-thirds of voters agreed with the statement that 'the Conservative Party looks after the interests of the rich, not ordinary people' (Policy Exchange, 2013). Similarly, in a context of sustained wage repression and falling living standards, the Conservatives were particularly vulnerable to Labour's charge that it had provoked a 'cost of living' crisis (Wood, 2013). Insofar as wages and living standards continued to decline throughout most of the parliament, the Coalition's 'One Nation' framing was vulnerable to the charge that it was little more than a smokescreen designed to provide cover for a programme which favoured the interests of the already well-off (Massie, 2015).

The Coalition therefore only mobilised its 'One Nation' framing to a limited extent. In addition, it simultaneously deployed a distinctive 'two nations' legitimation strategy which sought to 'mobilise the support of strategically significant sections of the population [whilst passing] the costs of adjustment onto other sectors' (Jessop, 1983; Jessop et al., 1988: 179). Two conditions must be in place if we are to characterise a political project as embodying a 'two nations' strategy. The first is that the strategy must rest upon a clear distinction between 'privileged' and 'marginalised' social groups. In broad terms, the Coalition's political programme identified two key social groups who would bear the burden of the spending cuts: working-age welfare recipients and public sector employees (Cameron, 2012; Dorey, 2015: 91). Passing the burden of adjustment onto these social groups was largely inevitable given the Coalition's economic strategy of securing deficit reduction through large spending cuts. The second feature of a 'two nations' project is that it constructs this as a 'moralised antagonism'—that is that it seeks to solicit the active support of the 'privileged' nation by convincing it that the marginalised group's social position (and in particular its parasitic relationship with the state) has deleterious effects on the nation as a whole. In the case of the Coalition government, it sought to contrast the 'privileges' of social groups supposedly reliant on the state with the position of social groups concentrated within the private sector. In this way, the Coalition sought to mobilise support from 'privileged' sections of the community (namely private sector employees and groups of workers who were discursively constructed as 'independent' from the state) in order to advance its austerity programme. In the following sections, this 'two nations' hegemonic project will be analysed in relation to two key policy areas: welfare restructuring and public sector employment retrenchment.

Welfare Restructuring and Real Wage Decline

The Coalition's austerity programme involved a 'bewildering array' of changes to the welfare system (Baumberg, 2012: 25; Hood & Phillips, 2015). The purpose here is not to detail the full complexity of these changes but rather to delineate the way in which this programme of retrenchment was sustained politically through the deployment of a broad 'two nations' legitimation strategy. Although classifications vary, spending on welfare is generally understood to account for approximately 30% of public expenditure in Britain. For example, whilst total government spending amounted to £695 billion in 2011–2012, £242 billion of this went on 'social protection', a spending category which includes working-age benefits and old age pensions (Burton, 2013: 2). From the beginning of the parliament, the Conservatives had placed reducing the size of the welfare bill at the centre of its deficit reduction strategy. In the June 2010 Budget, one-third of the savings proposed was to be achieved through cuts to spending on welfare (HM Treasury, 2010: 16).

The October 2010 Spending Review set out further welfare cuts of £7 billion per year over the course of the parliament (Cheesman, 2014; Ferry & Eckersley, 2012: 19). However, in the light of electoral considerations, the Conservatives chose to protect the value of old age pensions over the parliament, creating a 'triple lock' which would ensure that state pension payments would increase year-on-year by whichever had the highest value out of earnings or inflation. Since pensions account for approximately half of the total welfare bill, this meant that large welfare savings had to be found elsewhere (IFS, 2014b).

The principal area of welfare which became earmarked for cuts therefore became working-age benefits. In some respects, cutting working-age welfare may not have seemed to be a difficult a task for the Coalition. For instance, opinion polls confirmed that the public were largely in favour of reducing certain working-age benefits, with over 50% of survey respondents between 2010 and 2015 consistently stating that benefits for the unemployed were 'too high and discouraged work' (YouGov, 2013b). However, in terms of the total benefits bill, only 3% specifically went to unemployed households (IFS, 2014a: 8). This compares with 18% for the sick and disabled, 17% for in-work but low-income households and 18% towards families with children (ibid.). As such, broad swathes of the population were in fact in receipt of some kind of welfare support, whether in the form of housing benefit, tax credits, child benefits or other forms of fiscal transfer. This meant that the task of cutting the welfare bill remained fraught with political danger for the Coalition.

It is here, in the implementation and management of the Coalition's programme of welfare retrenchment, where we can identify a broad but distinctive 'two nations' legitimation strategy. A good example of this strategy can be seen if we consider the relationship between real wage decline, welfare restructuring and inequality in the post-crisis conjuncture. In a sense, there was a paradox at the heart of the debate around inequality in Britain in this period. On the one hand, inequality emerged as a key area of public debate in the aftermath of the 2008 crisis. Across the political spectrum, there was a growing recognition that rampant distributional inequities were economically imprudent and unsustainable. However, this re-emergence of concern with inequality occurred at precisely the moment when, on some measures at least, inequality fell in Britain. As the IFS demonstrated, the gini coefficient fell from 0.36 in 2007–2008 to 0.34 in 2012–2013 (IFS, 2014a: 34). This was the lowest level of income inequality recorded—at least on the gini measure—in Britain for over two decades.

Since the 2008 financial crash, there had been a period of unprecedented real wage decline, with in-work households losing approximately 8% of their incomes during this period. The result of this was that inequality measured in terms of the 'market income'—the distribution of income between those who derive their income from employment, self-employment and capital—did increase in the first three years of the downturn (Exell, 2013). Private firms effectively passed the burden of economic adjustment on to employees in the form of wage cuts and pay freezes, whilst the public sector simultaneously cut back on pay and on the size of its workforce (Green & Lavery, 2015). However, in the years immediately following the crisis, the income of *non-working households* remained relatively protected, largely because welfare payments are indexed to inflation and therefore act as 'automatic stabilisers' in periods of recession (IFS, 2014b: 3). As the income of non-working households fell less rapidly than the incomes of in-work households, this led to a decline in the overall level of income inequality between 2008 and 2013 (Lupton et al., 2015: 6; ibid.: 40).

This dynamic was of considerable political significance in the debate over austerity in Britain. The Coalition government—sensitive to opposition charges that its policies had precipitated a 'cost of living crisis'—argued that the fall in income inequality was proof that the burden of its austerity programme had been shared equitably across society. For example, in his 2014 Budget Speech, Osborne pointed out that, 'under this government income inequality is at its lowest level for 28 years', whilst during a PMQs in November 2013 Cameron argued that the fall in income inequality demonstrated that the Conservatives were committed to building a 'fairer country' (Cameron, 2013). However, there was a profound irony at the heart of this narrative (SPERI, 2015: 5–7). As was argued above, the decline in income inequality had been driven by a combination of declining median real wages occurring alongside the relative protection of non-working household incomes through the benefits and tax credit system. However, as of April 2013 the pace of cuts to benefits and tax credits was substantially accelerated, as the provisions of the Welfare Reform Act (2012) came into effect (HM Government, 2012). As a result of this legislation, the government introduced a number of reforms which disproportionately reduced the incomes of groups lower down the income scale. For example, it implemented a 'welfare cap' which set a limit on the total sum of benefits that working-age households could claim (Hamnett, 2014). However, households in the lower half of the income distribution were more dependent on benefits which had been 'capped' than households in the upper half of the income distribution. As a result, the welfare cap 'disproportionately targeted benefits claimed by the least well off' (Goulden, 2014). In addition, Osborne announced that most working-age benefits and tax credits would be up-rated by one per cent (below inflation) for the three years from April 2013 to April 2016, a measure which was estimated to achieve savings of £1.7 billion (IFS, 2014a: 9). Again, this had a disproportionate impact on households in the lower end of the income distribution who were more reliant on social security payments (ibid.: 33). The tax and benefit changes implemented between April 2013 and April 2015 therefore had a clearly regressive impact, such that households in the bottom four income deciles experienced a net loss to their incomes, whilst households in the upper deciles saw their incomes protected in both absolute and relative terms (IFS, 2014b: 54).

The result was that between 2010 and 2015, the overall impact of the Coalition's programme of tax and benefit reforms was broadly regressive. As one report put it:

> The poor bore the brunt of [the Coalition's] changes to direct taxes, tax credits and benefits from May 2010 to 2014-15. Up to 2014/15, the poorest twentieth lost nearly 3 per cent of their incomes on average from these changes (not allowing for VAT and other indirect taxes) and people in the next five-twentieths of the income distribution lost almost 2 per cent... [on the other hand] those in the top half of the distribution were net gainers from the changes. (Lupton et al., 2015: 5)

The tension in the Conservatives' narrative was clear: on the one hand, the government highlighted the fall in income inequality as evidence of the 'fairness' of its austerity programme; at the same time, through its programme of benefit and tax credit cuts it set about actively dismantling the very mechanisms which had produced this (small) reduction in income inequality in the first place. As a result, the initial drop in income inequality which occurred after the crisis began to go into reverse. Thus, in 2014 the IFS wrote that, 'on-going cuts to benefits and tax credits [will] reduce incomes towards the bottom... income inequality may well return to its pre-crisis level within the next few years' (IFS, 2014b: 56). Another report similarly suggests that, once the Coalition's tax and benefit changes were taken into account, net household income inequality as well as relative and absolute poverty were all set to increase substantially by 2020 (Brewer et al., 2012). As such, the decline in income inequality between 2008/2009 and 2012/2013 is best viewed as a temporary blip in an otherwise clear historical trajectory in Britain. The benefit and tax system for a short period of time protected the incomes of the poorest households and reduced relative inequality in the first few years of the post-crisis conjuncture. However, by 2012 this very mechanism had itself become politicised and identified as an object of retrenchment by the Coalition.

In what sense did this dynamic embody a 'two nations' hegemonic project? As was argued in Chapter 3, one of the key features of hegemonic projects is that they do not only seek to accommodate the preferences of the public in order to advance distinctive political projects; they also seek to strategically deploy ideas in order to shape public discourse in ways which support particular logics of social, political and economic restructuring (Hay, 1997). As we have seen, between 2008/2009 and 2012/2013, the welfare system protected the incomes of non-working households relative to wage earners. The outcome of this dynamic—a temporary drop in income inequality—was used by the Coalition to bolster its argument that its austerity programme was fairly distributing the pain of retrenchment. However, at the same time, the Conservatives sought to actively play upon the distinction between non-working households and wage earners in order to advance a distinctive programme of welfare retrenchment which would effectively reverse these gains. In broad terms, the Conservatives drew upon a long-standing distinction between the 'deserving' and 'undeserving' poor (or in the contemporary parlance 'strivers' v 'skivers') in order to frame its programme of welfare retrenchment (Garthwaite, 2011; Valentine & Harris, 2014). For example, in the White Paper *21st Century Welfare*, it was stated that:

> Any reforms should … establish a fairer relationship between the people who receive benefits and the people who pay for them and, as crucially, between the people on out of work benefits and the people who work in low paid jobs. (DWP, 2010: 5)

Similarly, in 2012, Osborne stated that:

> It's unfair that when that [working] person leaves their home early in the morning, they pull the door behind them, they're going off to do their job, they're looking at their next-door neighbour, the blinds are down, and that family is living a life on benefits. That is unfair … and we are going to tackle that as part of tackling this country's economic problems. (Hern, 2012)

This broad distinction between a 'deserving' and 'undeserving' poor of course has a long pedigree in Conservative thought and governing practice (Evans, 1997: 607; Hickson, 2009: 351). However, it is crucial to account for how the Conservatives' utilisation of this discourse in government involved more than an abstract appeal to traditional anti-welfarist principles. It also involved interpreting, narrating and framing its particular interventions in terms of specific conjunctural trends associated with the post-crisis context. It is here where the link between inequality, real wage decline and welfare retrenchment provides us with a good example of the Conservative-led government's 'two nations' legitimation strategy.

In January 2013, the Coalition aimed to drive its *Welfare Benefits Up-Rating Act* (2013) through parliament. As we saw previously, this aimed to impose a below inflation 'cap' of 1% on a range of benefits which working-age households could claim over a three-year period. The goal was to achieve savings of £270 million per annum from 2014 to 2015 onwards. However, crucially, the Conservatives did not only justify this on the grounds that it would contribute to deficit reduction. They also sought to frame this intervention in terms of 'fairness' and as a measure which showed that they were 'standing up for working people' (Mason, 2013). Specifically, the government argued that in a context of falling wages, it was unfair that welfare recipients should receive more than in-work households. In this way, the Conservatives sought to discursively construct themselves as the Party of 'hard working families' in order to gain a political advantage in key marginal seats and to make inroads into Labour's core vote. As the Labour Party voted against the measures, the Conservatives' responded with an advertising campaign which sought to portray Labour as 'soft' on welfare, making the point that Labour were 'voting to increase benefits by more than workers' wages' (Conservative Home, 2013). In this way, the Conservatives sought to portray Labour's policy as promoting the interests of feckless benefit claimants as opposed to hard-working families.

The Coalition's 'two nations' strategy therefore rested upon constructing a 'moralised antagonism' between a privileged group of 'workers' and a marginalised group of 'benefit claimants'. It then sought to mobilise support for its own approach by emphasising how its policies favoured the former over the latter. In particular, the government sought to present its policy as favouring those 'in work' as opposed to those on the unemployment register. For example, the Department for Work and Pensions impact assessment stressed that as a result of the policy, 'workless households will no longer receive more in benefits than the average weekly wage received by families in work' (DWP, 2012). Iain Duncan Smith justified the policy in similar terms by claiming that, 'for too many people, it pays more to languish on benefits than to enter work... [the policy would therefore ensure] fairness to those who work hard and pay into the system in the process' (Duncan Smith, 2013). The problem was that this dichotomy rested on a rhetorical rather than a factual opposition between 'workers' and 'benefit claimants'. In practice, the effect of the welfare cap was to reduce the incomes of 9.5 million households. Of these, only 2.5 million were out of work; 7 million of the affected households were in fact in low-paid employment (Mason, 2013). As such, the policy had the effect of reducing the incomes of broad swathes of the working population. However, the *framing* of the policy was designed to secure the support of precisely this social group. In this regard, the strategic deployment of a 'two nations' discourse was highly successful: by a three-to-one majority, the public (incorrectly) thought that the welfare cap would primarily hit the unemployed as opposed to low-paid workers (TUC, 2013a). In encouraging identification and mobilisation against a (largely constructed) 'workless' underclass, the Conservatives successfully secured broad-based support for a policy which might otherwise have failed. Partly as a result of this, on the eve of passing the legislation, 74% of the population were in favour of the cap as opposed to 11% who were against it (YouGov, 2013b).

Declining real wages and stagnant living standards posed a real threat to the Coalition's governing legitimacy over the post-crisis conjuncture. By 2012, Labour's 'cost of living' narrative had gained considerable political traction. By a margin of approximately 10%, voters thought that Labour were more likely to 'improve living standards' and to 'provide more jobs' than the Conservatives (YouGov, 2013a). However, we can see how through the deployment of its 'two nations' strategy, the Conservatives effectively bolstered support for its own political programme by channelling the discontent of in-work households downwards onto a (largely constructed) subaltern group of welfare dependent 'shirkers'. This strategy achieved three principal goals. First, it transformed the potential liability of sustained real wage decline into a political asset for the Conservatives. The government used the sustained drop in real wages as a means to justify welfare retrenchment and to build support for a policy which (ironically) would further retrench the after-tax incomes of low-paid workers. Second, it allowed the government to deflect blame for falling living standards onto welfare recipients. Third, taking these two dynamics together, the Conservatives could then mobilise support for further welfare retrenchment from a discursively constructed 'privileged' nation of hard-working tax payers. The fact that this process would unravel the very welfare protections which had facilitated the decline in income inequality in the first few years of the crisis and which the Conservatives had themselves held up as a symbol of the 'fairness' of its programme was, from the perspective of the strategic objectives of the government, irrelevant. The strategic deployment of a 'two nations' legitimation strategy and the construction of a 'moralised antagonism' between workers and working-age benefit claimants was effective in helping to advance the short- and medium-term political objectives of the Coalition government.

The 'Public-Private' Divide

The Coalition's austerity programme severely limited the strategies which it could deploy in order to solicit the support of subordinate social groups. With approximately 80% of deficit reduction to be secured through spending cuts, the government's economic strategy also ran the risk of producing a substantial public backlash against the cuts (Burnham, 2011) This was particularly so in the case of public sector employment. In its second and third terms, New Labour had significantly increased spending on public services, such that public sector employment increased by 700,000 between 2000 and 2010 (Cribb, Disney, & Sibieta, 2014). In contrast, the Coalition's programme of fiscal consolidation outlined cuts of 19% across non-protected departments (Ferry & Eckersley, 2012: 17). Since wages account for approximately 30% of all general government expenditure, one of the key tasks for government departments was to cut the size of their wage bills (Bozio & Disney, 2011: 163). The Coalition aimed to secure this through three principal mechanisms: through wage cuts, pensions reform and large-scale redundancies (Bach & Stroleny, 2013: 345). In this way, an economic crisis which had originated within the banking sector was reconstituted as a fiscal crisis of the state, with a significant portion of the burden of adjustment passed on to those working within the public sector (Burnham, 2011; Gamble, 2012: 61).

This strategy of public sector retrenchment came with two considerable political risks. First, the public sector is the most highly unionised section of the British workforce: it has a trade union density four times that of the private sector (Parry, 2011: 4). Although the power of organised labour had been increasingly marginalised since the late 1970s, its relative strength in the public sector remained a potential barrier to the Coalition (Eaton, 2010; Machin, 1997). This was evidenced in 2011 when 1.3 million working days were lost to strike activity primarily in the public sector—a figure which far exceeded previous trends throughout the 2000s. Second, there was a danger that large-scale public sector job losses would lead to an increase in unemployment, which could have compromised the government's deficit reduction programme and undermined its governing legitimacy. The key strategic objective of the Coalition government was therefore to contain the fallout from public sector retrenchment in both of these areas. As was the case with its programme of welfare restructuring, we can identify the utilisation of a broad 'two nations' legitimation strategy in order to achieve this objective.

The Coalition sought to bring about a large reduction in the size of the public sector workforce. In the June 2010 Budget, it was predicted that 490,000 jobs would go in the public sector by 2014–2015 in order to save £3.3 billion by the end of the parliament (Exell, 2010: 29; Grimshaw, 2013: 10). However, less than two years into the Coalition's period in office, 420,000 public sector job cuts had already been implemented (Grimshaw, 2013: 9). As a result, by 2012, the OBR had increased the level of overall job cuts it expected to see in the public sector to 740,000 by 2017 (OBR, 2012: 75). By 2013, this figure had increased further still—overall, the OBR projected a net loss of 1,000,000 public sector jobs between 2011 and 2018/2019 as the public spending squeeze was extended into the next parliament (OBR, 2013: 75). As the IFS remarked, this represented a cut to general government employment which was 'three times as large as those delivered in the early 1990s, and unprecedented in at least the last 50 years' (Cribb, Disney, et al., 2014: 36).

This massive reduction in the size of the general government workforce was paralleled by a qualitative restructuring of the employment relation within public workplaces. First, government departments sought to deliver large savings by initiating a sustained period of real wage cuts per head for public sector workers. Until March 2011, wage deals which had been agreed in the 2008–2011 Spending Review period were still current (Parry, 2011: 13). However, in the June 2010 Budget, a two-year pay freeze was announced which subsequently took effect between March 2011 and 2013. For the following three years (from 2013 to 2016), public sector pay increases were limited to one per cent, a percentage increase which was below the average rate of inflation (Bach & Stroleny, 2013: 345). As a result, throughout the 2010 to 2015 parliament and beyond, public sector workers experienced a prolonged period of real wage decline. Second, the Coalition sought to lower the value of public sector pensions. In the June 2010 Budget, the government moved to up-rate pensions by CPI (a measure which typically produces a lower rate of inflation because it excludes housing costs) rather than by the RPI. Combined with other reforms, the net effect of this was to reduce the value of public sector pensions by an average of 25% relative to previous schemes (Exell, 2010: 30). In addition, as of April 2012, public sector workers were required to pay on average 3% more in contributions to pension schemes than previously, whilst pensions were to be determined on a 'career average' rather than final salary basis (ibid.: 31). Thus, in terms of the size, pay and conditions of the public sector workforce, the Coalition initiated a sustained period of retrenchment (Hall, 2011). Furthermore, these cutbacks were not designed as a 'temporary' fix to the UK's fiscal problems. For example, in his 2014 Autumn Statement, Osborne acknowledged that public sector pay freezes had delivered £12 billion of savings over the parliament. However, he went on to note that, 'by continuing to restrain public sector pay we expect to deliver commensurate savings in the next Parliament until we have dealt with the. The Conservatives' strategy was therefore not just concerned with containing public sector employment in response to short-term considerations. Its programme sought to systematically de-privilege the public sector's position as a complementary component of Britain's finance-led growth model.

The Coalition's programme of public sector retrenchment bore the hallmarks of a classic 'two nations' hegemonic project. On the eve of the 2010 general election, Cameron stated, 'in some parts of the country the state accounts for a bigger share of the economy than it did in the communist countries in the old eastern bloc. This is clearly unsustainable' (BBC News, 2010). However, the task of implementing mass public sector redundancies and a decade-long period of pay constraint was not presented merely as an unavoidable or regrettable result of deficit reduction. Rather, reducing the size of public sector employment was presented as a core element of the Coalition's economic strategy to 'rebalance' the UK economy towards the private sector (Osborne, 2010). In this way, the government presented achieving large-scale public sector retrenchment as in accordance with the 'general' national interest. Opponents of this policy—in particular the large public sector trade unions—were characterised as pursuing 'sectional' interests at the expense of taxpayers. The Conservatives were clear that any public sector recalcitrance would be dealt with firmly. Oliver Letwin, a key member of the Cabinet who has been described as the 'architect' of the government's public sector reform programme, outlined the way in which the Conservatives would utilise the state in order to weaken public sector employees' bargaining position (Toynbee & Walker, 2015: 68). Speaking at the consultancy firm KPMG in 2011, he said that it was necessary for 'fear and discipline' to be instilled into public sector employees in order to drive up productivity rates. He added that large-scale public sector redundancies would be an 'inevitable and intended consequence' of government policy (Boffey, 2011).

By 2014, public sector workers had experienced a real terms pay cut of £2245 relative to 2010 (TUC, 2014). However, when trade unions formulated a response to this unprecedented decline in real wages, the Chancellor immediately presented them as acting against the 'national interest'. In response to mounting trade union pressure and the threat of public sector strikes, Osborne insisted that the Coalition's public sector reforms were, 'fair to both taxpayers and public servants. I would once again ask the unions why they are damaging our economy at a time like this – and putting jobs at risk' (Osborne, 2011). At the same time, the Conservatives outlined plans to place new minimum thresholds on strike ballots in order to further restrict industrial militancy. These plans, formalised in the run-up to the 2015 general election, have been described as, 'the most sweeping and radical tightening of the rules on industrial action seen since the Thatcher era of the 1980s, with a minimum 50 per cent ballot participation threshold alongside a requirement for unions in 'important public services' to obtain a minimum 40 per cent majority of all those eligible to vote' (Darlington & Dobson, 2015: 1). In this way, the Conservatives adopted a classic model of 'roll back' neoliberalisation: recalcitrant social groups were identified as barriers to market liberal expansion and state power was strategically deployed in order to drive through their marginalisation (Peck, 2010).

'Two nations' projects do not only seek to pass the costs of economic adjustment onto subordinate social groups, in this case onto public sector workers. They also seek to build a limited but durable social base of support for broader projects of social, economic and political restructuring (Jessop, 1990: 211). They do this by constructing 'moralised antagonisms' between the (perceived) interests of social groups 'privileged' by the dominant accumulation strategy and the interests of marginalised social forces. The Coalition's programme of public sector restructuring rested upon cultivating a moralised antagonism focused upon a 'public-private' distinction. By strategically deploying governing narratives which constructed and entrenched this 'public-private' dichotomy, the government aimed to secure support for public sector retrenchment from key sections of the social base, in particular from private sector workers.

We can see this dynamic at play in the way in which the Coalition justified its implementation of real wage cuts across the public sector. Here, the Conservatives sought to present public sector employees as 'privileged' relative to their private sector counterparts (Bach & Stroleny, 2013: 348). This dichotomy was strongly conditioned by strategic considerations. 'The government viewed the public sector workforce as key beneficiaries of the previous Labour government. Consequently, they assumed that public sector wage restraint would generate little public sympathy for the workforce during a severe recession' (ibid.: 345). Between 2008 and 2010, nominal public sector pay rose by 4.5% whilst nominal private sector pay rose by only 1% (Cribb, Emmerson, et al., 2014: 1). This had occurred because 'many public sector workers, including teachers, NHS workers and the police, [were] subject to three-year settlements from 2008 to 2011. These settlements were made shortly after the 2007 Comprehensive Spending Review, before the recession happened and before it was known that private sector earnings would stop growing' (Cribb, Emmerson, et al., 2014: 5). However, since real wages in the private sector declined so rapidly in the immediate post-crisis period, this meant that public sector pay packets were protected in relative terms (Bozio & Disney, 2011: 163).

The 'public-private' distinction was utilised by Osborne in order to justify a sustained period of public sector pay retrenchment. When the Chancellor announced that public sector pay increases would be limited to 1% over three years in the 2011 Autumn Statement, he drew attention to the fact that, 'public sector pay has risen at twice the rate of private sector pay over the last four years'. He then stated that, 'while I accept that a 1% average rise is tough; it is also fair to those who work to pay the taxes that will fund it' (Osborne, 2011). As was the case with respect to welfare retrenchment, novel distributional dynamics which had protected the incomes of certain social groups in relative terms in the immediate post-crisis context subsequently became politicised and identified as objects of retrenchment under the Coalition. The result was that the broader context—one of broadly sustained real wage decline across both the public and private sectors—was effectively depoliticised.

A large number of factors had contributed to real wage decline in this period. For example, as we saw in the previous chapter, 77% of net job creation between 2010 and 2013 had been in low pay sectors whilst the jobs recovery had been underpinned by a large increase in generally low-paid self-employment (TUC, 2013b). By deploying a moralised antagonism between private and public sector workers, the government took advantage of low pay growth to further retrench the conditions of workers in those sectors which for a short period of time had been insulated from the worst of the economic downturn. As Pierson has written, 'the contemporary politics of the welfare state is the politics of blame avoidance. Governments confronting the electoral imperatives of modern democracy will undertake retrenchment only when they discover ways to minimise the political costs involved' (Pierson, 1996: 179). In other circumstances, initiating a period of sustained public sector pay retrenchment may have been difficult. However, by mobilising the public–private distinction and by constructing the achievement of public sector pay cuts as in the 'national interest', the Coalition successfully avoided blame for its programme of retrenchment whilst at the same time securing support for its programme of delivering a 'private sector-led recovery'.

After a brief interregnum, pay in the private sector consistently grew faster than pay in the public sector from 2010 to 2014 (Cribb, Emmerson, et al., 2014: 1). As Grimshaw and Rubery have commented, 'in the course of the roll-out of public spending cuts since 2010 real pay cuts for full-time public sector workers have exceeded those for the private sector' (Grimshaw & Rubery, 2015: 212). Projections from the OBR suggested that this dynamic was set to continue into the future: for the period between 2014 and 2018, it projected that, 'pay will continue to grow faster in the private sector than in the public sector' (Cribb, Emmerson, et al., 2014: 1). This was no accident. It represented a conscious strategy on the part of the Coalition to systematically privilege private sector employment growth and to undercut public sector pay and conditions.

This attempt to secure 'rebalancing' between the public and private sector was an elemental feature of the Conservatives accumulation strategy. However, this dynamic was also replete with political considerations. As Jessop and his collaborators have argued in relation to Thatcherism, 'a 'two nations' hegemonic project aims, first, to expand the numbers of those in the privileged nation in areas where its privileges are well entrenched… and second, to widen the scope of their privileges' (Jessop et al., 1988: 179). In other words, although 'two nations' projects are *limited* in the sense that they direct material concessions and symbolic rewards to a 'privileged' section of the social base, they are also *expansive* in the sense that they seek to augment the size of those 'privileged' social groups in order to deliver future political support. It is here where the medium- to long-term political strategy of the Conservatives in the post-crisis conjuncture is evident. Specifically, the Conservatives sought to reduce the size of the (typically Labour voting) public sector whilst expanding the size of the (typically Conservative supporting) private sector. As Osborne's biographer has written, the Chancellor's 'grand strategy' involved:

> [T]he calculated use of policy to gradually expand the share of the electorate with a rational interest in voting for his party. Diminishing tax credits for the well off, scything the public sector pay role, capping child benefit. Osborne does not adopt these policies simply because they might boost the size of the electorate that has a rational interest in voting Tory, but that potential outcome very much occurs to him. (Ganesh, 2012: 264)

This political dynamic finds support in polling analysis from Peter Kellner, who wrote with respect to the 2015 General Election:

> There is a growing divergence between private and public sector workers [in terms of their voting behaviour]. The Tories led Labour by 17 points among people working in the private sector, while Labour lead by three points among public sector workers…if this gulf persists, it's good long-term news for the Conservatives, as private sector employment expands while the public sector contracts. (YouGov, 2014)

As this suggests, the Coalition's deployment of a 'two nations' hegemonic project in the area of public sector retrenchment fulfilled both short- and longer-term political objectives for the Conservatives. In the short term, it allowed the government to justify an unprecedented period of public sector wage retrenchment whilst displacing blame for this dynamic through an appeal to 'fairness'. In the longer term, it was hoped this would create a limited but durable base of support for 'balanced budgets' and public sector residualism in the future—a situation which, naturally, would favour the Conservatives.

Conclusion

The Coalition effectively broke with the 'One Nation' hegemonic project which had been deployed by New Labour in the pre-crisis conjuncture. In contrast, the Coalition deployed a distinctive 'two nations' hegemonic project. 'Two nations' strategies seek to build a limited but durable base of support for programmes of far-reaching social, economic and political reform through entrenching a series of 'moralised antagonisms' between distinct social groups. In the case of the Coalition, two case studies were offered to illustrate how its political programme utilised such a 'two nations' strategy in the post-crisis conjuncture. First, the relationship between welfare retrenchment and real wage decline was analysed. By constructing its policies as in favour of 'hard working families' as opposed to working-age benefit claimants, the Conservatives successfully managed to secure sufficient support for a policy of welfare retrenchment which actually impacted negatively primarily on the incomes of low-paid 'in-work' households. The Coalition's 'two nations' strategy also served to legitimise a policy of job cuts and wage freezes in the public sector which in other circumstances might have been very difficult to implement.

The Coalition's pursuit of a deep austerity programme was a high-risk strategy. It involved implementing large cuts to the incomes of broad swathes of the population (Stanley, 2016). It limited the Coalition's capacity to secure popular support through channelling resources to strategically significant groups. In this context, the Coalition's 'two nations' hegemonic project was relatively successfully. In a context of declining real wages, the Coalition managed to build a limited base of supporting by cultivating 'moralised antagonisms' between 'workers' and 'welfare claimants' on the one hand and private and public sector workers on the other. However, the Coalition's approach also came with considerable costs. New Labour's 'One Nation' hegemonic project had helped to stabilise British capitalism. Enhanced public expenditure redistributed resources and jobs to social groups and regions which might otherwise have been excluded from Britain's finance-led growth model. The Coalition's 'two nations' strategy systematically undercuts these stabilising mechanisms. As a result, deep structural weaknesses within British capitalism were re-embedded during the post-crisis conjuncture. The volatile politics of the Britain in the period after the Coalition revealed the limitations of its 'two nations' programme.

References

Atkins, J. (2015). "Together in the National Interest": The Rhetoric of Unity and the Formation of the Cameron—Clegg Government. *The Political Quarterly, 86*(1), 85–92.

Bach, S., & Stroleny, A. (2013). Public Service Employment Restructuring in the Crisis in the UK and Ireland: Social Partnership in Retreat. *European Journal of Industrial Relations, 19*(4), 341–357.

Bank of England. (2012). The Distributional Effects of Asset Purchases. *Bank of England Quarterly Bulletin 2012 Q3*. London.

Baumberg, B. (2012). Benefit Cuts, Welfare Reform and Inequality. *The Coalition Government and Income Inequality: Half-Term Report*. London.

BBC News. (2010). *NI's 100 Days Under the Coalition—BBC News*. BBC News Website. Retrieved December 15, 2015, from http://www.bbc.co.uk/news/uk-northern-ireland-politics-11004792.

Beech, M. (2011). A Tale of Two Liberalisms. In M. Beech & S. Lee (Eds.), *The Cameron-Clegg Government: Coalition Politics in an Age of Austerity* (pp. 267–279). Basingstoke: Palgrave Macmillan.

Boffey, D. (2011). Public Sector Workers Need "Discipline and Fear." *The Guardian*. London.

Bozio, A., & Disney, R. (2011). *Public Sector Pay and Pensions*. IFS Green Budget. Retrieved December 13, 2015, from http://www.ifs.org.uk/budgets/gb2011/11chap7.pdf.

Brewer, M., Dickerson, A., Gambin, L., Green, A., Joyce, R., & Wilson, R. (2012). *The Impact of Employment Changes on Poverty in 2020*. JRF—Joseph Rowntree Foundation. Retrieved December 12, 2015, from https://www.jrf.org.uk/report/impact-employment-changes-poverty-2020.

Bulpitt, J. (1986). The Discipline of the New Democracy: Mrs Thatcher's Domestic Statecraft. *Political Studies, 34*(1), 19–39.

Burnham, P. (2011). Towards a Political Theory of Crisis: Policy and Resistance Across Europe. *New Political Science, 33*(4), 493–507.

Burton, M. (2013). *The Politics of Public Sector Reform: From Thatcher to the Coalition*. Basingstoke: Palgrave Macmillan.

Cameron, D. (2010). *Conference Speech 2010: Together in the National Interest*. BBC News Website. Retrieved December 6, 2015, from http://www.bbc.co.uk/news/uk-politics-11485397.

Cameron, D. (2012). David Cameron's Welfare Speech. *The Telegraph*. London.

Cameron, D. (2013). *PMQs 6 November 2013. House of Commons Hansard Debates for 6 November 2013*. Retrieved December 9, 2015, from http://www.publications.parliament.uk/pa/cm201314/cmhansrd/cm131106/debtext/131106-0001.htm#column_231.

Cheesman, H. (2014). Cameron's Tories: Talking Conservative, Acting Radical. *Revue LISA/LISA E-Journal, 7*(8).

Cribb, J., Disney, R., & Sibieta, L. (2014). *The Public Sector Workforce: Past, Present and Future* (IFS Briefing Note BN145). London.

Cribb, J., Emmerson, C., & Sibieta, L. (2014). *Public Sector Pay in the UK*. London.

Crines, A. S. (2013). The Rhetoric of the Coalition: Governing in the National Interest? *Representation, 49*(2), 207–218.

Darlington, R., & Dobson, J. (2015). *The Conservative Government's Proposed Strike Ballot Thresholds: The Challenge to the Trade Unions*. Salford.

Dorey, P. (2015). A Farewell to Alms: Thatcherism's Legacy of Inequality. *British Politics, 10*(1), 79–98.

Dorey, P., & Garnett, M. (2012). No Such Thing as the "Big Society"? The Conservative Party's Unnecessary Search for "Narrative" in the 2010 General Election. *British Politics, 7*(4), 389–417.

Duncan Smith, I. (2013). *Speech to Capita Welfare Reform Conference*. Capital Welfare Reform Conference. Retrieved December 13, 2015, from http://www.ukpol.co.uk/2015/12/03/iain-duncan-smith-2013-speech-to-capita-welfare-reform-conference/.

DWP. (2010). *21st Century Welfare*. London.

DWP. (2012). *Benefit Cap (Housing Benefit) Regulations 2012: Impact Assessment for the Benefit Cap*. London.

Easton, M. (2011). *Fair's Fair*. BBC News Website. Retrieved December 8, 2015, from http://www.bbc.co.uk/blogs/thereporters/markeaston/2011/02/fairs_fair.html.

Eaton, G. (2010). Cameron Prepares to Go to War with the Trade Unions. *The New Statesman*. Retrieved December 14, 2015, from http://www.newstatesman.com/blogs/the-staggers/2010/07/cameron-unions-strike-assault.

Evans, S. (1997). Thatcher and the Victorians: A Suitable Case for Comparison? *History, 82*(268), 601–620.

Evans, S. (2010). "Mother"s Boy': David Cameron and Margaret Thatcher. *The British Journal of Politics & International Relations, 12*(3), 325–343.

Exell, R. (2010). The Spending Review and Public Sector Jobs. *Radical Statistics, 103,* 25–34.

Exell, R. (2013). *Inequality, Social Security and the Recession.* TUC Touchstone Blog. Retrieved December 8, 2015, from http://touchstoneblog.org.uk/2013/05/inequality-social-security-and-the-recession/.

Ferry, L., & Eckersley, P. (2012). Budgeting and Governing for Deficit Reduction in the UK Public Sector: Act 2 "The Annual Budget". *Public Money & Management, 32*(2), 119–126.

Gamble, A. (2011). Project Cameron. *Public Policy Research, 18*(3), 173–178.

Gamble, A. (2012). Economic Policy. In T. Heppell & D. Seawright (Eds.), *Cameron and the Conservatives: The Transition to Coalition Government* (pp. 59–73). Basingstoke: Palgrave Macmillan.

Ganesh, J. (2012). *George Osborne: The Austerity Chancellor.* London: Biteback Publishing.

Garthwaite, K. (2011). "The Language of Shirkers and Scroungers?" Talking About Illness, Disability and Coalition Welfare Reform. *Disability & Society, 26*(3), 369–372.

Goulden, C. (2014). *Budget 2014: Welfare Cap Protects Wealthier Claimants, Not Those in Greatest Need.* Joseph Rowntree Foundation Blog. Retrieved December 10, 2015, from https://www.jrf.org.uk/blog/budget-2014-welfare-cap-protects-wealthier-claimants-not-those-greatest-need.

Green, J., & Lavery, S. (2015). The Regressive Recovery: Distribution, Inequality and State Power in Britain's Post-crisis Political Economy. *New Political Economy, 20*(6), 894–923.

Griffiths, S. (2015). Statecraft as a Straightjacket: A Reply to Gamble and Hayton. *Parliamentary Affairs, 68*(4), 735–743.

Grimshaw, D. (2013). Austerity, Privatization and Levelling Down. In D. Vaughan-Whitehead (Ed.), *Public Sector Shock* (pp. 576–626). Geneva: Edward Elgar.

Grimshaw, D., & Rubery, J. (2015). Neoliberalism 2.0: Crisis and Austerity in the UK. In S. Lehndorff (Ed.), *Divisive Integration: The Triumph of Failed Ideas in Europe.* Brussels: ETUI.

Hall, S. (1979, January). The Great Moving Right Show. *Marxism Today,* 14–20.

Hall, S. (2011). The Neo-Liberal Revolution. *Cultural Studies, 25*(6), 705–728.

Hall, S., & Jaques, M. (1983). *The Politics of Thatcherism.* London: Lawrence and Wishart.

Hamnett, C. (2014). Shrinking the Welfare State: The Structure, Geography and Impact of British Government Benefit Cuts. *Transactions of the Institute of British Geographers, 39*(4), 490–503.

Hay, C. (1996a). Narrating Crisis: The Discursive Construction of the 'Winter of Discontent'. *Sociology, 30*(2), 253–277.
Hay, C. (1996b). *Re-stating Social and Political Change*. Milton Keynes: Open University Press.
Hay, C. (1997). State of the Art: Divided by a Common Language: Political Theory and the Concept of Power. *Politics, 17*(1), 45–52.
Hay, C. (1999). Crisis and the Structural Transformation of the State: Interrogating the Process of Change. *The British Journal of Politics and International Relations, 1*(3), 317–344.
Hayton, R. (2013). Conservative Party Statecraft and the Politics of Coalition. *Parliamentary Affairs, 67*(1), 6–24.
Hern, A. (2012). George Osborne Doesn't Like it if Your Blinds are Down in the Morning. *New Statesman*. Retrieved November 12, 2018, from https://www.newstatesman.com/blogs/star-spangled-staggers/2012/10/george-osborne-doesnt-it-if-your-blinds-are-down-morning.
Hickson, K. (2009). Conservatism and the Poor: Conservative Party Attitudes to Poverty and Inequality Since the 1970s. *British Politics, 4*(3), 341–362.
HM Government. (2012). *Welfare Reform Act 2012*.
HM Treasury. (2010). *Spending Review 2010*. London.
Hood, A., & Phillips, D. (2015). *Benefit Spending and Reforms: The Coalition Government's Record*. London.
Hope, C., & Winnett, R. (2012, January 9). Downing Street: Broadest Shoulders Must Carry Tax Burden. *The Telegraph*.
IFS. (2010). *New IFS Research Challenges Chancellor's "Progressive Budget" Claim*. London.
IFS. (2014a). *A Survey of the GB Benefit System*. IFS Election Briefing.
IFS. (2014b). *What Is Welfare Spending?* Institute for Fiscal Studies (IFS). London.
Jessop, B. (1983). Accumulation Strategies, State Forms, and Hegemonic Projects. *Kapitalstat, 10*, 89–111.
Jessop, B. (1990). *State Theory: Putting the Capitalist State in Its Place*. Cambridge: Polity Press.
Jessop, B., Bonnett, K., Bromley, S., & Ling, T. (1988). *Thatcherism: A Tale of Two Nations*. Cambridge: Polity Press.
Keegan, W. (2014). *Mr Osborne's Economic Experiment*. London: Searching Finance Limited.
Kerr, P., Byrne, C., & Foster, E. (2011). Theorising Cameronism. *Political Studies Review, 9*(2), 193–207.
Lakin, M. (2013). The Ideology of the Coalition: More "Muscular" Than "Liberal"? *British Politics, 8*(4), 476–490.
Lee, S. (2011a). No Plan B: The Coalition Agenda for Cutting the Deficit and Rebalancing the Economy. In S. Lee & M. Beech (Eds.), *The Cameron-Clegg*

Government: Coalition Politics in an Age of Austerity (pp. 3–23). Basingstoke: Palgrave Macmillan.

Lee, S. (2011b). "We Are All in This Together": The Coalition Agenda for British Modernization. In S. Lee & M. Beech (Eds.), *The Cameron-Clegg Government: Coalition Politics in an Age of Austerity* (pp. 3–23). Basingstoke: Palgrave Macmillan.

Lupton, R., Burchardt, T., Fitzgerald, A., Hills, J., McKnight, A., Obolenskaya, P., & Vizard, P. (2015). *The Coalition's Social Policy Record*. Social Policy in a Cold Climate. London.

Machin, S. (1997). The Decline of Labour Market Institutions and the Rise in Wage Inequality in Britain. *European Economic Review, 41*(3–5), 647–657.

Marsh, D., & Rhodes, R. A. W. (1995). Evaluating Thatcherism: Over the Moon or as Sick as a Parrot? *Politics, 15*(1), 49–54.

Mason, R. (2013, January 8). Will the Benefit Squeeze Hit the "Strivers" or the "Skivers with Their Blinds Down"? *The Telegraph*.

Massie, A. (2015, April). Why Aren't the Tories Winning? Because They Are Seen as the Party of the Rich. *The Spectator*.

McAnulla, S. (2010). Heirs to Blair's Third Way? David Cameron's Triangulating Conservatism. *British Politics, 5*(3), 286–314.

OBR. (2012). *Economic and Fiscal Outlook—*. London.

OBR. (2013). *Economic and Fiscal Outlook 2013*. London.

OBR. (2014). *Economic and Fiscal Outlook—December 2014*. London.

Osborne, G. (2010). *Comprehensive Spending Review 2010. House of Commons Hansard Debates for 20 Oct 2010*. Retrieved December 6, 2015, from http://www.publications.parliament.uk/pa/cm201011/cmhansrd/cm101020/debtext/101020-0001.htm.

Osborne, G. (2011). Autumn Statement 2011: George Osborne's Speech. *The Telegraph*. Retrieved November 3, 2015, from http://www.telegraph.co.uk/finance/budget/8923191/Autumn-Statement-2011-George-Osbornes-speech.html.

Parry, R. (2011, July 4–6). *The Public Sector Workforce in Recession 2010–11—The Course of Policy Development in the Euro Area and the UK*. Paper for the Annual Conference of the Social Policy Association (pp. 1–16). Lincoln.

Peck, J. (2010). *Constructions of Neoliberal Reason*. Oxford: Oxford University Press.

Pierson, P. (1996). The New Politics of the Welfare State. *World Politics, 48*(2), 143–179.

Policy Exchange. (2013). *What's Wrong with the Tory Party?* Retrieved December 7, 2015, from http://www.policyexchange.org.uk/media-centre/blogs/category/item/what-s-wrong-with-the-tory-party.

SPERI. (2015). *Inequality Redux*. Sheffield Political Economy Research Institute (SPERI) Paper, 22. Sheffield.

Stanley, L. (2016). Legitimacy Gaps, Taxpayer Conflict, and the Politics of Austerity in the UK. *The British Journal of Politics and International Relations, 18*(2), 389–406.

Taylor-Gooby, P., & Stoker, G. (2011). The Coalition Programme: A New Vision for Britain or Politics as Usual? *The Political Quarterly, 82*(1), 4–15.

Toynbee, P., & Walker, D. (2015). *Cameron's Coup: Anatomy of a Revolution.* London: Faber & Faber.

TUC. (2013a). *Support for Benefit Cuts Dependent on Ignorance, TUC-Commissioned Poll Finds.* Trade Union Congress (TUC). Retrieved December 13, 2015, from https://www.tuc.org.uk/social-issues/child-poverty/welfare-and-benefits/tax-credits/support-benefit-cuts-dependent.

TUC. (2013b). *The UK's Low Pay Recovery.* Trade Union Congress (TUC). Retrieved November 2, 2015, from https://www.tuc.org.uk/sites/default/files/Lowpayreport.pdf.

TUC. (2014). *Public Sector Workers Lose Out on £2,245 Under This Government, Says TUC.* TUC Press Release. Retrieved December 14, 2015, from https://www.tuc.org.uk/industrial-issues/public-sector/pay-fair-campaign/public-sector-workers-lose-out-%C2%A32245-under.

Valentine, G., & Harris, C. (2014). Strivers vs Skivers: Class Prejudice and the Demonisation of Dependency in Everyday Life. *Geoforum, 53*, 84–92.

Wood, S. (2013). Explaining One Nation Labour. *The Political Quarterly, 84*(3), 317–320.

YouGov. (2013a). *Conservative for Economy, Labour for Living Standards?* YouGov. Retrieved December 13, 2015, from https://yougov.co.uk/news/2013/10/10/conservative-economy-labour-living-standards/.

YouGov. (2013b). *YouGov/Sunday Times Survey Results.* London.

YouGov. (2014). *General Election 2015: How Britain Really Voted.* YouGov Website. Retrieved December 15, 2015, from https://yougov.co.uk/news/2015/06/08/general-election-2015-how-britain-really-voted/.

CHAPTER 7

After the Coalition: Towards a Transformation or Consolidation of British Capitalism?

Since the 2008 crisis, anti-establishment forces have grown in strength across the Western world. In Europe, right-wing nationalist parties, such as the Alternative für Deutschland (AFD) and the French National Front challenged for power. Other groupings, such as the Austrian Freedom Party, the Lega Nord in Italy and Viktor Orbán's Fidesz in Hungary, have assumed governmental office. Populist social movements and parties on the Left also grew in strength (Mouffe, 2018). Podemos, a left party which emerged out the 15-M anti-austerity coalition in Spain, rose to prominence in 2014. In Greece, Syriza became the government in 2015 with a mandate to resist the deep cuts which had been pushed on it by the EU. Beyond Europe, the rise of 'populism' was symbolized by the election of Donald Trump to the White House in December 2016. Trump's promise to 'Make America Great Again' was based on a programme which combined anti-immigrant rhetoric, protectionist trade policies and a break from the traditional network of alliances which had characterised American leadership throughout the twentieth century. The populist upsurge continues to reconfigure domestic politics across the West and even threatens to challenge the prevailing global order.

Britain's parliamentary democracy is often presented as a model of constitutional stability, relatively immune from the recurrent patterns of political turmoil which grip its continental European neighbours. The post-crisis world has changed that. Britain emerged as one of the focal points in the rise of global populism (Blyth & Matthijs, 2017).

S. Lavery, *British Capitalism After the Crisis*, Building a Sustainable Political Economy: SPERI Research & Policy, https://doi.org/10.1007/978-3-030-04046-8_7

Three post-crisis developments fundamentally reconfigured British politics. First, in June 2016, Britain voted to leave the EU. The vote for 'Brexit' ended 40 years of European membership and sent shock waves throughout Britain and around Europe. Second, in the aftermath of the EU referendum, a new government under Theresa May emerged. The May government committed to a 'hard Brexit', which meant leaving the Single Market and Customs Union, ending free movement and ending the jurisdiction of the European Court of Justice (ECJ). In its early stages, the May government combined this with a highly interventionist economic programme, designed to break with Cameron's social and economic liberalism and to forge a new social compact across Britain (Pabst, 2017). Third, under the leadership of Jeremy Corbyn, the Labour Party underwent a process of radical reconfiguration. Corbyn led his Party into the 2017 general election on a populist left programme committed to reversing austerity, boosting mass public investment and re-nationalising key industries. Despite failing to secure a parliamentary majority, Corbyn's Labour experienced a huge surge in the popular vote, securing its largest vote share since 2001 and a net increase of 30 seats. A new era of post-crisis British politics had emerged.

Post-crisis British Politics

The instabilities unleashed from 2016 onwards came as a shock because it seemed that the fallout from the 2008 crisis had finally been contained. By 2015, Britain's finance-led growth model had effectively been re-established. Cameron returned to government with a majority in May 2015, promising to continue along the path of deficit reduction whilst consolidating the Conservative's position as the leading force in British politics. Despite the depth and severity of the 2008 crisis, it appeared that British capitalism had been stabilised. The rise of Brexit, May and Corbyn blew this complacency apart. These developments took place against a number of long and medium-term structural shifts within British capitalism (Jessop, 2016). From a long-term perspective, each embodied a backlash against four decades of sustained neoliberal restructuring (Bailey, 2018; Hopkin, 2017). The collapse of Britain's manufacturing base, rising regional inequalities, sustained real wage cuts and a steady increase in migrant labour all fuelled the conditions for a populist backlash in Britain. The long decomposition of democratic capitalism and the corresponding rise of post-democratic forms of governance had generated increasingly polarised polities (Streeck, 2017). Latent antagonisms between creditors and debtors and the 'winners' and 'losers' of globalisation proliferated.

The 2008 crisis intensified many of these trends. Brexit, May and Corbyn are all of course distinct political forms with their own unique histories and future trajectories. But, in a sense, they all embody a distinctive form of *post-crisis politics* in Britain. Each emerged out of the deep structural malaise of British capitalism which had set in during the post-crisis conjuncture. In addition, each sought to build its base of support by pledging to transform British capitalism. The campaign for Brexit drew heavily on a protectionist political economy, promising to radically restrict net migration into the UK whilst increasing spending on key public services (Hopkin, 2017). The May government's early embrace of a 'hard' Brexit and economic interventionism consciously sought to break with Cameron's liberalism and to carve out a new position for Britain in the world economy (Pabst, 2017). Labour's left populist economic programme sought to reverse austerity and to radically reconfigure power relations in British society. The Coalition had presided over an orthodox liberal response to 2008, initiating a politics of deficit reduction and public expenditure cuts. The emergence of post-crisis British politics after Brexit began the unravelling of this project. The following sections trace the origins and development of Brexit, May and Corbyn, before considering their possible impact on the future trajectory of British capitalism.

The Politics of Brexit

The UK's vote for Brexit was underpinned by a number of long- and medium-term factors. Historically, Britain had displayed an 'exceptionalism' in relation to the European continent, expressed through its distinctive common law system, its constitutional tradition of parliamentary sovereignty and its status as a (post-)imperial centre of global capitalism. Since the late 1980s, as the European integration process gathered pace, the Conservative Party became the main conduit for British Euroscepticism. Whilst the Thatcher government broadly embraced the prospect of increasing trade in Europe through the creation of the Single Market, large sections of the Party remained opposed to transferring sovereignty to Brussels. The eurosceptic challenge crystallised in the early 1990s over the Major government's signing of the Maastricht Treaty (Buller, 2000). Major managed to face-off his backbench 'Maastricht rebels', securing an 'opt-out' from the EU's 'Social Chapter' and from the future single European currency. However, with a parliamentary majority of only twenty-one and, Major's authority was fatally undermined.

David Cameron assumed the Conservative leadership on a platform of 'modernisation'. One of the central planks of Cameron's modernisation project was that his Party needed to overcome its divisions over Europe. Cameron initially sought to appease his eurosceptic backbenchers by promising to veto the Lisbon Treaty and by withdrawing from the European People's Party (EPP), the mainstream Conservative grouping within the European Parliament. However, like Major before him, Cameron soon found that he could not contain destabilising Euroscepticism within his own ranks. In December 2011, eighty-one eurosceptic Conservative MPs defied a three-line whip and voted in support of holding an EU referendum. At the same time, the UK Independence Party (UKIP) was making significant gains in the polls, threatening the Conservative's prospects of re-election. In this context, Cameron felt he had no option but to commit to holding a referendum on EU membership in the following parliament. At his ill-fated 2013 Bloomberg speech, Cameron committed to holding an 'in-out' referendum in the next parliament.

Cameron unexpectedly secured a parliamentary majority in the May 2015 general election. Given the manifesto commitment, Cameron announced that a referendum on the UK's EU membership would be held before the end of 2017, once he had sought to 'renegotiate' the terms of the UK's membership with Brussels. After securing limited concessions from the Commission, Cameron confirmed in January 2016 that he would lead the 'Remain' campaign. The referendum campaign began in earnest. Remain deployed the strategy which had worked for the Conservatives in the 2010 and 2015 elections. This focused almost exclusively on the theme of the 'economic risk' which Brexit posed to the British economy. Osborne and the Treasury took centre stage in this approach, briefing that Brexit would lead to a sharp economic downturn and would result in every household in Britain losing £4300. Osborne, alongside former Labour Chancellor Alistair Darling, outlined the deep expenditure cuts which would be necessary if Britain voted to leave the EU, a move which critics branded a 'punishment budget'. In addition, the Remain campaign organised briefings from business and global institutions which warned of the dire economic consequences of Brexit.

Within the first day of the campaign, the CEOs of a third of FTSE 100 firms had written to the Times warning of the economic peril of Brexit. This was followed by numerous interventions by international elite institutions—including the IMF, the OECD and the US president—which cautioned against a 'leave' vote. This relentless focus on 'economic risk' led Leave campaigners to dub the Remain campaign 'Project Fear'. Nonetheless, Remain stuck to its core economic message throughout the campaign, wagering that the British electorate would not vote to imperil its economic interests.

The official campaign to leave the EU—'Vote Leave'—had the backing of six senior cabinet ministers and a large section of the Parliamentary Conservative Party. Its central theme was that Brexit would allow Britain to reclaim sovereignty from Brussels. This was immortalised in the slogan 'Take Back Control'. This was not presented as an abstract appeal to reclaim parliamentary sovereignty, however. The Leave campaign focused on how Brexit would concretely allow Britain to assume control of its 'money, its laws and its borders', by ending British contributions to the EU budget, ending the jurisdiction of the ECJ and by limiting immigration, respectively. The official Leave campaign operated in parallel with the unofficial campaign, led by Aaron Banks and Nigel Farage. 'Leave. EU' put the issue of immigration front and centre, infamously suggesting that EU membership would lead to a flood of Syrian and African migrants entering the UK whilst stoking fears that Turkey's accession to the EU was imminent. Initially, the official Leave campaign was reluctant to run a negative campaign focused on the issue of immigration, for fear of alienating floating voters. However, the lead strategist of Vote Leave, Dominic Cummings, was deeply aware of the potency of weaponising immigration as a core campaign issue. Cummings' strategy was to not focus on immigration early on in order to 'win the right to be heard by polite society' (Shipman, 2017: 49). However, on 26 May the ONS published figures which showed that net migration to the UK had been 333,000 in 2015. In the following weeks, Vote Leave pivoted towards restricting immigration as their core message.

After six months of campaigning, on 23 June 2016, 52% of the British electorate voted to leave the EU. The result sent shock waves throughout Britain and Europe. Sterling plummeted and the Bank of England adopted emergency measures to shore up the British economy. Cameron resigned the following morning. Labour MPs, angered by Corbyn's alleged lacklustre embrace of the Remain campaign, initiated an attempt to oust him as the leader of the Labour Party. In Scotland, which had voted strongly in favour of Remain, the First Minister Nicola Sturgeon suggested that Brexit could lead to a second independence referendum. The fractious politics of Brexit had begun. It would continue to consume the country for years to come.

The vote for Brexit was underpinned by a number of long- and medium-term factors. In each case, the context of the 2008 crisis exacerbated existing tensions and bolstered the momentum behind the Leave campaign. The first medium-term factor which lay behind Brexit was the issue of immigration. In 2004, the EU underwent a significant enlargement, drawing-in countries from Central and Eastern Europe, including Poland, Hungary and the Czech Republic. Existing member states had the option to impose transitional controls which would have limited immigration from the accession states for a five-year period. However, the Blair government eschewed this option (Thompson, 2017). This was driven by the calculation that allowing Eastern Europeans into Britain would increase labour market competition and help to contain wage costs. Furthermore, the Home Office had expected that labour in-flows from these countries would be as low as 5,000 per year (Evans & Menon, 2017: 14). The actual figure was ten-times higher. From the mid-2000s onwards, immigration rocketed as an issue in British public opinion and, increasingly, the issue of EU membership became linked to the issue (ibid.: 18). The rise in immigration and growing public dissatisfaction with the EU therefore predated the 2008 crisis. But the downturn in the world economy and the paroxysms which were to grip the Eurozone after 2010 were crucial in sharpening hostility to EU immigration in Britain. Between 2010 and 2016, growth and employment were consistently higher in Britain than in EU member states, particularly in comparison with the Southern and Eastern European countries. As a result, Britain emerged as the 'employer of last resort', along with Germany, for unemployed European workers (Thompson, 2017). The result was that by 2014, 1.5 million Eastern European workers lived in the UK. The 2008 crisis had played a key role in driving up immigration in Britain, creating the grounds for the backlash which crystallised with the Brexit vote.

The Coalition's austerity programme also played a critical role in creating the conditions for the Leave vote. Public expenditure cuts under the Coalition had disproportionately fallen on lower income areas. Whilst local authority spending fell by 23.4% on average between 2010 and 2015, poorer areas experienced cuts of up to 46.3% whilst more prosperous areas experienced cuts of 6.2% (Becker, Fetzer, & Novy, 2017: 13).

To take one specific example, the Welfare Reform Act resulted in a £914 cut per head in Blackpool compared to £177 in the City of London (Fetzer, 2018: 18). There is a strong correlation between areas which experienced high levels of public expenditure cuts under the Coalition and areas which voted to 'leave' in the EU referendum (Harrop, 2016). Indeed, one academic study based on an aggregate study of expenditure cuts and voting patterns in the referendum, concluded that Leave support 'could have could have been up to 9.5 percentage points lower...had the austerity shock not happened' (Fetzer, 2018). This wider context of austerity shaped the EU referendum campaign in two distinct ways. First, it weakened the 'economic risk' argument pushed by the Treasury and the Remain campaign. The warning that Brexit would result in a sharp contraction in living standards rang hollow in areas which had experienced close to a decade of falling real wages and deep public expenditure cuts (Watson, 2018). The Leave campaign also sought to capitalise on public anger at austerity, promising that reclaiming EU budget contributions would allow Britain to redirect funds to vital services such as the NHS. Brexit of course enjoyed support from more affluent areas and was shaped by numerous other factors including age, education and long-held social values. But the post-crisis context of sustained fiscal austerity played a key role in mobilising the Leave vote, ultimately facilitating the UK's exit from the EU.

The May Government

On the morning after the EU referendum, Cameron resigned as Prime Minister. Within three weeks, Theresa May had taken the keys to 10 Downing Street. During the referendum, May had officially backed Remain but had kept a low profile throughout the campaign. This, along with her extensive ministerial experience and her perceived competence, allowed her to position herself as the 'unity' candidate, capable of bringing her Party and the country together (Quinn, 2018). May won the backing of a majority of MPs in the first stage of the leadership contest. After Andrea Leadsom pulled out, May assumed the premiership unopposed on 13 July 2016.

May's social and economic programme, from the outset, embodied a distinctive form of post-crisis politics. Upon becoming Prime Minister, May initiated a decisive break with the legacy of the Cameron government. Osborne, whose position had been fatally compromised during the referendum campaign, was unceremoniously sacked. May began sharply differentiating her government from the Cameron era. This was exemplified both by her embrace of Brexit and her attempt to carve out a new governing narrative and economic strategy organised around a form of 'post-liberal interventionism' (Pabst, 2017). May consciously wove these two issues together, stating that, 'the EU referendum result was an instruction to change the way our country works, and the people for whom it works, forever' (The Conservative Party, 2017). On the steps of Downing Street, May framed the referendum result as the expression of deep dissatisfaction in the country. May's economic interventionist programme pivoted on a critique of Cameron's social and economic liberalism and the inequities this had generated.

May's governing programme was profoundly shaped by the question of Brexit. Forty per cent of her parliamentary party had backed Brexit as had the majority of the Conservative membership. She set out to immediately quell eurosceptic unrest within her own ranks. In her first cabinet reshuffle, she promptly appointed prominent Leave campaigners to key positions. David Davis became minister for the new Department for Exiting the European Union, Boris Johnson became foreign secretary, Liam Fox trade secretary and Chris Grayling headed up the Department of Transport. Rhetorically, May underlined her commitment to delivering on the result of the referendum. In her speech announcing her candidacy for the leadership, May for the first time deployed a phrase which would be repeated *ad nauseum* in the opening months of her premiership: 'Brexit means Brexit'. This phrase was at once purposive and ambiguous. It sent a signal to the Conservative party and the country that May was serious about respecting the referendum result. There would be 'no attempts to remain inside the EU, no attempts to rejoin it through the back door, and no second referendum' (May, 2016d). The phrase was also of course a tautology. It bought May valuable time to reconfigure her cabinet, unify her Party and shape her Brexit strategy without getting caught up in immediate turf wars over the precise form of her Brexit programme.

By October 2017, pressure on May to be clearer about her preferred form of Brexit mounted (Allen, 2018: 113). In Birmingham at the Conservative Party Conference, May delivered a speech which added important details to her Brexit vision, stating that 'we are not leaving the European Union only to give up control of immigration again. And we are not leaving only to return to the jurisdiction of the European Court of Justice' (May, 2016a). These words strongly indicated that May was committed to leaving the Single Market and by implication was committed to embracing a so-called hard Brexit. The direction of travel was confirmed in January 2017, when May delivered her Lancaster House speech. In this landmark intervention, May explicitly stated that her government was committed to leaving both the Single Market and the Customs Union, would end free movement and the jurisdiction of the ECJ and would negotiate a new free trade deal (May, 2017a). The broad contours of May's Brexit programme were set. The government was committed to reclaiming British sovereignty over 'money, laws and immigration', delivering on some of the key commitments which had been made during the referendum campaign.

The second plank of May's governing programme involved the formulation of a distinctive 'post-liberal conservatism' which aimed to decisively break from the legacy of the Cameron years (Pabst, 2017). One core plank of Cameron's 'modernisation' efforts had involved attempting to shift the Party towards the 'social liberal' values of key Tory target seats (Hayton, 2018). May positioned herself early on as a traditionalist Tory, bringing her in line with the bulk of her own backbench MPs and the Party membership (ibid.). In her 2016 conference speech, she took aim at 'metropolitan' politicians and commentators, telling the party faithful that, 'they find your patriotism distasteful, your concerns about immigration parochial, your views about crime illiberal, your attachment to your job security inconvenient' (May, 2016c). She continued, with the now infamous line, 'if you believe you're a citizen of the world, you're a citizen of nowhere' (ibid.). In January 2017, May built on this theme, decrying the 'cult of individualism' that had taken hold in British society whilst highlighting the pernicious impact which globalisation had had on social ties and communitarian values (May, 2017b). May stated that her government would therefore reject a 'laissez-faire liberalism that leaves people to get by on their own' (ibid.). In its place, an interventionist strategy oriented towards 'righting the wrongs' of market liberal society would be adopted.

May's embrace of interventionism profoundly shaped her vision of the British economy. Osborne's accumulation strategy had embraced a market liberal philosophy of deficit reduction, balanced budgets and private sector-led recovery. May sought to sharply distinguish her approach from this strand of market liberalism (Pabst, 2017: 501). Other forces within her cabinet—most notably her Chancellor, Phillip Hammond—represented the 'Treasury view'. But in the early years of the May government, liberal orthodoxies were partially subordinated to her new interventionist programme. May's economic philosophy was rooted in a critique of the excesses of globalisation. She pointed to how unbridled markets had eroded social ties and communitarian values. Building on the themes of her inaugural statement as Prime Minister, she framed her pitch in terms of the so-called left behinds of globalisation, stating:

> If you're from an ordinary working class family, life is much harder than many people in Westminster realise…you have a job but you don't always have job security. You have your own home, but you worry about paying the mortgage […] over recent years these people have felt locked out of the political and social discourse in Britain. If they voiced their concerns, their views were shut down. Decisions made in faraway places didn't always seem to be the right decisions for them. They saw their community changing, but didn't remember being consulted – or agreeing to – that change. They looked at the changing world – the onset of globalisation and the advances in technology – and worried about what the future held for their children and grandchildren. (May, 2016b)

These concerns with unbridled globalism were not entirely novel. A strand of 'Blue Collar' or 'One Nation' conservatism which critiqued the destabilising social impact of markets had long informed elements of Conservative thought and political practice (Gamble, 2014). But what distinguished May's interventionist ethos was that it was bolstered with a 'more explicit political economy' (Pabst, 2017). May advanced numerous policy commitments which flanked her emergent interventionist economic discourse. She called for workers to be represented on company boards, for limits on shareholder pay and placed the development of a new industrial strategy as the flagship economic initiative of her government (Allen, 2018). These policy commitments were flanked by a broader 'attack on financial elites and tax-dodging multinationals' (Pabst, 2017: 504). During her 2016 conference speech, she highlighted inequities which had emerged from the Bank of England's policy of 'loose' monetary policy, pointing to its inequitable distributional effects. She stated that 'change has to come', a comment which was widely interpreted as an implicit challenge to the Bank's independence. At the same time, May's home secretary Amber Rudd floated the notion that businesses would be responsible for keeping lists of immigrant workers. Carolyn Fairburn, Director-General of the CBI, warned in the aftermath of May's 2016 conference speech that the government was 'closing the door' on business.

May's interventionist political economy was profoundly shaped by electoral calculations. For decades, large chunks of Britain's ex-industrial periphery—in the North of England, Wales and the Midlands—had remained out of bounds for the Conservative Party. Brexit exposed deep divisions in Britain's electoral geography. The vote revealed a cleavage between those who had been 'left behind' by globalisation and those in primarily metropolitan areas that were comfortable with the change it had wrought. In the wake of the referendum, a new pathway to power seemed to be opening up for the Conservatives. Two factors were critical here. First, in the aftermath of the referendum vote, UKIP was pitched into turmoil. May's move towards a 'hard Brexit' position early on in her premiership had deprived the Party of its central political purpose. UKIP collapsed into infighting and saw a rapid decline in its polling fortunes. UKIP had in the 2015 election secured second place in 44 Labour heartland constituencies. The Conservatives would aim to colonise the collapse of its vote and displace Labour's dominance in its heartlands. The second factor underpinning May's strategy was the perception that the Labour Party was vulnerable. Of Labour's 229 seats held in 2015, 149 had voted in favour of Brexit (Heath & Goodwin, 2017). Furthermore, under Jeremy Corbyn, Labour appeared particularly vulnerable. A poll in August 2016 had suggested that may was more popular with Labour supporters than Jeremy Corbyn (Evans & Menon, 2017: 98). May's pathway to enhancing her majority was to retain the seats which Cameron had won in 2015 whilst making significant inroads into the Labour vote (Heath & Goodwin, 2017). In early 2017, May's pivot seemed to be working. During the fortnight prior to her calling an election, polls put the Conservative party on an average of 42.8% compared to Labour on 25.5% (ibid.: 345). But the expected electoral rout was not to pass. A third form of post-crisis politics—largely written-off since 2015—emerged as a bulwark against May's advance. This was the Labour Party under the left populist leadership of Jeremy Corbyn.

The Corbyn Opposition

Since the 1980s, the Labour left had been effectively marginalised within the structures of the Party (Panitch & Leys, 2001). Tony Blair consolidated this process, concentrating policymaking and patronage powers within the leadership whilst removing some of the left's core policy commitments, most notably 'Clause Four' which had committed Labour to the cause of nationalisation. During this time, Corbyn remained an obscure MP on the backbenches, alongside John McDonnell and Diane Abbot. The rise of Corbyn to the leadership of Labour was remarkable. Its immediate origins lay in internal Party rule changes which had been implemented under Ed Miliband. Traditionally, Labour leaders were selected under a 'block vote' system, whereby members, affiliated trade unions and MPs were involved in electing the Party leader. During his leadership, Miliband came under pressure from within the Party to shift to a 'one Member, one Vote' system. Miliband also moved to an 'open primary' model, whereby 'registered supporters' of Labour could pay a small fee and vote in leadership elections. This internal reconfiguration had ironically been pushed by the Right of the Party, who hoped that by widening Labour's internal electoral base, the power of the trade unions within the party structure could be further eroded.

After Labour's defeat in the 2015 general election, Miliband resigned and the new leadership rules were followed in the subsequent leadership election. In order to appear on the ballot, candidates required the support of at least 35 MPs. Corbyn secured the requisite number of votes to make it onto the ballot paper, in large part due to the support of MPs who did not support Corbyn's leadership bid, but hoped to 'widen the debate' during the campaign. However, the 'outsider' candidate quickly emerged as the surprise front runner. Corbyn toured the country and galvanised a wide base of support amongst the membership. New members flooded into the Party—500,000 joined during the leadership campaign—enthused by Corbyn's anti-austerity message and his commitment to move Labour firmly to the left. On 12 September 2015, Corbyn won the leadership election with 60% of the vote. An avowedly socialist MP, backed by an influx of new members and the organising muscle of the new grassroots campaigning force Momentum, had become.

The real battle had only just begun. Corbyn began by appointing his shadow cabinet, appointing ally John McDonnell to be Chancellor whilst drawing MPs from across the Party into his new leadership team. The first eighteen months of Corbyn's leadership were tumultuous. A large section of the Parliamentary Labour Party was opposed to Corbyn's leadership. Sometimes this was due to policy, for example, in relation to Corbyn's long-standing opposition to NATO or his lukewarm acceptance of the EU. Other disputes revolved around the claim that Corbyn's values were incompatible with securing electoral victory. Corbyn's competence as leader was persistently questioned. Parliamentary opposition to the Corbyn leadership culminated in the aftermath of the EU referendum. The Leader's office had not actively embraced the Remain campaign. There were even suggestions that Corbyn's office, under the influence of communications director, Seamus Milne, had actively obstructed the 'Labour In' campaign. In the turmoil after the Brexit vote, Labour MPs moved and mobilised in a coup attempt against Corbyn. The bulk of his shadow cabinet tendered their resignations, in a coordinated attempt to maximise pressure on the leader's office. A vote of no confidence was subsequently held and 172 MPs—80% of the Parliamentary Labour Party—voted in favour of the motion. Corbyn was under immense pressure. But he could draw on his the mandate and support which he had secured from outside the PLP, namely from key trade unions including Unite and the newly expanded membership. New campaign groups, such as Momentum, mobilised in his defence. A second leadership challenge, from Owen Smith, was comprehensively defeated. Corbyn secured 62% of the vote and re-established his mandate to lead the Labour Party. The first eighteen months of the Corbyn leadership had been shaped by a relentless fight for survival. Within a year, after the 2017 general election, the internal politics of Labour would shift dramatically.

The 2017 General Election

On 31 March 2017, May followed through on her commitment and triggered Article 50. The UK's exit from the EU had formally begun. In its immediate aftermath, May focused her sights on domestic politics. Since the launch of her leadership campaign, May had ruled out an election prior 2020. In this way, she avoided destabilising speculation such as that which had damaged Gordon Brown at the beginning of his premiership (Theakston, 2011: 401). But by early 2017, the logic behind holding an early election was proving to be irresistible. Corbyn's Labour, dogged by constant unrest amongst the PLP, was far behind in the polls. In March 2017, Labour was polling 25% compared to the Conservatives who were on 43%. Corbyn's leadership ratings were poor, such that one poll in late 2016 revealed that May was more popular than Corbyn amongst Labour supporters. Two months earlier, the Conservatives had won the Copeland constituency in a by-election, a seat which Labour had held for decades. May's team were also concerned that delaying an election until 2020 would weaken the government's negotiating hand during the Article 50 negotiations (Shipman, 2017: 188). Furthermore, there were good internal party political reasons to push for an early election. The majority which May had inherited from Cameron was slim, meaning that she remained constrained by blocs of MPs—not least the well-organised group of eurosceptics under the European Research Group (ERG)—who could limit her room for manoeuvre. Buoyant in the polls and seemingly assured of a landslide electoral victory, the usually cautious May gambled. On April 18, 2017, she called a snap general election. It was a gamble which would backfire spectacularly.

May claimed that her choice to call an election was driven by a desire to secure a mandate for her vision of Brexit. But the central rationale behind her decision was the opportunity to decisively defeat the Corbyn-led Labour Party and to bolster her majority. In pursuing this objective, the Conservative campaign was organised around two central themes. First, seeking to capitalise on May's personal approval ratings over Corbyn, the Conservative campaign focused intensely around the personality of May, deploying the slogan that only she could provide the 'Strong and Stable' leadership which Britain required. Second, the campaign built upon the themes which May and Nick Timothy had cultivated since her bid for the Tory leadership. This involved blending together an apparent commitment to a hard Brexit—prioritising immigration control over Single Market membership—with an interventionist economic programme designed to support those who had been 'left behind' (Lynch & Whitaker, 2018: 40). The Conservative manifesto sought to achieve this through a series of policy proposals, including 'promises to cap energy prices, increase the national living wage, develop a new industrial strategy, support grammar schools, give workers more input into the governance of companies, and end the free movement of EU nationals' (Heath & Goodwin, 2017: 347). This combination of an embrace of 'hard Brexit' with an interventionist economic platform was designed to capture a large number of leave-voting Labour seats whilst retaining the seats which Cameron had secured in 2015.

The Conservative strategy quickly ran into serious difficulties. From the very beginning, there was an internal split within the campaign between Timothy, who wanted to present the election as one of transformation and 'change', and the approach of electoral consultant Lynton Crosby who wished to focus on the themes of 'stability' and 'continuity'. May's effective coronation as Prime Minister meant that she had never been tested heading-up a political campaign. Doubts began to emerge early on about her skills as a political campaigner. The former home secretary struggled to connect with voters through her set piece speeches and policy interventions, earning her the unflattering epithet of the 'Maybot' during the campaign. A series of unforced strategic errors also served to derail the campaign early on. The Conservative manifesto, penned by Nick Timothy, sought to capture the political philosophy of Mayism, building on the themes which the Prime Minister had laid out early on in her premiership. But it was incredibly short on 'retail' policies which could appeal to the electorate. Worse still, the specific headline policies it did advance proved to be hugely unpopular. The manifesto plan for addressing the 'challenges of an ageing society', for example, required homeowners to sell their houses in order to finance the cost of their social care. This quickly became dubbed the 'Dementia Tax' by both the media and Labour, in reference to the negative impact the policy could have on elderly citizens suffering from the condition. May at first defended the policy but then was forced to U-turn, fatally undermining the campaign's 'Strong and Stable' motif.

Labour was initially ill-prepared when May announced there would be a 'snap' election. The Party did not yet have candidates selected in many target seats, with the election only seven weeks away. There were also divisions within the Party machine in terms of how to fight the election. Party staffers, led by long-standing election chief Patrick Heneghan, sought to embark upon a 'defensive' campaign, concentrating resources in seats liable to swings in favour of the Tories. Sections of the leader's office and the broader constellation of grass-roots campaign organisations, such as Momentum, countenanced a more offensive campaign where energies would also be focused on key Tory marginals.

Notwithstanding these internal difficulties, during the Easter parliamentary recess, Labour began to roll out its pitch to the electorate. Over 12 days, the Party unleashed a policy 'blitz', where it advanced eight distinctive policy ideas designed to build support for Corbynite initiatives. These included raising the minimum wage to £10 an hour, implementing universal free school meals for primary school children and raising the top rate of income tax from 45 to 50%. Polls revealed that these policies were popular with the electorate. The following week, Corbyn built upon this platform, launching the official Labour campaign. Corbyn's speech positioned himself and Labour as underdogs, fighting an insurgency against entrenched economic and political interests. Mobilising a left populist rhetoric, Corbyn stated, 'it is the establishment versus the people and it is our historic duty to make sure that the people prevail… we don't accept that it is natural for Britain to be governed by a ruling elite, the City and the tax-dodgers' (Corbyn, 2017).

Labour's policy platform was outlined in the Party's election manifesto, entitled *For the Many, Not the Few,* which was launched on 16 May in Bradford (The Labour Party, 2017). The manifesto's core theme was that Labour would engage in a far-reaching programme of reform, designed to transfer social, economic and political power from elites to working people. Labour's headline macroeconomic pledge was that seven years of Conservative austerity would be reversed. The manifesto promised an extra £30 billion for the NHS, equivalent to annual increases of 7%. £25 billion was set aside for the school's budget, reversing Conservative cuts to education. On welfare, Labour was more constrained, but did pledge to scrap the sanctions regime and the 'bedroom tax' and to reinstate housing benefit for under-21s. The Party also committed to putting 10,000 new policy officers on the street—a policy with which proved particularly potent in the context of two terror attacks during the campaign—at a cost of £2.7 billion. These spending commitments were to be paid for out of tax rises on the top 5% of income earners as well as increases in corporation tax. The Labour manifesto was underpinned by the 'Fiscal Credibility Rule'—based on work by the economists Jonathan Portes and Simon-Wren Lewis and endorsed by McDonnell's economic adviser, James Meadway—which promised to balance current spending over a five-year cycle, borrowing only to finance long-term investment. This allowed Labour to claim that its manifesto was 'fully-costed' and economically responsible whilst at the same time 'radical' in its ambition to overturn years of Conservative cuts.

Rebalancing the British economy was a central theme of *For the Many, Not the Few*, exemplified by the central place which industrial strategy assumed within it. The Party committed to setting up a National Investment Bank which would have capital of £250 billion to be invested over the following ten years. This would be supported by an underlying system of regional banks, charged with funnelling investment into local SMEs. On the back of this, Labour promised to ensure that 3% of GDP was invested and research and development by 2030, whilst at the same time committing to securing 60% of Britain's energy needs in renewable energy in this same time frame. As well as 'rebalancing' through industrial strategy, the manifesto sought to initiate a transformation in the ownership structure of the British economy. Privatisation of the major utilities was identified as a major policy failure. Water prices had increased by 40% since they had fallen into private hands (Blackburn, 2018: 14). The manifesto pledged to bring the private utilities—water, rail, utilities—back under public control. McDonnell claimed that this could be financed initially through borrowing at record low interest rates but that, over the long term, the overall cost to the taxpayer would be negligible since the utilities were profit-making entities. Labour's commitment to reversing privatisation was flanked by complementary initiatives designed to produce a greater 'democratic control' of the economy. A growing body of thought within Labour pushed for 'economic democracy', whereby local authorities and cooperative groups would assume a greater role in the ownership structures and management of regional economies. This was exemplified most clearly in the 'Preston Model', an approach taken from Cleveland in the USA and pioneered by Preston City Council, which sought through the procurement process to support local businesses and cooperative groupings. This approach fed into to the Manifesto, which committed to double the number of cooperatives and to give employees 'first buyer' rights when the company they worked for went up for sale.

On the back of its left populist programme, Labour launched a ground offensive across the country. Drawing upon the 500,000 new members and supporters which had joined the Party since 2015, Corbyn toured the country and drew huge crowds to campaign events. This, coupled, with the implosion of the Conservative campaign and May's poor performance on the campaign trail, led to a shift in the pre-election polls. Labour cut its polling deficit substantially. Corbyn's approval ratings increased rapidly, albeit from a low base, as May's plummeted. Nonetheless, polls immediately prior to the election still suggested that a Conservative majority was likely.

On the day of the 2017 election at 10 p.m., the BBC announced the result of the official exit poll. The projection sent shock waves around the country. Instead of enhancing her majority, the poll predicted that May had squandered it. The results which came in throughout the evening confirmed the exit poll projection. The Conservatives emerged as the largest Party with 317 seats, but this was 13 fewer than they had achieved in the 2015 election. Labour, on the other hand, increased its seats by 30 to 232 seats. This was enough to deprive the Tories of a majority and to bring about the second hung parliament in Britain in less than a decade. In the absence of an overall majority, May was forced into a supply and confidence arrangement with the Democratic Unionist Party (DUP).

The bedrock of the Conservative strategy was that the UKIP vote would collapse. They were right on this point. UKIP's national vote share fell from 13.8 to 1.8%. However, this did not translate into significant gains which the Tories had expected. Large swathes of the UKIP vote did switch to the Conservatives, leading to big swings to the ruling party in key constituencies. However, Corbyn's Labour Party managed to secure a significant proportion of these UKIP switchers and also successfully mobilised traditional non-voters. Labour's three-line whip to vote through Article 50 had neutralised Brexit as an issue its heartlands. As a result, the swing to the Conservatives in these Labour constituencies was contained. On average, in constituencies which had voted for Leave, the Tories registered only a small swing of 0.8% compared to Labour (Heath & Goodwin, 2017). The result was that the Conservatives only gained six seats from Labour, a figure which was far short of the predicted surge. May's pivot towards 'hard Brexit' also alienated voters in middle-class constituencies which had voted 'Remain' in the referendum. In constituencies where the Leave Vote was less than forty-five per cent, Labour secured a swing from the Conservatives of around 7%. This led to Labour gains in unlikely places such as South Kensington and Canterbury, as a large bloc of traditional non-voting groups, most notably the young, rallied to the Corbyn cause.

The fallout from the 2017 general election profoundly reconfigured the terrain of British politics. Theresa May had moved from a position of apparent unassailability to one of extreme weakness. Core elements of her early interventionist strategy were dropped whilst she was forced to sack her two closest aides, Timothy and Hill, who had shaped her path to power. The future of Brexit looked increasingly uncertain. On the one hand, the parliamentary arithmetic looked to favour a hard Brexit. The ERG could use its position to extract concessions from the now weakened May whilst the reliance on DUP votes further limited her room for manoeuvre. On the other hand, the election resulted in the re-assertion of the power of parliament where there was no overall majority in favour of a hard Brexit. Far from securing a mandate for Brexit, May was now fatally compromised in her ability to shape it. The huge surge of support for Corbyn had consolidated his position within the Labour Party. The 'soft left' of the PLP quickly fell into line whilst the staunchest opponents of Corbyn—the group of 40 or so MPs on the right of the Party—became increasingly marginalised. The Labour campaign had reshaped the national debate on the future of British capitalism. In the aftermath of the election, May is reported to have said, 'austerity is now over'. The terrain of post-crisis British politics had been radically reconfigured. Navigating this terrain is now the central challenge for rival forces seeking to shape the future trajectory of post-crisis British politics.

Towards a Consolidation or Transformation of British Capitalism?

The 2008 financial crisis exposed the profound structural weaknesses of neoliberal capitalism. Deregulated financial markets had unleashed chaos throughout the global economy. Western states—far from being 'powerless' in an age of free capital flows—recapitalised their financial systems and transformed the downturn from a 'banking crisis' into a 'sovereign debt' crisis (Burnham, 2011). In this context, many observers expected that a new policy paradigm might emerge which would displace the dominant neoliberal model. However, in the immediate aftermath of the crash, this shift did not materialise. Neoliberal ideas and practices proved markedly resilient across the West (Schmidt & Thatcher, 2013). In the Eurozone, creditor states doubled down on austerity, enshrining fiscal discipline in new supranational mechanisms. In Britain, the Coalition advanced an orthodox liberal policy of public expenditure cuts and deficit reduction, seeking to lay the foundations for a private sector recovery. The pre-crisis order had survived the crisis. Continuity had prevailed.

Or so it seemed. The history of capitalist crises can offer some important lessons here. The first relates to the temporality of structural change. It is true that the crises of the 1930s and 1970s generated far-reaching transformations across Western capitalism. But these shifts took a long time to materialise. The best part of two decades separated the 1929 stock market crash and the rise of the Bretton Woods settlement. The first signs that the post-war Keynesian compact was under pressure emerged in the 1960s, as profit rates began to stagnate and as Anglo-American finance escaped the fetters of national regulations through the Eurodollar markets (Green, 2015). However, the transition to a new regime of global neoliberalism took another twenty years to emerge (Coates, 2018). Expectations that 2008 would herald a rapid transition away from the neoliberal regime were therefore premature. The second lesson of the 1930s and

1970s crises is that domestic politics within national states is often a key driver of capitalist transformation. The 1930s crisis was exacerbated by the operation of the gold standard, which required rapid deflations—cuts to incomes and prices—in order to maintain stable exchange rates (Eichengreen & Temin, 1997). However, throughout the first quarter of the twentieth century, the organised working class had become increasingly powerful. National governments could only deflate their economies so far before they provoked bouts of destabilising labour militancy. This undermined the core operating principle of the gold standard. The lesson was that the quest for international currency stability could only push national democratic systems—and their newly enfranchised working classes—so far. This lesson fed into the design of the Bretton Woods settlement, which sought to insulate the policymaking autonomy of national states from the whims of the money markets. Domestic politics therefore played a key role in re-shaping the post-war global order.

These lessons can help us to conceptualise continuity and change in the post-crisis conjuncture. Whilst there is evidence of neoliberal continuity in the decade since the 2008 crisis, important reconfigurations have also emerged. Domestic politics across the West has been shaped by the rise of 'populisms' of the left and the right. These populist upsurges have potentially far-reaching consequences for the global order (Blyth & Matthijs, 2017). As Gamble has written, 'for the first time since 2008, the crisis has assumed a markedly political form, with a challenge to the political and economic assumptions of the international market order' (Gamble, 2016: 119). The election of Donald Trump in December 2016 was emblematic of this shift. Upon taking office, Trump initiated a partial withdrawal from the network of strategic alliances with other Western states which had shaped US foreign policy throughout the twentieth century. Trump flirted with protectionist trade policy and sought to tear up multilateral trade deals which the USA had sponsored in the heyday of neoliberal globalisation. In Europe, the surge of right-wing populism has generated new problems for policymakers in Brussels, threatening the integrity of the Schengen zone, the principle of free movement and even the EU project itself. The central myth of the pre-crisis era—that 'globalisation' was both inevitable and universally beneficial—was directly challenged by the populist upsurge.

Post-crisis British politics should be understood in this wider global context. The emergence of Brexit, May and Corbyn fit into a wider pattern of populist upheaval across the advanced capitalist world. Each of these developments of course has its own distinct historical origins, as outlined in the previous sections. But each also emerged within the specific context of Britain's post-crisis conjuncture. Deep public expenditure cuts, stagnant real wages and the proliferation of insecure work intensified the squeeze on living standards for broad swathes of the population. The 'losers' from globalisation—typically concentrated in Britain's provincial towns, the UK's ex-industrial regions and neglected coastal areas—endured the sharp edge of the Coalition's austerity programme. Local government cuts and welfare restructuring disproportionately affected these areas. At the same time, a predominantly urban youth struggled with an increasingly precarious labour market and exclusionary housing market. Public sector workers had endured a sustained period of deep wage cuts. Schools and hospitals struggled in a context of severe spending constraint and growing demographic challenges. Small businesses faced tight credit constraints. The limitations of the Coalition's 'two nations' legitimation strategy were emerging. Collapsing living standards and constrained economic growth had given rise to a large and volatile bloc of disenchanted voters.

Post-crisis British politics was increasingly shaped around the need to secure the support of this fractious social bloc. The Leave campaign's focus on Labour's ex-industrial heartlands, May's pitch to the 'just about managing' working classes and Corbyn's anti-austerity programme all sought, in their own ways, to appeal to this social base. In so doing, all three promised to initiate a sharp break with the trajectory of post-crisis British capitalism.

Two different pathways for British capitalism have now emerged in the post-crisis conjuncture. On the one hand, we could see a *transformation* of British capitalism. Forces associated with Brexit, May and Corbyn all agitate for different forms of transformation. What unites these disparate forces is a will to radically re-shape the British economy, albeit in markedly different directions. British politics has polarised and the electoral terrain is volatile. The conditions for a shift beyond Britain's financialised growth model have arguably never been riper. On the other hand, attempts to restructure British capitalism face profound structural constraints. The prospect of a *consolidation* of British capitalism is another possible pathway out of the present conjuncture. In this scenario, the populist upsurge is contained, and Britain returns to its status quo position. This, itself, would likely be only a transitory solution, given the deep structural weaknesses of British capitalism. Nonetheless, a temporary containment of British capitalism's structural crisis is possible. In the remainder of this chapter, possible future trajectories for Brexit, May and Corbyn are outlined. Whether these lead to a transformation or consolidation of British capitalism remains an open question.

Let us begin with the question of Brexit. The triggering of Article 50 confirmed that Britain would formally leave the EU in March 2019. But the shape of the future relationship between Britain and the EU was still to be settled. A number of future relationships were possible. The UK could formally leave the EU but remain in the Single Market and the Customs Union, via membership of the European Economic Area (EEA). This 'Norway option' would mean that the UK remained fully aligned with EU legislation which would ensure a high level of access to the Single Market. However, this would mean the UK would have to continue to allow free movement, would be subject to the jurisdiction of the ECJ and would still be required to pay contributions to the EU budget. May's commitment to ending all three made this option highly unlikely. A second option was for the UK to formally leave the Single Market and Customs Union but to remain closely aligned to EU legislation across a number of key areas. This would be complemented by a free trade deal—often described as 'Canada Plus'—which would allow significant access to the Single Market whilst allowing the UK to strike trade deals with third countries. This form of relationship was the favoured negotiating position of May which she brokered with her cabinet in the 'Chequers agreement' of July 2018. A third option was to embrace a so-called hard Brexit. This involves leaving the EU but with no free trade deal in place. In this instance, the UK would revert to WTO rules in relation to EU trade, which would allow the UK to strike independent trade deals but would mean a significant increase in tariff and non-tariff barriers between the two blocs.

At the time of writing, the ultimate 'shape' of the final Brexit deal, let alone its long-term impact on the British economy, is unknown. That said, it is possible to chart future scenarios and to assess the extent to which Brexit is likely to precipitate a transformation in British capitalism. The most 'transformative' vision advanced by Brexiteers is the

'No Deal' option. This would likely result in a significant shock to the British economy. The reversion to WTO rules would generate new tariff and non-tariff barriers between the UK and the EU. Access to the Single Market would be greatly restricted. In this scenario, the UK would need to strike comprehensive trade deals with countries outside of the EU. This would likely prove to be an incredibly difficult task. Brexiteers often point to the prospect of striking new trade deals with the 'emerging' economies such as Brazil, Russia, India and China. However, spatial proximity remains a key determinant of trade. Britain currently trades more with Ireland than it does with all the BRICs combined (Harris, 2014). A comprehensive free trade deal with the USA is often touted as a key opportunity presented by Brexit, but it has been calculated that such an outcome would add only 0.2% to Britain's overall GDP (House of Commons, 2018). The 'no deal' Brexit option therefore comes with very significant economic and political risks.

However, for its advocates on the right wing of the Conservative Party, a 'hard' Brexit also presents a unique opportunity. 'No deal' Brexiteers argue that EU regulations, such as its environmental protections, it's social and employment policy and product standards, act as a drag on the competitiveness of the British economy. 'No deal' advocates therefore embrace the opportunities which regulatory divergence would generate. Britain could pare back its social and employment protections and seek to regain competitiveness through under-cutting the regulatory standards of its EU neighbours. In this way, labour market competitiveness could be enhanced. The UK's financial services sector could be made more competitive still by consolidating its position as a lightly regulated 'offshore' hub. The City of London could emerge as a 'Singapore-on-Thames' surrounded by a hypercompetitive and deregulated labour market regime (CITYPERC, 2017). Under this 'no deal' scenario, British capitalism would be transformed into a low regulation hub on the edge of the European market, integrated into global capital flows whilst unencumbered by regulatory constraints from its EU neighbours.

This 'no deal' scenario fits with the globalist wing of the Conservative Party which favours a return to Britain's position as a great trading nation, unencumbered by the perceived protectionist bent of the EU. However, profound obstacles are likely to frustrate the deregulatory vision of Brexit. First, whilst the vocal ERG back the prospect of 'no deal' as a serious option, it is not clear that a majority of Conservative

MPs agree with this position. Furthermore, it is unlikely that there is a parliamentary majority which would back a 'no deal' scenario. The other problem faced by this wing of the Conservative Party is that one central plank of the Brexit campaign was to appeal to lower income voters with promises of extra spending for the NHS and public services. The proposal to advance a deregulatory Brexit—eroding employment rights and environmental protections whilst loosening restrictions on the City—is unlikely to appeal to this social bloc. Any future government seeking to carve out a niche in the global economy through radical deregulation would be likely to face huge opposition. In addition, powerful forces within British society—not least the bulk of large, organised British business interests—has lobbied hard to avoid a so-called cliff edge Brexit. Immediately after the Brexit vote, the CBI made it clear that its preferred position was to retain a high level of regulatory alignment with the EU in order to avoid disruption. Together these dynamics suggest that the 'no deal' Singapore on Thames model is unlikely to succeed in the medium- to long-term.

A more likely outcome is that a high level of regulatory alignment with the EU will continue (Baker & Lavery, 2018). Whilst the UK's membership will formally end in March 2019, institutional arrangements will be put in place which will de facto ensure continued alignment. The result, however, would be the UK moving from becoming a 'rule-taker', subject to EU legislation but unable to actively shape EU law in line with its interests. It is unlikely, then, that Brexit on its own will usher in a transformation of British capitalism. Instead, Britain is likely to remain partially linked to European structures, albeit with a lower level of access to the Single Market and lacking 'voice' in the formulation of EU policy. The overall impact of this is likely to be relatively constrained growth and a further weakening of tax receipts. In these conditions, Brexit is likely to sharpen the fiscal crisis of the British state. This in turn will reduce the redistributive capacity of British governments. A referendum which was delivered on the back of promises to the 'left behind' of globalisation is therefore likely to undermine their position further. Future bouts of political instability and conflict over the European question are the likely consequence.

Theresa May entered 10 Downing Street promising to fundamentally reconfigure the way the British economy operated. In its early guise, under the direction of Timothy, May's approach purposively equated the vote for Brexit with the proposition that large swathes of the public felt excluded from Britain's economic model. May's early embrace of statist interventionism was designed to address these twin concerns. The economic and social liberalism of Cameron and Osborne were quickly and deliberately eschewed. In its place, new policy commitments were embraced in the spheres of industrial policy, executive pay and worker representation on company boards. May critiqued 'rootless' elites and put predatory employers 'on notice'. These moves were flanked by a commitment to 'hard' Brexit, which would end free movement, the jurisdiction of the ECJ and budget contributions. This political philosophy drew on Timothy's version of 'blue collar' Conservatism. But it was underpinned by a political strategy: to cannibalise UKIP votes and displace Labour in its own ex-industrial heartlands. However, just as May's early stance was borne of politics, it died by politics too. The 2017 general election exposed the frailty both of May as a leader and of her early strategy more broadly. Labour was displaced in only six constituencies by the Conservatives whilst a surge of Remain voters punished May's pivot towards a hard Brexit. A leader who in early 2017 seemed unassailable had within months slipped into becoming one of the weakest Prime Ministers in British political history.

The transformative promise of May's early programme died on the election night of 2017. She was forced to sack Timothy and Hill, the two advisors who had facilitated her rise to the premiership and had shaped her early political programme. With no parliamentary majority and a perilously weakened mandate, May was put on notice by the Conservative parliamentary party. In the days following the election, May told a meeting held by the 1992 backbench committee of Tory MPs 'I will serve as long as you want me'. Central planks of May's interventionist programme were attacked and dismantled by members of her cabinet. Savid Javid, the Communities minister, reprimanded May's economic policy platform, stating that 'now is an opportunity to dump all those anti-business policies that we had in our manifesto' (Javid, cited in Shipman, 2017: 458). May's ability to shape the government's position on Brexit was also hugely compromised by the election result. On the one hand, her weakened parliamentary numbers empowered the ERG. A small rebellion of Eurosceptic MPs could force her hand on key European issues and could even render her position untenable. Her reliance on DUP votes also hemmed her in on Brexit, as the Leave-supporting, Northern Irish Party had a number of key red lines on the issue. On the other hand, May had called the election as a mandate to 'deliver' her version of Brexit. The electorate decisively denied her this mandate, casting the future shape of Brexit into doubt. The post-election cross-party parliamentary arithmetic made it difficult for May to deliver the kind of 'hard' Brexit she had initially courted.

The transformation of British capitalism which May had promised early on in her premiership was now replaced by a quotidian fight for survival. Her one strength was that no obvious contender for the leadership was in place or had sufficient support from Conservative MPs. The March 2019 'Article 50' deadline to leave the EU was fast approaching, meaning that holding a new leadership election would be incredibly difficult. Furthermore, the Tories feared that a divisive leadership campaign could lead to a general election and even a future Corbyn government. May therefore hobbled on in office. Had she enhanced her majority in 2017, the architect of her political philosophy, Nick Timothy, would have remained in post. It is likely that she would have sacked one key opponent of her interventionism—the Chancellor, Phillip Hammond—and would have set about implementing her 'blue collar' conservative programme. British capitalism may yet have been re-shaped in line with a re-vitalised nativist Conservatism. Instead, 'Mayism' as a political project became a ship without a captain. Suffice to say that perilous waters lie ahead.

Since the launch of his leadership campaign in 2015, Jeremy Corbyn set out to reconfigure the Labour Party internally and to fundamentally transform the structures of British capitalism. Corbyn's headline economic policy commitment was to reverse over seven years of Conservative-led austerity. Large tax rises on corporations and the top 5% of income earners would facilitate greater funding for schools and hospitals. The major utilities such as water, gas and the railway system would be brought back under public control. Increased borrowing would finance a £250 billion National Investment Bank, charged with revitalising the country's economic base. Alternative models of ownership, based on boosting the cooperative sector and encouraging localised procurement strategies, were floated as alternatives to Britain's model of shareholder capitalism (O'Neill & Guinan, 2018). With the 2017 general election result, Corbyn consolidated his position as leader of the Labour Party. The prospect of Corbyn eventually becoming Prime Minister had moved from being unthinkable to possible. The former head of the Civil Service, Bob Kerslake, advised the Labour leader's office on how to prepare for government. In the event that Corbyn did not stand at the next election or lost it and was forced to resign, the Left within the Labour Party had secured enough power to ensure that a future 'Corbynite' candidate could prevail.

The prospect of a future left populist Labour government has therefore emerged as a real prospect. However, a government of this form would face profound barriers to delivering on a left programme for government. A future Labour government would have to develop a political strategy for overcoming these obstacles. Two barriers to such a programme can be identified. The first barrier is internal and concerns the structures of the British state. At the heart of Corbyn's economic programme is the objective of 're-industrialisation'. But cultivating a renaissance of export-led growth cannot be conjured out of a hat. Deep and sustained intervention by the state, in line with a comprehensives industrial strategy is necessary. The problem is that history teaches us that key centres of power within the British state tend to militate against programmes of this nature. In particular, the Treasury has time and again aborted attempts at state-led re-industrialisation. The NEDCs of the 1960s, the offspring of the Wilson government, were marginalised by the Treasury and its prioritisation of budgetary balance. More recently, as Martin Craig has demonstrated, nascent attempts to build a 'Green Investment Bank' were stillborn after intervention by 11 Downing Street (Craig, 2016). A future Labour government would therefore have to develop a political strategy oriented towards fundamentally reconfiguring the institutional architecture of the British state. There is not space to outline what such a reconfiguration might look like here, other than to highlight one proposal for Treasury reform which colleagues at SPERI advanced in 2017 (Berry, Gamble, Hay, Payne, & Hunt, 2016).

The second impediment to a future Corbyn government is external and is embodied in the structure of the world economy. The heart of McDonnell's programme is broadly left Keynesian in orientation, insofar as it advocates borrowing to finance infrastructure investment and seeks to ensure that wages keep up with productivity growth. These policies would provide welcome relief from years of under-investment and punishing fiscal austerity. But Keynesian policies today face a radically altered international environment compared to when they were originally implemented during the post-war settlement. Successive decades of capital account liberalisation have created numerous 'exit options' for capital. Both the USA and the UK run huge current account deficits, which renders them vulnerable to outflows of foreign investment. Bondholders increasingly exert structural power over government policy. Ownership of the public debt has become increasingly concentrated in the hands of wealthy asset-holders, raising important distributional questions about the impact of expansionary fiscal policy (Hager, 2015). A renewed Keynesian drive today faces a structurally altered and markedly hostile international environment. Any left Keynesian strategy needs to take this obstacle very seriously indeed.

These barriers are not in principle insurmountable. Indeed, capital's ability to 'exit' is often exaggerated, as earlier research by Hay and Rosamond has demonstrated (Hay & Rosamond, 2002). But there is little doubt that any future left government would face intense international economic pressures. A key strategic question, then, is how to deal with this hostile international terrain. A strategic response must operate on two levels. First, there is a need to develop a serious plan for countering the disciplinary power of an 'investment strike'. One way to do this is to develop the institutional capacity to implement capital controls. Unthinkable in the recent past, the key role which capital controls can play in insulating democracy from the whims of international creditors is becoming increasingly mainstream on the centre-left (Blakeley, 2018). A Labour government would also have to cultivate support for capital controls at the 'everyday' level amongst the population at large. This is not an impossible task, but it requires serious work. The right has a powerful narrative on capital controls which conjures up images of tourists at borders having to deal with tight restrictions on their holiday money. One challenge for the left is to develop a compelling counter-narrative. There is historical precedent here. During the Bretton Woods era, there was a consensus that constraining 'hot money'—volatile, speculative capital flows—was an eminently sensible thing to do (Frieden, 2006). A parallel contemporary narrative would emphasise the high social costs of allowing uncontrolled and destabilising rent-seeking into the national economy.

Corbyn's Labour has identified deep structural flaws in British capitalism. Its central political premise is that an opportunity has opened-up since the 2008 global financial crisis to build support for a populist left programme capable of overcoming these structural weaknesses. But profound internal and external barriers continue to delimit the Labour Party's room for manoeuvre. The task for Labour in the coming years is to develop a political strategy capable of overcoming these constraints, whilst building and maintaining a wide social base of support. This is a difficult task, fraught with political danger. But it is one that will have to be executed if a successful left transformation of British capitalism is to be initiated.

Conclusion

Since the 2008 crisis, a populist insurgency has gripped the advanced capitalist world. Anti-establishment forces on the left and the right have destabilised domestic political systems. Collectively, the rise of these populist movements threatens to undermine the foundations of the global order. Britain embodies a pivotal sphere within this global reconfiguration. After Cameron's Conservative Party secured a majority in the 2015 election, it seemed that stability had been restored. But destabilising currents were bubbling under the surface. The vote for Brexit, the May government's interventionist programme and the rise of Corbyn's Labour all emerged from within the post-crisis conjuncture. Public expenditure cuts, low growth, growing labour market precarity and falling living standards combined to produce a volatile and disenchanted electorate. A distinctive form of post-crisis British politics had emerged.

Brexiteers, May and Corbyn all sought to draw upon the tide of public anger which had grown since the 2008 crash. Immigration from Eastern Europe had surged since the Eurozone crisis. Brexiteers deftly combined public anxieties about rising immigration with promises to fund public services in order to secure a Leave vote in the EU referendum. The May government saw the referendum result as an opportunity to colonise Labour heartlands, pivoting towards a 'hard Brexit' whilst embracing an anti-cosmopolitan brand of statist interventionism. Corbyn's Labour pledged to reverse years of austerity. On the back of its left populist manifesto, Corbyn's Labour Party mobilised a large surge in turnout in the 2017 election which deprived May of her majority. The Coalition had contained the fallout from the 2008 crisis, re-establishing Britain's finance-led growth model whilst pivoting to a 'two nations' legitimation strategy. But this containment was only temporary. After the 2015 general, a new political terrain emerged in Britain, shaped by the distinctive post-crisis politics of Brexit, May and Corbyn.

The future trajectory of British politics is highly uncertain. The deep structural weaknesses of British capitalism have been laid bare. Policies which in recent decades would have been unthinkable—the return of public ownership, the imposition of capital controls, the de-financialisation of the British economy—have entered into mainstream debate. The volatile and unpredictable character of British politics means that the conditions for a transformation of British capitalism are in place. But profound structural barriers to reform endure. A deregulatory Brexit, favoured by some on the Conservative Right, is unlikely to command sufficient parliamentary or public support. The May government's early radicalism has been neutered by her electoral failure. Political survival rather than transformation has become her main preoccupation. Labour's left programme faces serious internal and external constraints, not least the likely hostility of the Treasury to its economic policies and the prospect of international capital flight. All this takes place against a background of growing global uncertainty. A prolonged phase of sustained low growth seems likely across the advanced capitalist states. The White House under Trump is disentangling the US state from its traditional commitment to liberal order. Growing trade protectionism, currency instability and geopolitical unrest will be the likely consequence. Deep phases of capitalist crisis have historically ushered in far-reaching systemic changes. The 'transformation' of capitalism after 2008 has not yet occurred. The form of exit from the crisis is still being shaped by volatile and unpredictable forces. Ultimately, the shape of capitalism after the crisis will not be determined by 'structural' forces alone. *Politics* will shape the transition to the new regime. Britain is one key centre in this emergent global shift. Shaping its future trajectory is a crucial task, both intellectually and politically.

References

Allen, N. (2018). "Brexit Means Brexit": Theresa May and Post-referendum British Politics. *British Politics, 13*(1), 105–120.

Bailey, D. J. (2018). Misperceiving Matters, Again: Stagnating Neoliberalism, Brexit and the Pathological Responses of Britain's Political Elite. *British Politics, 13*(1), 48–64.

Baker, A., & Lavery, S. (2018). Brexit and Future Model of British Capitalsm. In P. Diamond, P. Nedergaard, B. Rosamond, & C. Lequesne (Eds.), *The Routledge Handbook of the Politics of Brexit*. London: Routledge.

Becker, S. O., Fetzer, T., & Novy, D. (2017). Who Voted for Brexit? A Comprehensive District-Level Analysis. *Economic Policy, 32*(92), 601–650.

Berry, C., Gamble, A., Hay, C., Payne, A., & Hunt, T. (2016). *Reforming the Treasury, Reorienting British Capitalism* (Working Paper No. 21). Sheffield: Sheffield Political Economy Research Institute.

Blackburn, R. (2018). The Corbyn Project. *New Left Review*.

Blakeley, G. (2018). *On Borrowed Time: Finance and the UK's Current Account Deficit*. London: Institute for Public Policy Research.

Blyth, M., & Matthijs, M. (2017). Black Swans, Lame Ducks, and the Mystery of IPE's Missing Macroeconomy. *Review of International Political Economy, 24*, 203–231.

Buller, J. (2000). *National Statecraft and European Integration*. London: A & C Black.

Burnham, P. (2011). Towards a Political Theory of Crisis: Policy and Resistance Across Europe. *New Political Science, 33*(4), 493–507.

CITYPERC. (2017). *A Singapore on the Thames*. Retrieved from https://www.city.ac.uk/__data/assets/pdf_file/0005/356558/CPRMay2017.pdf.

Coates, D. (2018). *Flawed Capitalism: The Anglo-American Condition and Its Resolution*. Newcastle: Agenda.

Corbyn, J. (2017). Jeremy Corbyn First Speech of the 2017 General Election Campaign. *The Labour Party*. Retrieved August 15, 2018, from https://labour.org.uk/press/jeremy-corbyn-first-speech-of-the-2017-general/.

Craig, M. (2016). *"Treasury Control" and the British Enviornmental State* (SPERI Paper No. 39). Sheffield: Sheffield Political Economy Research Institute.

Eichengreen, B., & Temin, P. (1997). The Gold Standard and the Great Depression. *Contemporary European History, 9*(2), 183–187.

Evans, G., & Menon, A. (2017). *Brexit and British Politics*. Cambridge: Polity Press.

Fetzer, T. (2018). *Did Austerity Cause Brexit?* (Warwick Paper No. 381). Retrieved from https://ideas.repec.org/p/ces/ceswps/_7159.html.

Frieden, J. A. (2006). *Global Capitalism: Its Fall and Rise in the Twentieth Century*. New York: W. W. Norton.

Gamble, A. (2014). *The Conservative Nation*. London: Routledge.

Gamble, A. (2016). The Crisis Gets Political. In C. Hay & T. Hunt (Eds.), *The Coming Crisis* (pp. 113–119). Basingstoke: Palgrave.

Green, J. (2015). Anglo-American Development, the Euromarkets, and the Deeper Origins of Neoliberal Deregulation. *Review of International Studies, 42*(3), 425–449.

Hager, S. B. (2015). Corporate Ownership of the Public Debt: Mapping the New Aristocracy of Finance. *Socio-Economic Review, 13*(3), 505–523.

Harris, J. (2014). This Way to the Brexit: What Would Happen if Britain Left the EU? *The Guardian*. Retrieved August 14, 2018, from https://www.theguardian.com/politics/2014/oct/10/this-way-to-brexit-what-would-happen-if-britain-left-eu.

Harrop, A. (2016). Support for Brexit Linked to Unequal Public Spending. *The Fabian Society*. Retrieved August 14, 2018, from https://fabians.org.uk/support-for-brexit-linked-to-unequal-public-spending/.

Hay, C., & Rosamond, B. (2002). Globalization, European Integration and the Discursive Construction of Economic Imperatives. *Journal of European Public Policy, 9*(2), 147–167.

Hayton, R. (2018). British Conservatism After the Vote for Brexit: The Ideological Legacy of David Cameron. *The British Journal of Politics and International Relations, 20*(1), 223–238.

Heath, O., & Goodwin, M. (2017). The 2017 General Election, Brexit and the Return to Two-Party Politics: An Aggregate-Level Analysis of the Result. *The Political Quarterly, 88*(3), 345–358.

Hopkin, J. (2017). When Polanyi met Farage: Market Fundamentalism, Economic Nationalism, and Britain's Exit from the European Union. *The British Journal of Politics and International Relations*. https://doi.org/10.1177/1369148117710894.

House of Commons. (2018). *UK-US Trade Relations—International Trade Committee—House of Commons*. Retrieved August 14, 2018, from https://publications.parliament.uk/pa/cm201719/cmselect/cmintrade/481/48103.htm.

Jessop, B. (2016). The Organic Crisis of the British State: Putting Brexit in Its Place. *Globalizations*, 1–9. https://doi.org/10.1080/14747731.2016.1228783.

Lynch, P., & Whitaker, R. (2018). All Brexiteers Now? Brexit, the Conservatives and Party Change. *British Politics, 13*(1), 31–47.

May, T. (2016a). Britain After Brexit: A Vision of a Global Britain. *Speech to the 2016 Conservative Party Conference*. Retrieved August 14, 2018, from http://press.conservatives.com/post/151239411635/prime-minister-britain-after-brexit-a-vision-of.

May, T. (2016b). *Statement from the New Prime Minister Theresa May*. Retrieved August 14, 2018, from https://www.gov.uk/government/speeches/statement-from-the-new-prime-minister-theresa-may.

May, T. (2016c). The New Centre Ground: Theresa May's 2016 Conference Speech. *The Financial Times*. Retrieved August 14, 2018, from https://www.ft.com/content/ffb25e84-8af2-11e6-8aa5-f79f5696c731.

May, T. (2016d). *Theresa May—2016 Speech to Launch Leadership Campaign*. Retrieved August 14, 2018, from http://www.ukpol.co.uk/theresa-may-2016-speech-to-launch-leadership-campaign/.

May, T. (2017a). *The Government's Negotiating Objectives for Exiting the EU*. Retrieved August 14, 2018, from https://www.gov.uk/government/speeches/the-governments-negotiating-objectives-for-exiting-the-eu-pm-speech.

May, T. (2017b). *The Shared Society: Prime Minister's Speech at the Charity Commission Annual Meeting*. Retrieved August 14, 2018, from https://www.gov.uk/government/speeches/the-shared-society-prime-ministers-speech-at-the-charity-commission-annual-meeting.

Mouffe, C. (2018). *For a Left Populism*. London: Verso.

O'Neill, M., & Guinan, J. (2018). The Institutional Turn: Labour's New Political Economy. *Renewal, 26*(2), 5–16.

Pabst, A. (2017). Postliberalism: The New Centre Ground of British Politics. *The Political Quarterly, 88*(3), 500–509.

Panitch, L., & Leys, C. (2001). *The End of Parliamentary Socialism: From New Left to New Labour*. London: Verso.

Quinn, T. (2018). The Conservative Party's Leadership Election of 2016: Choosing a Leader in Government. *British Politics*, 1–23. https://doi.org/10.1057/s41293-018-0071-2.

Schmidt, V., & Thatcher, M. (2013). *Resilient Liberalism in Europe's Political Economy*. Cambridge: Cambridge University Press.

Shipman, T. (2017). *Fall Out: A Year of Political Mayhem*. London: William Collins.

Streeck, W. (2017). Return of the Repressed. *New Left Review*.

The Conservative Party. (2017). *Our Plan for Britain*. Retrieved August 14, 2018, from https://www.conservatives.com/sharethefacts/2017/03/our_plan_for_britain/.

The Labour Party. (2017). *For the Many, Not the Few*.

Theakston, K. (2011). Gordon Brown as Prime Minister: Political Skills and Leadership Style. *British Politics, 6*(1), 78–100.

Thompson, H. (2017). Inevitability and Contingency: The Political Economy of Brexit. *The British Journal of Politics and International Relations*. https://doi.org/10.1177/1369148117710431.

Watson, M. (2018). Brexit, the Left Behind and the Let Down: The Political Abstraction of "the Economy" and the UK's EU Referendum. *British Politics, 13*(1), 17–30.

CHAPTER 8

Conclusion

The twentieth century witnessed two great moments of capitalist crisis, the Great Depression of the 1930s and the stagflation of the 1970s. Both of these crises led, eventually, to a profound structural change in the world economy. The 2008 crisis embodied a 'shock' of similar proportions. However, in the immediate aftermath of the crash, a transition to a new regime of global capitalism did not materialise. Neoliberal ideas and practices proved markedly resilient. That said, one decade after the crisis, there are signs of an emergent shift within the advanced capitalist economies. A new regime of 'loose' monetary policy—sustained low interest rates and Quantitative Easing—has emerged (Green & Lavery, 2018). At the same time, populist forces on the left and right have grown in strength, challenging incumbent parties and even threatening the core principles of the global order. The post-crisis conjuncture has been an era of both continuity and change. It has produced a period of phase of profound volatility and instability (Hay & Hunt, 2017). The future trajectory of global capitalism remains uncertain.

The global downturn following the 2008 crisis impacted upon national states differentially. This book has focused on the case of post-crisis British capitalism. Its central question has been to ask to what extent British capitalism after the crisis embodies a *continuation of* or a *rupture with* the regime which was in place in the pre-crisis conjuncture. In order to answer this question, the book has engaged in a comparison of the political-economic strategies pursued by the New Labour and the Coalition governments, respectively. In the light of this analysis, we can identify

S. Lavery, *British Capitalism After the Crisis*, Building a Sustainable Political Economy: SPERI Research & Policy, https://doi.org/10.1007/978-3-030-04046-8_8

important instances of both continuity and change within post-crisis British capitalism. Whilst the Coalition effectively re-established the conditions for a renewed wave of finance-led growth in Britain, it effectively broke with the legitimation strategy which New Labour had deployed in the pre-crisis conjuncture. The result was that deep structural weaknesses remained embedded at the heart of post-crisis British capitalism. These structural weaknesses are likely to shape its developmental trajectory into the future.

The argument of this book has proceeded in a number of distinct steps. First, the 'growth model perspective', which argued that Britain's economy was underpinned by a dynamic of 'privatised Keynesianism', was critically reviewed and developed (Crouch, 2011; Finlayson, 2008; see also Streeck, 2014). Whilst this growth model perspective provides us with a good account of some of the structural imbalances at the heart of Britain's pre-crisis model of capitalism, it is also limited in a number of important respects. In particular, it advances a *limited conception of the state* which tends to privilege analytically forms of state intervention which were 'functional' to the financialisation of British capitalism. In addition, it cannot provide a compelling explanation of how Britain's pre-crisis growth model was *stabilised* throughout the pre-crisis conjuncture. In order to overcome these weaknesses, two theoretical approaches were drawn upon and further developed. Regulationist perspectives draw to the ways in which growth models are embedded within 'extra-economic' institutional attention complexes which can serve to stabilise economic development over time. Neo-Marxist theories of the state provide us with a framework through which to conceptualise the ways in which the state is typically oriented towards securing a range of different social and political objectives simultaneously. Drawing on these approaches, the limitations of the 'growth model perspective' can be overcome. In particular, whilst the growth model perspective provides us with a good account of the *accumulation strategies* advanced by policymakers, the book has argued that this should be complemented by an account of the *legitimation strategies*—or 'hegemonic projects'—pursued by state managers as they attempt to secure support for their favoured programme of development. By introducing this analytical distinction between *accumulation strategies* and *legitimation strategies*, a more compelling framework for comparing the political economy of New Labour and the Coalition can be advanced.

The pre-crisis conjuncture was a period of stable and consistent economic expansion in Britain. During this period, New Labour established a distinctive hybrid regime of development. New Labour advanced a finance-led accumulation strategy which both consolidated the position of the financial sector within Britain and which further extended the price mechanism into a diverse range of social spheres. However, this accumulation strategy was paralleled by a distinctive—albeit limited and provisional—'One Nation' legitimation strategy or 'hegemonic project'. From 2000 onwards, New Labour engaged in the largest increase in spending on public services of any post-war British government. It also implemented a range of redistributive social policies which channelled state revenues to social groups who might otherwise have been excluded from the dominant finance-led growth model. However, these (limited) forms of redistribution were not driven by a 'logic' which was internal to the finance-led growth model. Rather, they were driven by a range of political considerations, including the Labour Party's attempt to consolidate and entrench a continued base of support for its social and economic programme.

This has two implications for the existing literature. First, in contrast to many accounts of New Labour—which tend to focus on the question of whether the Party's programme was in essence 'neoliberal' or 'social democratic'—New Labour's political economy assumed a distinctive *hybrid form*. Britain's pre-crisis model of capitalism combined elements of marketisation *and* state-led redistribution which effectively—but only temporarily—secured the conditions for stable economic expansion before the 2008 crash. Second, and relatedly, the state was not simply 'rolled back' under New Labour. It was simultaneously 'rolled out' and expanded in a number of different ways (Peck, 2010). Public sector and state-led employment increased markedly throughout the pre-crisis conjuncture, whilst tax subsidies for in-work households increased to a significant extent. Crucially, this hybrid regime of development played a key role in stabilising British capitalism throughout the pre-crisis conjuncture. New Labour's expansion of public expenditure played an important role in reducing relative poverty, constraining the growth of income inequality and (partially) mitigating the uneven development of British capitalism (Joyce & Sibieta, 2013).

The 2008 financial crisis fatally undermined New Labour's hybrid regime of social and economic development. As lending dried up and as asset prices began to plummet, Britain's finance-led growth model went into a tailspin. Growth fell, tax revenues slumped and the benefits bill increased as workers were pushed onto the unemployment register. Subsequently, the public finances deteriorated, with the public debt and the budget deficit increasing markedly as a proportion of GDP between 2008 and 2010. It was in this context that the Conservative Party—under the leadership of Cameron and Osborne—took the initiative and consolidated their position over Brown's embattled Labour government. The core rationale of the Conservatives' new social and economic programme was simple: to 'sort out the mess that Labour left behind', a commitment which was confirmed in the June 2010 Budget as Osborne committed to eliminating Britain's large budget deficit—primarily through spending cuts—within one parliament. A remarkable shift had therefore taken place. Whereas in 2007, the Conservatives in opposition had committed to match Labour's public expenditure plans, by 2010 the new government had effectively committed to reducing non-protected departmental budgets by around a fifth. A new regime of fiscal consolidation and welfare retrenchment had begun to take shape.

This book has traced the emergence and evolution of the Coalition's political-economic strategy in office. However, it has sought to do this from a particular perspective. Specifically, it has contextualised the evolution of the Coalition's political economy in relation to New Labour's hybrid regime of social and economic development. This provides us with a framework against which to judge the extent to which Britain's post-crisis model of capitalism represented a *continuation of* or a *rupture with* the model of capitalism which had been in place in the pre-crisis conjuncture. By the end of the 2010–2015 parliament, the Coalition had effectively re-established the conditions for a renewed wave of finance-led growth in Britain, albeit after a transitionary period and in a slightly modified form. Despite its discursive commitment to 'rebalancing' the British economy sectorally and geographically, the Coalition did not secure a restructuring of Britain's finance-led growth model (Berry & Hay, 2016). When GDP growth returned in the spring of 2013, it was driven by consumption and by an expansion in the services sector. Britain's large trade deficit endured whilst its current account deficit reached a post-war high of six per cent in 2015. Industrial production fell, manufacturing exports remained weak and investment continued to be biased towards commercial and residential property. Although household debt as a proportion of GDP remained below its pre-crisis peak in 2015, it was projected to surpass that level in the following parliament.

The Coalition did not move Britain away from the finance-led growth model which had predominated throughout the pre-crisis conjuncture. Deep structural weaknesses endured within post-crisis British capitalism.

However, the 2013 economic recovery did not simply reflect a return to 'privatised Keynesianism' Mark II. Some of the key mechanisms which had been in place throughout the first wave of privatised Keynesian expansion—high rates of MEW and high levels of net lending to households—were simply not in place during the initial return to growth. The boost in consumption in this period was driven by a decline in the savings ratio rather than exclusively by a rapid increase in private debt. This alternative source of demand had been largely exhausted by the end of the parliament insofar as the savings ratio had fallen back to pre-crisis levels. Household debt-to-GDP ratios were also on an upward trajectory whilst real wage growth continued to be markedly constrained. In addition, government policies such as Help to Buy aimed explicitly to re-establish features of Britain's pre-crisis growth model, for example, in the form of high loan-to-value ratios and increased levels of mortgage debt. As such, the period of putative economic recovery between 2013 and 2015 is perhaps best viewed as an *interregnum* period within which the basic conditions for a renewed wave of finance-led growth became firmly re-established within Britain.

Whilst the Coalition effectively re-established the finance-led growth model which had been in place under New Labour, substantial change was also in evidence throughout the post-crisis conjuncture. In particular, the Coalition broke with the *legitimation strategy* which New Labour had deployed in government. In contrast to New Labour, which had sought to expand its base of support by advancing a 'One Nation' hegemonic project, the Coalition pursued a distinctive 'two nations' strategy which sought to secure a limited but durable base of support amongst strategically significant sections of the population (Jessop, 1990: 216). The defining feature of a 'two nations' project is that it seeks to build what were termed *moralised antagonisms* between different social groups. In particular, two nations strategies seek to construct the interests of one social group as fundamentally in conflict with another. In this way, state actors can seek to build a limited base of support for their favoured developmental programme by actively mobilising one social coalition against a subordinate 'Other'. We can identify the emergence of this strategy in two policy areas in the post-crisis conjuncture: in the Coalition's programme of welfare restructuring and in its programme of public sector retrenchment.

The period immediately after the crash generated a series of novel distributional trends in Britain. Real wages collapsed to an unprecedented extent. This meant that the incomes of 'non-working' households were protected relative to 'in-work' households. Public sector pay was also protected relative to private sector pay due to pay agreements struck before the crisis in 2007. The Coalition advanced a particular construction of these distributional dynamics in order to build support for its programme of welfare retrenchment and public sector cuts. In particular, the Coalition sought to entrench a *moralised antagonism* between 'welfare claimants' and 'workers' on the one hand and 'public' and 'private' sector workers on the other. In each case, the Coalition turned what could have been a profound liability—the rapid decline in real wages and the corresponding drop in living standards over which it had presided—into a political asset. In particular, it utilised this novel distributional context to justify large cuts to the welfare bill and to public sector pay and employment levels. Under other conditions, these policies may have proven incredibly difficult to implement.

This argument has two important implications for the existing literature. First, it suggests an important link between the Coalition's *accumulation strategy* on the one hand and the range of *legitimation strategies* which it could deploy in office on the other. Although governments can attempt to secure the popular support in a variety of ways, the kind of strategies which they can pursue will be strongly conditioned by the prevailing economic context (Gramsci, 1971: 161). Whilst the Coalition's commitment to eliminate the budget deficit in one parliament may have given it a decisive political advantage over the Labour Party in terms of its economic credibility, this strategic orientation came at a considerable cost. Its prioritisation of deficit reduction limited its capacity to secure real terms public expenditure increases or to offer tax cuts to middle-income earners. Thus, whilst 'austerity' may be a powerful idea which can resonate with the belief systems of 'everyday' actors (Konings, 2015; Stanley, 2014), its potency as a political strategy should not be overstated. The Coalition attempted to portray its *Welfare Benefits Up-Rating Bill* as a policy which would 'make work pay' insofar as it would reduce the level of benefits received relative to average earnings. However, as was shown in Chapter 6, this policy in fact primarily reduced the incomes of *in-work households*. The extent to which governments can 'frame' a policy as benefiting a given social group (in this case 'workers') whilst at the same time imposing real terms losses on large sections of this social group therefore remains an open question.

Second, it is important to *historicise* the Coalition's 'two nations' project in relation to the regime of development which preceded it. New Labour's 'One Nation' legitimation strategy had important distributional consequences. It resulted in an increase in public sector and state-backed employment and in a substantial rise in tax credits paid to low-income households. Whilst this helped to maintain New Labour's legitimacy in office, it also produced a series of path dependencies which endured into the post-crisis conjuncture. The relative protection of public sector pay and out-of-work benefits in the immediate post-crisis period—and the budgetary implications which this had—were therefore unintended consequences of New Labour's political and economic programme. As such, the Coalition's room for manoeuvre was not only limited by the economic strategy which it pursued in office; it was shaped by the institutional legacies of previous rounds of market liberal restructuring in Britain (Peck, 2010). This underscores the critical importance of tracing processes of continuity and change in advanced capitalist states historically. The politics of austerity are not just imposed 'from above' by international creditor institutions or by the 'logic' of the global capitalist system (Robinson, 2001). Rather, the manner in which fiscal consolidation processes unfold is also strongly shaped and conditioned by the novel institutional frameworks which are in place within distinct national configurations of capitalism. The Coalition's 'two nations' hegemonic project and its economic strategy should be viewed in this light, as a strategic programme which aimed to negotiate a series of distributional trends and path dependencies which were specific to British capitalism in the post-crisis conjuncture.

By the time the Coalition government had disbanded in 2015, a series of structural weaknesses and imbalances had been re-embedded within post-crisis British capitalism. These are likely to strongly condition Britain's developmental trajectory into the future. The Coalition did not successfully move Britain away from the finance-led growth model which had been in place throughout the pre-crisis conjuncture. However—as outlined by proponents of the growth perspective—this model of development renders the British economy vulnerable to a future downturn on a number of fronts. By 2015, Britain was running a current account deficit of 6% of GDP: the highest since records began in 1955 (Perraton, 2015). Insofar as international creditors are happy to finance this deficit, it should not present a problem to policymakers. The risk is that if there is a bout of global economic uncertainty—and there is ample evidence of rising instability within the global economy at present (SPERI, 2016)—then investors may choose to take flight and precipitate a run on Sterling. Britain's yawning current account deficit and the Coalition's failure to correct this imbalance through increasing export earnings therefore represents a point of clear vulnerability within post-crisis British capitalism. Sustained real wage repression produces imbalances and structural asymmetries within advanced capitalist states. In particular, it can act as a barrier to aggregate demand formation and can encourage destabilising bouts of credit growth amongst low-income households (Montgomerie & Büdenbender, 2014; Onaran, 2014). By 2015, Britain had experienced real wage cuts of 10%. This represented the largest decline in real wages of any European country other than Greece and the largest sustained drop in earnings in Britain since the nineteenth century. This suggests that a core driver of imbalance in the pre-crisis conjuncture has not only been re-established in the post-crisis conjuncture; it has intensified.

High levels of income inequality and a low 'wage share' have been identified as key drivers of financialisation and structural imbalance within advanced capitalist economies (Stockhammer, 2013). The Coalition's economic recovery was secured through the deployment of a range of policies which look likely to entrench distributional inequities further still. As the Bank of England's own analysis has shown, its huge programme of QE has primarily benefited households in the top 5% of the income distribution. Similarly, sustained low interest rates have benefited homeowners, with mortgage interest rates falling by 37% between 2008 and 2013 (IFS, 2014). As a result, Britain's post-crisis return to growth embodied a 'recovery through regressive redistribution'—a state-led process of social and economic restructuring which combines 'loose' monetary policy with sustained real wage repression and public sector retrenchment (Green & Lavery, 2015). Some of the key distributional asymmetries and structural imbalances associated with Britain's finance-led model of capitalism have been re-embedded or have even intensified throughout the post-crisis conjuncture.

The story of British capitalism after the crisis is therefore primarily a story of continuity. Long-standing structural weaknesses in the British economy remain. Indeed, after almost a decade of austerity and stagnant growth, many of British capitalism's weaknesses have intensified (Lavery, 2018). But these continuities should not blind us to important underlying political shifts which have also emerged in the post-crisis conjuncture. A populist insurgency began to take hold in this era across the Western world (Brubaker, 2017). From Budapest to Washington, from

Helsinki to Rome, anti-establishment movements of the left and right began to reconfigure domestic political systems. Populist forces even threatened to undermine the core principles of the global liberal order. Britain has emerged as a pivotal sphere within this wider global populist shift. This was exemplified by Britain's vote to leave the EU, the interventionist programme of Theresa May's government in its early stages and the left populism of the Labour Party under Jeremy Corbyn. Each of these developments emerged from within and was shaped by the volatile politics of the post-crisis conjuncture. Each advanced programmes which, in their own ways, promised to transform British capitalism. Whether such a transformation is likely to occur of course remains an open question. Profound structural barriers to reform remain in place, both within the internal structures of the British state and economy and externally in relation to the world economy. Any force seeking to transform British capitalism will have to be capable of overcoming these barriers whilst maintaining a sufficient level of popular support. This is an extremely difficult task. But it is also a crucial one, both intellectually and politically.

References

Berry, C., & Hay, C. (2016). The Great British "Rebalancing" Act: The Construction and Implementation of an Economic Imperative for Exceptional Times. *The British Journal of Politics & International Relations, 18*(1), 3–25.

Brubaker, R. (2017). Why Populism? *Theory and Society, 46*(5), 357–385.

Crouch, C. (2011). *The Strange Non-death of Neoliberalism.* Cambridge: Polity Press.

Finlayson, A. (2008). Characterizing New Labour: The Case of the Child Trust Fund. *Public Administration, 86*(1), 95–110.

Gramsci, A. (1971). *Prison Notebooks.* London: Lawrence and Wishart.

Green, J., & Lavery, S. (2015). The Regressive Recovery: Distribution, Inequality and State Power in Britain's Post-crisis Political Economy. *New Political Economy, 20*(6), 894–923.

Green, J., & Lavery, S. (2018). After Neoliberalisation? Monetary Indiscipline, Crisis and the State. *Transactions of the Institute of British Geographers, 43*(1), 79–94.

Hay, C., & Hunt, T. (2017). *The Coming Crisis.* Basingstoke: Palgrave Macmillan.

IFS. (2014). *Living Standards, Poverty and Inequality in the UK: 2014.* London: Institute for Fiscal Studies.

Jessop, B. (1990). *State Theory: Putting the Capitalist State in Its Place.* Cambridge: Polity Press.
Joyce, R., & Sibieta, L. (2013). An Assessment of Labour's Record on Income Inequality and Poverty. *Oxford Review of Economic Policy, 29*(1), 178–202.
Konings, M. (2015). The Spirit of Austerity. *Journal of Cultural Economy, 9*(1), 86–100.
Lavery, S. (2018). The Legitimation of Post-crisis Capitalism in the United Kingdom: Real Wage Decline, Finance-Led Growth and the State. *New Political Economy, 23*(1), 27–45.
Montgomerie, J., & Büdenbender, M. (2014, October). Round the Houses: Homeownership and Failures of Asset-Based Welfare in the United Kingdom. *New Political Economy*, 1–20. https://doi.org/10.1080/13563467.2014.951429.
Onaran, O. (2014). *State Intervention for Wage-Led Development.* London: Class Online.
Peck, J. (2010). *Constructions of Neoliberal Reason.* Oxford: Oxford University Press.
Perraton, J. (2015). *The UK Balance of Payments: In the "Red Signal" Zone?* Sheffield Political Economy Research Institute (SPERI) Blog. Retrieved February 20, 2016, from http://speri.dept.shef.ac.uk/2015/02/03/uk-balance-payments-red-signal-zone/.
Robinson, W. I. (2001). Social Theory and Globalization: The Rise of a Transnational State. *Theory and Society, 30*(2), 157–200.
SPERI. (2016). *The Coming Crisis.* Sheffield Political Economy Research Institute (SPERI) Blog. Retrieved from http://speri.dept.shef.ac.uk/category/the-coming-crisis/.
Stanley, L. (2014). "We"re Reaping What We Sowed': Everyday Crisis Narratives and Acquiescence to the Age of Austerity. *New Political Economy, 19*(6), 895–917.
Stockhammer, E. (2013). Rising Inequality as a Cause of the Present Crisis. *Cambridge Journal of Economics*, 1–24. https://doi.org/10.1093/cje/bet052.
Streeck, W. (2014). *Buying Time: The Delayed Crisis of Democratic Capitalism.* London: Verso.

Index

S. Lavery, *British Capitalism After the Crisis*, Building a Sustainable Political Economy: SPERI Research & Policy, https://doi.org/10.1007/978-3-030-04046-8

The manufacturer's authorised representative in the EU is Springer Nature Customer Service Centre GmbH, Europaplatz 3, 69115 Heidelberg, Germany. If you have any concerns regarding our products, please contact ProductSafety@springernature.com

Printed and bound by CPI Group (UK) Ltd, Croydon, CR0 4YY
22/09/2026
02221063-0002